Polygons: Cultural Diversities and Intersections
General Editor: **Lieve Spaas**, *Professor of French Cultural Studies, Kingston University*

Volume 1: *Reynard the Fox: Social Engagement and Cultural Metamorphoses in the Beast Epic from the Middle Ages to the Present*
Edited by Kenneth Varty

Volume 2: *Echoes of Narcissus*
Edited by Lieve Spaas in association with Trista Selous

Volume 3: *Human Nature and the French Revolution: From the Enlightenment to the Napoleonic Code*
Xavier Martin, translated from the French by Patrick Corcoran

Volume 4: *Secret Spaces, Forbidden Places: Rethinking Culture*
Edited by Fran Lloyd and Catherine O'Brien

Volume 5: *Relative Points of View: Linguistic Representations of Culture*
Edited by Magda Stroinska

Volume 6: *Expanding Suburbia: Reviewing Suburban Narratives*
Edited by Roger Webster

SECRET SPACES
FORBIDDEN PLACES

Rethinking Culture

Edited by Fran Lloyd
and Catherine O'Brien

Berghahn Books
New York • Oxford

First published in 2000 by

Berghahn Books
www.BerghahnBooks.com

Editorial offices:
604 West 115th Street, New York, NY 10025, USA
3 NewTec Place, Magdalen Road, Oxford OX4 1RE, UK

Library of Congress Cataloging-in-Publication Data

British Library Cataloguing in Publication Data
A catalogue record for this book is available from the British Library.

Printed in the United States on acid-free paper.

ISBN 1-57181-788-3 (hardback)
ISBN 1-57181-789-1 (paperback)

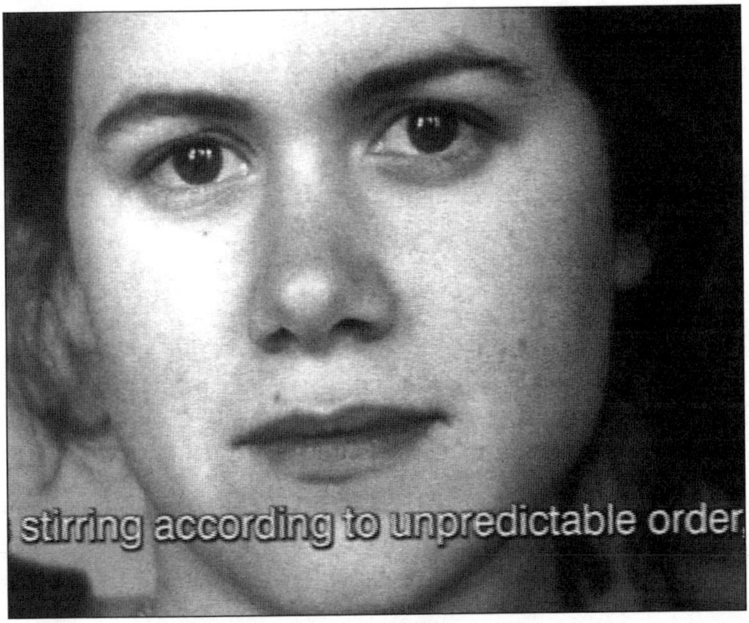
stirring according to unpredictable order,

Gilly Booth, *Continuum*, 1999.
Still from 16mm film commissioned for
Secret Spaces/Forbidden Places. Courtesy of artist.

CONTENTS

List of Illustrations

Acknowledgements

This publication would not have been possible without the support and efforts of numerous people and institutions. We should, therefore, like to thank all of the contributors for all their efforts.

We should like to take this opportunity to acknowledge all those who attended and contributed to the *Secret Spaces/Forbidden Places* symposium – held at atmospheric Herstmonceux Castle in East Sussex – which was the inspiration for this publication. Thanks to those institutions that offered financial support to colleagues attending the conference, especially Kingston University.

Many thanks to the various artists, writers, galleries and institutions who have given copyright permission. In particular, Máighréad Medbh and the Feminist Collective for permission to quote from *Easter 1991* © Máighréad Medbh, published in *The Feminist Review*, 44, 1993; Paula Meehan for permission to use quotations from *Don't Speak to Me of Martyrs* (1991) © Paula Meehan; and the very helpful staff at Poetry Ireland, Dublin Castle.

Our particular thanks go to Trista Selous for translating articles in chapters 2, 3, 6 and 8 from the original French.

Special thanks to Alison Wilding for patiently answering many questions, for mentioning the long lost twin of *Untitled*, and for allowing us to publish the image. Thanks also to Hilary Beyer for her wonderful transcription skills, and to colleagues and students at Kingston University who have been engaged in new ways of thinking about culture.

Much appreciation is owed to Lieve Spaas, the editor of the series, to Bryn Williams for his skilful copyediting, and to Mark Daniels and Marion Berghahn at Berghahn Books.

Personal thanks to Tom Ennis for his enduring patience, good humour and sense of perspective.

Finally, personal thanks to Patrick Warren and Luke, Camille, Duncan, Nathan and Saskia, for being a continuous source of support, encouragement and joy during this process.

Fran Lloyd and Catherine O'Brien

INTRODUCTION

Spaces, Places, Sites/Sights of the Secret and Forbidden

The defining characteristic of this book is multiplicity and interdisciplinarity. By bringing together writers from various academic backgrounds and different geographies, this study reveals that the cartography of secret spaces and forbidden places extends far beyond physical locations and is present in domains as disparate as art, language, literature, philosophy, cinema, memory, and social and political life. By theorising new positions, new gazes and multiple viewpoints on the secret and the forbidden, the aim is to uncover what has been hidden, displaced, repressed or suppressed in the spaces of cultural and political history, whether contemporaneously or with hindsight.

Secret Spaces, Forbidden Places encompasses both the suggestion of space as an interactive social sphere through which power and presence is either negotiated or claimed by diverse cultural groupings, and of place as located site/sight. With a focus on multiple positionings, within and across these social and cultural spaces, the essays in this collection are particularly concerned with the way in which the secret and the forbidden have been constructed at different moments in cultural histories, and how these can be rethought from the multiple perspectives of the present. The emphasis on the specificities of located experiences, articulated through diverse cultural practices, provides a powerful means of recovering, rediscovering and reclaiming historical visibility on both an individual and collective level.

Grouped around three main areas – the literary spaces of desire, politics of the forbidden and the visual spaces of art, memory and place – the essays explore how the secret and forbidden intersect and are constructed through and against the regulatory social systems embedded in such accepted notions as: the private and the public, the interior and exterior, and the male and female. The concepts of secrecy and prohibition are not the preserve of any one philosophy, religious belief or political system and can be found in the formulation of our sense of belonging to a particular territory, whether a geographical place or a mental space.

Mapping the secret and the forbidden is a formidable project. The secret may include the suppression of truth, the concealment of information or the preservation of desires or dark knowledge, whether by individuals, groups or governments. Inhabiting the city's labyrinths, embedded in the body, buried in the vaults of the archive or the deep recesses of the mind, the secret is both the space and the site through which, and upon which, the forbidden operates. Once the secret becomes forbidden and is therefore vigilantly guarded, the protective barriers signal its existence to the uninitiated.

Whether controlled by the symbolic orders of language, or the law of the father and/or the nation, the forbidden excludes certain groupings or individuals, marked by difference. It may be manifest by the refusal of entry into specific geographies or domains, the exile from designated spaces or sites/sights, or the taboos that create social or cultural prohibitions. The forbidden is carefully policed at its boundaries, and transgression frequently carries a heavy price within the multiple spaces and places of culture.

The Politics of Visibility

Not surprisingly, the issue of visibility and invisibility is a thread that runs through many of the essays in this collection. To be visible is to be seen, to be located in time and space, as both embodied subject and object. Yet visibility is also associated with the controlling gaze, and the regulatory systems of power and knowledge which work differently both within and across the proscribed boundaries of different cultures and groupings.

The writers identify a range of gazes across disparate and previously unconnected sites, from the Protestant spaces of seventeenth-century Holland through to the totalitarian regimes of the twentieth century, via literature, politics, language and visual representation. In her analysis of tenth-century Japanese literature, Valerie Henitiuk reveals the gaze of the 'Mother of Michitsuna' in a society where catching sight of a woman's body was tantamount to visual rape (chapter 1); desiring gazes inside and outside the eroticised space of the bedroom are considered by Tony Williams in his survey of nineteenth-century French novels by Balzac, Sand, Flaubert and Zola (chapter 4); and the misregistration between eye and gaze, together with the concept of the Lacanian 'hole', is explored by Chris Horrocks in his discussion of Duchamp's *Given* (chapter 17).

Xavier Martin argues (chapter 8) that the inception of Enlightenment thought in France was premised on the absolute power of visibility, its accompanying systems of physiognomical classification and the desire to 'master' the external world for the greater good. The resultant policing of the boundaries of both the individual and the state, both internally and externally, and the accompanying desire for transparency and order subsequently became key underlying tenets of Western modernity. Most visible within the spaces of the city, as several of the essays show, these tenets continue through to the present day in cultural areas as diverse as monument-making and the control of language in contemporary France.

Invisibility may be to have no position, no place; to be absent in time and space, disenfranchised and disempowered – whether through language, visual representation, or political and social agency. The effects of this are evident for various groupings, marked out by difference through gender, race, or sexuality. However, in the face of a totalising system, a powerful elite, a patriarchal order or a potential attacker, invisibility may become a place of safety; a secret space that protects and obscures one from the controlling gaze, at home or abroad. In his study of the multiple Jewish and gay communities in the Marais in Paris, Gordon Phillips foregrounds the historical necessity of such hidden spaces while posing questions about the freedoms that such spaces afford (chapter 9). Clarissa Wilks and Noëlle Brick explore how language works to exclude along the lines of gender, race, ethnicity and sexuality, yet also creates spaces in which exiled groups can flourish (chapter 13), and, in Andrea Rinke's analysis of Evelyn Schmidt's *The Bicycle* (chapter 12) where the female as outsider doubles as both the real and the symbolic site of marginalisation and subversion, we see how invisibility became a form of protection in postwar East Germany. Several of the essays focus on such contradictions, ranging across geographies and political regimes which are usually separated and seen as oppositional, rather than sharing similar, albeit differently structured, controlling systems.

For various reasons, artists and writers may construct secret spaces in which to operate where the sites of creativity are visible only to the gaze of the producer, and the light of the public gaze may kill the burgeoning seed. Agnès Cardinal reveals the alternative, private worlds created in the notebooks of Adolf Wölfli, the ink drawings of Madge Gill, and the secret diary of Verena Stefan's mother – a chronicle of forty years of family life, hidden in a linen chest (chapter 7). Both the desire for fame and the fear of discovery is shown in Stendhal's use of codes, pseudonyms and elision in his texts, where there is slippage between image and word in what Jean-Jacques Hamm describes as 'the place that has no name', and the personal search for revelation of the secret and the forbidden is continually frustrated and deferred (chapter 3). And Franciska Skutta's analysis of adolescent sexuality in the works of Jean Cocteau and Antal Szerb (chapter 6) reveals the private space behind the bedroom door to be refuge, prison and destructive force.

Inclusion and Exclusion

Operating differently, at different times, the secret and the forbidden are inextricably bound up with exclusion and inclusion. The secret, known only by a small section of the elected or selected, necessarily excludes others, while the forbidden demarcates the boundaries of what is permissible or prohibited, acceptable or undesirable, within specific domains. Questions of who is included/excluded within a particular realm, by whom, against or through what, and for what purposes, are therefore crucial ones. The essays demonstrate that power is continuously negotiated and controlled across boundaries and margins through the secret and the forbidden, raising the intriguing but frightening question of how reality may be constructed and manipulated. In a number of essays, we find the control of truth under totalitarian regimes. The production of a celluloid 'ideal France' in the wake of the events of Vichy is assessed by Suzanne Langlois as she explores censorship dossiers in French film archives (chapter 10), revealing that light shed on one aspect of the past leads to the edge of another shadow.

Although the secret spaces of power frequently reside at the centre of a culture, assuming a set of norms that exclude others, it has also become clear in recent years that these norms are under pressure from the margins in numerous ways. Whether the 'norm' be patriarchal society or an Eastern Bloc dictatorship after the Second World War, the following essays focus on how the people on the 'periphery' – who may be women, homosexuals, ethnic minorities, the people of Karelia exiled from their homeland, or the opponents of oppression – negotiate their positionings through the secret and the forbidden.

Women writers may customarily privilege interior space, with the traditional binary division of male-dominated public spheres confining women to the privacy of the domestic sphere, but these spatial divisions are constantly infringed. While the domestic, the feminine sphere of the home, has tended to be constructed as a place of sanctuary and of being 'offstage', it is now clear that the private is also constructed and negotiated by the public, and the multiple points of identification and dis-identification with the home include gender difference, race, ethnicity and sexuality. Various essays point to how the privatisation of the gendered domestic space is a relatively recent development, emerging, with the Enlightenment, amongst the dominant classes (of course, it never was or has been a private space for others).

Building upon previous research which identified the operation of the spaces of 'femininity' and 'masculinity', and the limitations of a formal mapping of the 'conceptual city', several of the essays demonstrate how such divisions, operative for certain classes, sexualities, etc. can be transgressed and negotiated in numerous ways.

In her reflection on the nature of domestic virtue in de Hooch's *A Woman with a Broom and Pail in a Courtyard*, Jorella Andrews shows a woman poised on the threshold between activity and receptivity (chapter 15). Victoria Korzeniowska introduces us to narratives of self-discovery in Jean Giraudoux's fiction, where the anonymity of the city allowed women to lead secret lives, finding a 'personal space' only in public (chapter 5). Those heroines who do question the gendered segregation of space introduce disorder, which destabilises the accepted spatial equilibrium and reconfigures space for their own purposes. As Andrew Stephenson shows in his review of the short story 'Pamela in Piccadilly', such acts force a reassessment not only of the impact of performative space on eroticised spectatorship (chapter 16), but also of the way in which individuals or groups may step out through the Other, as in the case of Pamela's father, who is introduced to the 'inner dualities' of art by his daughter – reversing traditional generational and sexual hierarchies.

Much has been written recently on the effects of displacement, of exile and the crossing of cultural and territorial boundaries, and feminist theorists in particular have seen such 'deterritorialisation' as a potentially productive site for women artists and writers. Nevertheless, one does not have to leave one's homeland to be displaced – practices of exclusion operate at all levels of society, including the personal. While exclusion may lead to alienation, marginality may, as several of the essays show, be an important factor that enables self-discovery.

Bodies/Boundaries/Identities

Whether conceived in terms of the visible/invisible, inclusion/exclusion, or multiple gazes, what is central to the operation of the secret and the forbidden is the regulation of bodies of difference at the levels of the individual, the group and the nation. Gendered, sexed, raced, classed and ethnicised bodies are both the site/sight of the secret and the forbidden, and the space of their embodiment and negotiation. In effect, the body is both a major site of regulation and of transgression.

Regulation implies a norm, an assumed set of values which, as the essays show, are constantly under threat and unstable. The essays in this collection give an insight into the complex and contradictory processes by which the forbidden places and secret spaces that bodies occupy become visible. Secrets slip out, they cross boundaries, and what may be forbidden in one space or place may be permissible in another. More importantly, at certain key moments, before attempts to police and reinstate the *status quo* via surveillance of the public and private, bodies that have been excluded through the multiple and fractured lines of gender, race, religion, class, ethnicity, generation or sexuality, have negotiated visibility.

As a number of the authors note, however, such transgression of boundaries may exert a punishment, particularly for the female transgressor, regarded by the misogynist as a deceptive masquerader. As Tivadar Gorilovics reminds us in the many retellings of the story of Bluebeard (chapter 2), the secret chamber contains the corpses of women who attempted to resist male threats. Prohibitions lead human beings to risk their lives because of the powerful seduction exerted by curiosity and the desire for omniscience.

The violation of the body at the level of personal, group or national identities is always one of the most disturbing forms of transgression. Sue Malvern's essay (chapter 20) shows the impotent and guilty gaze that is confronted with the inexpressible horror of rape, and the victim's knowledge that 'I am awake in the place where women die'. But as seen in Anu Hirsiaho's analysis of Irish feminist poetry and the nation state (chapter 14), the works of Alison Wilding (chapter 19) and Jenny Holzer (chapter 20), the female body has been used by women as a refusal of stereotypes and normative roles, where the shifting meanings of the secret and the forbidden can be explored.

The essays on *Visual Spaces* show the way multiple meanings are negotiated against the dominant masculinist culture, but also question the premise of the gaze, of visuality and its relationship to language and embodiment. These undercut the bias in logocentric thought to understand space purely in visual terms and to ignore the relationship of space to tactile experience, whether from a phenomenological experience of subjectivity through the changing body, or alternative ways of understanding through paradox, as in the essays on de Hooch (chapter 15) and Wilding (chapter 19).

Identities are not monolithic, uniformly constituted or reducible to singular categories, whether by religion, language, geography or gender. Like all identities, they are produced by the different ways in which embodied subjects are positioned and position themselves along multiple lines, according to gender, race, religion, ethnicity, generation, sexuality (and so forth) at specific historical junctures. The essays in this collection give an insight into the complex and contradictory process by which forbidden places and secret spaces become open and visible, and vice versa.

In the third millennium, questions about memory have become of paramount importance. Much recent writing has concentrated, for example, on the issues surrounding various forms of public and private memory, national and group memory (particularly in relation to the traumatic effects of the Holocaust), and their relationship to accepted histories and to what is forgotten.

Magda Stroińska's personal witness of propaganda manipulation in postwar Poland (chapter 11) and Marja Keränen's testimony to life in exile on the Finnish/Russian border (chapter 18) are exponents of the politics of memory; and Sue

Malvern considers how war memorials are founded on amnesia as well as remembrance (chapter 20).

Finally, the emphasis on language and imaging foregrounds culture as an active site of the renegotiation of bodies, boundaries and identities, and their multiple meanings, both for the artist/writer and the audience/spectator. Far from being embodied by dead texts, objects or images, with predetermined and fixed meanings, culture is part of the production of knowledge which is constantly open to new meanings, negotiated through points of identification and difference. These acts of performativity imply that the making of culture can be an act of discovery in the present, through the processes of remembering, rethinking and reexamining, rather than the establishment of predetermined meanings. Thus, while recognising the complexities and the weight of social and historical positioning, approaching culture as an act of discovery offers the possibility of creating anew, of remaking identities and of envisioning change.

As these essays show, the secret and the forbidden constantly change and shift ground – and it is only by being conscious of what ground they hold that the territory may be revealed, eroded and transformed.

Fran Lloyd and Catherine O'Brien

PART I

THE LITERARY SPACES OF DESIRE

Chapter 1

Walls, Curtains and Screens: Spatio-Sexual Metaphor in the *Kagerô nikki*

Valerie Henitiuk

> Most men's clubs confine women to a special room, or annexe, and exclude them from other apartments, whether on the principle observed at St. Sofia that they are impure, or whether on the principle observed at Pompeii that they are too pure, is matter for speculation.
>
> Virginia Woolf, *Three Guineas*

Literature written by women has often tended to privilege interior space, and the examples afforded by Japan are no exception. Typical upper-class women of Japan's Heian period (eighth to twelfth century) spent their entire lives confined behind walls and doors, curtains and screens, all but immobilised in multiple layers of clothing. Nonetheless, from the depths of this isolation, Michitsuna no Haha (literally, the Mother of Michitsuna) and others were able to produce the diaries, poems, and romances that form the Classical Japanese literary canon.[1] In the three books that make up the *Kagerô nikki*, Michitsuna no Haha [2] records her married life, providing an extensive collection of *waka* poetry (she was and is acknowledged among the finest poets of her age) and exploring her various psychological states, particularly with regard to the impact of the Heian polygynous system.

Such texts as the *Kagerô nikki* are intimately concerned with the private sphere – the inner, emotional landscape of the female author and protagonist – and are thereby fertile ground for images of enclosure and violation. Although nominally structured around matrilineal inheritance and uxorilocal marriage, the social architecture was jealously controlled by the patriarchy. As valuable commodities in marriage politics, with the Fujiwara males plotting to marry their daughters into the Imperial family and thus produce grandsons who could become emperors, women had to be kept secure and virginal. Even among the lower aristocracy not in line for the throne, wives, mistresses, and daughters were, as a rule, closely guarded and expected to remain hidden from men in the outside world. Consequently, scenes of impassioned lovers fighting their way through tangled, overgrown gardens, past outer and inner gates, and finally penetrating the female inner sanctum are the stock in trade of Heian literature. Because the very act of being seen is tantamount to accepting a man as one's lover, visibility becomes a metaphor for exposure and virtual rape. As an *ie no onna* (literally, housewoman, one not employed at court), Michitsuna no Haha lives under constant threat of a wide range of violations – physical, visual, and aural – of her integrity. A dialectic of violation and retreat is played out in the metaphorical body of her diary, revealing unambiguous images concerned with spatial and corporeal integrity. This essay will examine how interiority is identified with the feminine, and the way in which the author of the *Kagerô nikki* resists, or offers a posture of resistance, to any violation of her private space by her husband and others.

While the sobriquet 'Michitsuna's Mother' conceals our author's identity, it nonetheless insists on the essential fact of her femininity. It must be underscored that literature by women in Japan, far from being marginalised, actually forms the foundations of the literary canon. Women such as Murasaki Shikibu and Sei Shônagon are among the most celebrated Japanese writers of either gender, and have profoundly influenced literature throughout that country's history. Among the Heian elite, rival male factions each sought to enhance their own prestige by attracting the most accomplished writers to serve as ladies-in-waiting to their female relatives. Accordingly, women were encouraged to express themselves in a variety of literary forms, including poems, letters, and prose narratives such as romances and diaries.

These women were subject to a twofold restriction that they paradoxically managed to turn to full advantage. First, similarly to the use of Latin by educated men throughout much of European history, the men at the Heian court employed Chinese in their writings. Women were generally required by custom and education to write in their native Japanese, using the new *onna-de* (literally, woman's hand) syllabary of *hiragana*. While this script was far from the exclusive preserve of the female sex (men did use it in corresponding with their lovers, for example), it was nonetheless highly gendered. The women thus enjoyed the freedom and ease of writing in their mother tongue, rather than in a second language, and created unforgettable characters and situations. Second, the patriarchal social structure also restricted Heian women to writing primarily within the private sphere. Therefore, they focused on detailed examinations of interpersonal behaviour rather than on more broad based historical or political discussions. Their works deal primarily with the psychological response of individuals to the subtleties of intimate relationships, and do so with immense beauty and power.

For females in the Heian period, as in much of history, the integrity of their person was precarious in the extreme. A matrilineal society, with homes and property inherited along the female line, would seem to imply a strong notion of security for women. Nonetheless, if we consider the comparatively flimsy constructions of traditional Japanese housing (wood, paper and straw rather than brick or concrete, for instance), the validity of taking the woman-owned house as a guarantee of safety becomes compromised. More than one critic has rightly commented on 'the insubstantiality of Heian residential architecture and the penetrability of courtyard gardens' (Coats, 1993: 56), and, indeed, the intruder motif is central to *The Tale of Genji* and other works of the period. A woman without a nearby influential male to protect her real estate and, by extension, herself, is constantly exposed to violation on numerous fronts. And once she has attracted a protector, her unending task becomes the retention of his loyalty, for any abandoned woman has not only been insulted by one man's rejection but finds herself open to potential abuse at the hands of others. The *Kagerô nikki* constitutes 'an unvarnished account of what happens when a girl without powerful family backing embarks on a marriage with a man who can divorce her simply by ceasing to visit or communicate with her' (McCullough, 1990: 73). Far from wholeheartedly embarking on this union, our author is fully cognisant of the frightening loss of autonomy it represents.

From the very start of their relationship, Kaneie's attentions are presented as unwelcome and more than mildly threatening. It should be noted that this politically powerful man was already involved with several other wives and mistresses, in accordance with the custom of the day. Despite her initial rebuffs, 'he sends a retainer riding on a horse to pound on [her] gate.[3] Rather than interpreting this aggression positively as the actions of an ardent lover, Michitsuna no Haha attempts to reject and ignore her suitor. When required by family and friends to respond with a poem, she does not pretend to offer him any encouragement: 'do not flutter a voice that / will be quite to no avail' (KD: 59). Although the text is admittedly ambiguous on this score, it is likely that she would prefer celibacy to marriage with this man, who is elsewhere depicted 'as a forceful, arrogant man, insensitive to the feelings of others' (McCullough, 1990: 71). While continuing to view Kaneie's suit as a hostile invasion of her independence, our narrator ends by accepting him, and this diary reveals the ample opportunity she has to experience his insensitivity thereafter.

Perversely enough, for Kaneie, the barriers she erects in her resistance (actual and postured) serve merely to heighten his interest and desire. Michitsuna no Haha is not simply playing hard to get, however. She would prefer what has been called the 'luxury ... reserved for the well-born' (Peel, 1993: 114): a form of indirectness where all interpersonal communication takes place primarily via the elegant and highly mediated written word rather than direct and potentially clumsy physical contact.[4] As one discussion of Richardson's *Clarissa* notes, 'letters, like rooms and dresses, protect and present and enclose the self' (Brownstein, 1994: 60). This is not to suggest that our author does not grow to love her husband and desire his attentions, for at least some of this rejection and withdrawal is in fact a conceit of the resisting female that had developed within their society. Regardless, the metaphors embedded in this text suggest that her resistance is frequently sincere.

On several occasions, Kaneie is pictured as encroaching violently upon Michitsuna no Haha's space, in intrusions described so as to prompt the reader to see them virtually as assault, sexual or otherwise. For example:

> On the evening of the second, he suddenly appeared ... he shouts all over the house. I am startled and feel anger boil up,

> then pushing away this attendant, pulling that one toward him ..., then imitating me in a simpering way, he upsets my attendants. I was quite struck dumb, and, sitting across from him, I must have ended up looking drained and completely beaten. (KD: 215–17)

And later:

> Suddenly he bursts in, takes the incense burner and other usual implements for the day's observances and scatters them about, takes my rosary and throws it up on a high shelf, and otherwise behaves in a wild manner. It was astounding. (KD: 259)

The above images resemble those of an invading force pillaging conquered territory, riding roughshod over an enemy now completely in its power. As well, it is significant that the second passage involves religious paraphernalia – he is in effect ransacking a place of worship[5] and striking at a person's most intimate aspect, her spirituality. This latter invasion is, nevertheless, not without its redeeming qualities. Michitsuna no Haha underscores the contradictions inherent in interpersonal relationships by having the scene lead to a day spent in welcome intimacy between husband and wife.

On another occasion, their young son is co-opted into a joint violation of the narrator's space and stated intentions. Toying mercilessly with Michitsuna's parental loyalties, Kaneie uses the boy as an instrument of torment against his wife:

> 'If that is how it is, one way or another, it is for you to decide. If she will leave, then let's have the carriage drawn up.' Before [Kaneie] had finished saying this, my son leaped up and just began to gather all the things scattered around, wrapping them up, stuffing into bags the things that needed packing and stowing it all away in the carriage. Then he took down the curtains and folded up other things, roughly packing it all away. I sat there dazed. (KD: 253)

The son is learning how to oppress and control women, and as he appropriates her space and belongings, his mother is forced to recognise her offspring's membership in and identification with the patriarchy.

A strong, independent woman (at least for her time), Michitsuna no Haha does exhibit genuine protest in a number of ways. She employs discouraging facial expressions and blanket refusals to see him to indicate when Kaneie's visits are unwanted: 'With a look on my face of *what are you doing here*, I did not welcome him in, and finding things very uncomfortable, he left' [Original Emphasis] (KD: 81), and 'since I did not go out from my inner chamber to meet him, it was painful for him to stay, so he left' (KD: 93–4). She also frequently attempts to protect her boundaries by placing partitions between them (see Arntzen, 1997: 219, 215, 255). Nevertheless, the fact that these efforts at self-insulation accomplish little is explicitly recognised: 'Just as he entered, I drew a rather poor screen in front of me; while it hid a bit of me, it was really quite useless' (KD: 253). One night, she goes so far as deliberately to refuse him access to her home: 'just before dawn ... there was a knocking on my gate. Thinking that it must be him, I felt wretched, and as I did not have the gate opened, he went off to that other place' (KD: 71) – that place being the home of a recently acquired mistress. It requires no difficult feat of imagination to interpret this passage as a metaphor for a woman preserving her bodily integrity against harassing sexual overtures. The gate does not remain locked every night, however, and none of the omnipresent physical barriers – walls, curtains, or screens – provide any effective defence in the long run.

It is instructive to consider Michitsuna no Haha's all-consuming hatred of her rival from the perspective of the female self-identification with her home. It should be noted in this context that our author designates her husband's mistress as the Machi Alley woman – following the traditional manner in which a woman was identified by the street where she lived. By writing to this other woman while in his wife's house, or even by just leaving the letter lying about there for her to find, Kaneie has all but physically introduced his new lover into his wife's space. Figuratively speaking, through the mediation of the male, this rival has successfully invaded the sphere that Michitsuna no Haha claims as exclusively her own, and this infidelity thus constitutes a violation of her territory in a way none of the others do.[6] Our narrator is under no illusion that she is the only woman in Kaneie's life; it is the betrayal of her spatial integrity on this occasion that shocks and deeply pains her.

Even when Kaneie absents himself from her house, he manages to give the impression of violating Michitsuna no Haha on an auditory level. She is forced to endure the rattling of wheels as her husband and his entourage travel to Machi Alley or elsewhere: 'It was such a racket, so painful to my ears, and did he really have to pass right by my gate?' (KD: 81). The author obsesses about hearing him on the outskirts of her property, to the point where she 'could not help hearing him clear his throat as he passed by' (KD: 77). The normal barriers are revealed as fatally permeable to tormenting noise: 'at night, the sounds of the carriages rumbling outside would set my heart pounding' (KD: 195). Neither are they adequate to isolate her from rumours of his affairs and her ensuing emotional devastation: 'Hearing such whispered gossip, I feel so unhappy; the fall of each evening is just wretched' (KD: 79). The theme of aural violations of her spatial integrity as a particularly insidious form of torture is returned to time and time again in this diary. Considering how little visual input she normally enjoys, locked away in what Ivan Morris terms 'her twilight world of curtains, screens, and thick silk hangings' (1985: 217), it comes as no surprise that the Heian woman would privilege her other senses. One can easily picture the narrator sitting helplessly with her hands over her ears, trying to block out the sounds of Kaneie going elsewhere with his 'usual ostentatious fuss' (KD: 229), or alternatively the dead silence that indicates he is not coming at all on a given evening, and share the 'searing pain' (KD: 229) of her humiliation.

The arrival of Tônori, who comes to offer courtship to the adopted daughter, offers yet another example of the vulnerability of the female space to libidinous males. He bombards their house with pleading correspondence until finally allowed to visit. Michitsuna no Haha attempts to keep him at bay and, denying she is even at home, leaves him sitting alone on the veranda. Nonetheless, the man is not so easily deterred; coming again another night, he makes his way past the veranda into the gallery room. In an implicit recognition of this act of trespass, Tônori pauses to have his respects conveyed to his hostess. Michitsuna no Haha acknowledges this delicacy with her reply, mocking and yet not ungracious: 'He has my leave to come and speak in this place that he has been so interested in' (KD: 341), and invites him to sit with her son in an inner room. A lamp is lit for the two men, and Tônori talks with Michitsuna while the narrator remains discretely apart in a curtained enclosure: 'Within, I made not a sound.' Michitsuna no Haha eventually enters into conversation with the suitor herself, secure in the belief that the external light renders her invisible. Upon this guest's departure, however, she realises that 'the light placed on the veranda had gone out sometime before' (KD: 343) and that she was thus exposed to his gaze (albeit as nothing more than a dim shadow) by a lamp 'placed behind something within'. She is 'appalled' by even this meagre visual violation, for in her society, such seemingly inconsequential exposure is fraught with meaning:

> By the Heian period, the visibility of women was extremely restricted. For a woman to allow her face to be seen by a man was tantamount to accepting him as a lover. The romantic literary consequence was the *kaimami*, in which the unseen hero steals a glimpse of a lady through a gap in the fence or an opening in her curtains, a deed that could be termed visual rape. (Field, 1987: 123)

In an attitude common to all of her upper-class contemporaries, Michitsuna no Haha prides herself on normally allowing no breach whereby the voyeuristic male could surreptitiously invade her privacy.

While peeping toms are a constant danger, the complementary image of the woman within, seeing unseen, is used to great advantage by many Japanese writers of the period. This is not to deny that such scenes appear sparingly in the literature, and presumably in real life as well, given that other people do not always cooperate by coming within visual range of women who are unable to roam freely in the outside world. Regardless, this particular diary does offer a number of descriptions of the narrator looking at the outside world from her home, an ox-drawn carriage, or the various temples and shrines she visits (see Arntzen, 1997: 153, 159, 197–201).

Ironically, despite the fact that real power is ineluctably enshrined in the masculine, a woman's segregated, interior position awards her possession of the gaze and thus the status of subject rather than object. Field makes the point that, with certain limitations, 'women were always able to see – that is, look through and out' (Field, 1987: 337) the curtains, screens, and shades set up to conceal them. The degree of visibility the Heian female enjoyed depended, of course, on the lighting conditions and the willingness of gentlemen to come calling. The view from within nonetheless claims the inner space, shielded from the external bustle and glare, as inherently feminine. Invisibility reserves a certain amount of power for a woman, something she is wise enough not to surrender lightly.

During a subsequent visit by Tônori, he becomes emboldened enough to demand 'the satisfaction of waiting on [Michitsuna no Haha] within [her] curtains' (KD: 347) and actually raises his hand to the said curtain with the intention of forcing his way inside. Numerous incidents of swooning females yielding passively before similar intrusions can be found throughout *The Tale of Genji*, for example. It is an indication of our narrator's hard-earned sense of self that she is able to fend off her daughter's supposed suitor with, in contrast, astounding presence of mind. She is able to stand her ground precisely because she is conscious of it being *her ground*. She defuses the situation by responding coolly to Tônori's impertinent proposition, and he has no choice but to apologise and beat a hasty retreat from the space both acknowledge to be hers.

Seeing to the maintenance of their wives' and concubines' homes comprised an important part of the duties of Heian husbands and lovers. Accordingly, the narrator explicitly equates Kaneie's neglect of her property with neglect of her person:

> my house, with no one to take it in hand, falls into a worse and worse state of disrepair. And that my husband can come and go without noticing a thing makes me feel especially forlorn; when I think that it must indicate a lack of deep regard for me, a thousand weeds of worry grow rank in my mind. (KD: 135)

The fact that he allows her 'rundown house [to be] overrun with mugwort' (KD: 135) demonstrates how little this wife occupies Kaneie's thoughts. The disintegration can also be taken as a metaphor for the physical ageing that leads to the inevitable fading of a female's youthful beauty, and thus her devaluation in the patriarchal system. It has been pointed out that 'the decay and destruction of architectural settings symbolises for several characters the loss of power and prestige' (Coats, 1993: 58). It is easy to imagine the impact such blatant neglect by the male would have for this woman and others whose identity is inextricably bound up with their homes.

In the latter part of Book One, Michitsuna no Haha pays a highly unconventional visit to her husband's home. This escapade has somewhat erotic overtones as the woman assumes the masculine role, venturing not only into the outside world but also directly into the personal space of another. The pleasure she feels in travelling secretly to Kaneie's residence and herself acting the intruder is intense. On another, somewhat more straightforward level, naturally, the fact that he desires her presence so much that he has her brought to him is immensely flattering and satisfies her notion of ideal love. In a translator's note, Sonja Arntzen comments that 'her visit to his place is clearly one of the most romantic episodes in her marriage' (Arntzen, 1997: 126). Similarly, despite herself, the narrator indulges in romantic conjecture where she dreams of being asked to relinquish her autonomy entirely and share a dwelling with her husband: '*ah, truly, that splendid place he is building – but … even though he says, "I want to show it to you soon," things will turn out as they will*' [Original Emphasis] (KD: 175). When this fantasy proves unfounded, however, she quickly acknowledges its inappropriateness for someone with her fierce territorial bent: 'as for me, just as I thought, I am to remain where I am and I suppose that's best' (KD: 191).

It is important to note that, while the *shinden* (literally, sleeping hall, but used as a generic term for the residential architecture of the aristocracy) may be viewed as a repressive domicile within which women are immured, it far more frequently serves as a feminine refuge in mid-Heian prose. Figuring prominently in nineteenth-century English novels written by women is a claustrophobic 'female figure … trapped – even buried – in the architecture of a patriarchal society, and imagining, dreaming, or actually devising escape routes, roads past walls … to the glittering town outside' (Gilbert and Gubar, 1979: 313). Conversely, a woman in tenth-century Japan knows that she will find security of person only within the walls, in a withdrawal into her personal sphere. Critic Norma Field has commented that many examples of pilgrimages to famous shrines such as Uji are metaphorically retreats to *uchi*, the inner self. Although Michitsuna no Haha does once burst out of her home in a powerful image of escape (the start of her Ishiyama pilgrimage), she generally opts instead to retreat farther inside some sort of enclosure in an effort to escape the ever-intrusive male.[7] It is worth noting that when Kaneie offers to come and meet her after her pilgrimage to Hase, she responds as follows: 'I am thinking of going … even deeper into the mountains' (KD: 157). While it may be overly literal to read this particular line as a clear statement of rejection, the very telling comment made during the aforementioned pilgrimage to Ishiyama Temple supports the general idea: '"They say the entrance to that valley draws you in and you never get out. It's a dangerous place." Hearing things like this, I thought, *without even intending it, if only I could be drawn in and swallowed up*' [Original Emphasis] (KD: 211).

A cloistered life, that of the nun she yearns to become, is consistently and increasingly desperately the objective sought by the narrator. Given that the interior is *her* space, it functions as sanctuary rather than imprisonment, offering Michitsuna no Haha some protection from the belligerent male gaze and behaviour to which she would otherwise be subjected by both family and strangers. The 'sheer need to announce a departure from the world of men' (Field, 1987: 190) is an important part of her desire to retreat into a mountain temple and take the tonsure.

Turning her back on the public world, which is not after all the world she knows, our author's outlook 'revolves around the private life, her only sphere of activity' (Miyake, 1989: 96). Not for the average married woman is the 'external, outward-gazing world of the male courtier, the active world of people coming and going, the arena of public poetry recitations at banquets, court events, and other social gatherings' (Miyake, 1989: 95). Instead, mid-Heian women's literature shares a common focus on 'the hidden, inner space of a woman's sexual feelings' (Bundy, 1991: 85) as it examines the imbalance inherent to social relationships. As Lynne K. Miyake comments: 'Sitting at home (or in her little niche provided for her at court), isolated, and often waiting longingly for her lover, the woman turned her gaze inward and recorded the workings of her soul' (Miyake, 1989: 90). Writers and readers have frequently been taught to consider the exterior, peopled by men, as hostile to the female half of the species, which helps explain why women have tended to turn their attention to the interior, domestic sphere. Of course, the equation 'home = refuge' does not preclude the simultaneous associations of the life-sentence that must be served there. For, in allowing the male into her space, willingly or not, Michitsuna's Mother has simultaneously allowed him to take a place in her heart and life, and thus feels pain when he neglects her. Our narrator is forced to spend years in a more or less solitary state of anticipation, hoping against hope that Kaneie will deign to come by. To a Western reader, the parallel with such characters as Jane Austen's unmarried Bennet sisters, doomed to sit decorously in their drawing room awaiting suitors who may or may not appear, is striking.[8] Regardless, while the domestic sphere does play this contradictory role of jail and sanctuary, it is the latter that is privileged throughout this text.

Michitsuna no Haha plays repeatedly with the motifs of intrusion and retreat in her *Kagerô nikki*, describing scenes that depict variously successful threats to her spatial and bodily integrity. Like other female characters in this literature, she makes use of her physical surroundings to define and protect herself, eternally seeking to resist penetration of her boundaries by Kaneie and others. From beginning to end, interiority is unambiguously aligned with the feminine, and functions as a metaphor for the ever-vulnerable female body. Entrenched within the refuge of her home, Michitsuna no Haha wages this struggle to shield herself from the intrusive behaviour of the male, both physically and visually. While occasionally successful in winning a battle against the hostile patriarchal forces of her society, she is doomed ultimately to lose the war over respect for her personal, private space.

Notes

1. This is not to deny that other important writers such as Sei Shônagon and Murasaki Shikibu spent several years serving as ladies-in-waiting to an empress and were thus hardly in a position of isolation. Nonetheless, there is evidence that the latter had completed at least part of her masterpiece *The Tale of Genji* while still in private life. In addition, court service lasted a finite term, and the fact remains that women were allowed far less intercourse with the world at large than their male counterparts.
2. Michitsuna is the author's son by her husband, Kaneie. During the Heian period, it was considered improper to record the names of women, other than empresses, imperial consorts, and so on. Women authors of the time have normally thus come down to posterity by the names and/or titles of their male relations, as, for example, with Takasue's Daughter, author of *The Floating Bridge of Dreams*, and Sei Shônagon (Sei = Sino-Japanese reading of family name 'Kiyowara'; Shônagon = her father's title), author of *The Pillow Book*. This rule also holds true for Murasaki Shikibu, since while 'Murasaki' is borrowed from one of her characters, 'Shikibu' was a title her father held at one point in his career.
3. S. Arntzen, trans., *The Kagerô Diary* [*Kagerô nikki*], 57. All further quotations from this translation will be abbreviated as KD, followed by page number in this edition.
4. Although there is no space in this paper for such an endeavour, it would be of great interest to examine the use Michitsuna no Haha makes of her poetry in establishing and maintaining relationships, on the one hand, and, on the other, keeping people at a distance.
5. Much later, of course, Freud was to explain churches as a dream metaphor for female genitalia, offering support for interpreting this scene as a figurative rape.
6. Michitsuna no Haha's willingness to discuss openly with her husband matters concerning his principal wife Tokihime may be offered as an argument against this interpretation. However, since Tokihime preceded our author into Kaneie's life, she has always been considered a given fact rather than a newly introduced threat. Similarly, in the scene where the narrator shares a laugh with Kaneie over some infelicitous poetry composed by another of his lovers (see Arntzen, 1997: 287), the element of threat to their marital relationship is again lacking.
7. The following comment by Roselee Bundy is of interest in this context: 'In the city, the Mother of Michitsuna lived on the fringes of Kaneie's life, sequestered in her house. In her residence in the temple, she makes herself

the center of all action and the story's main protagonist' (Bundy, 1991: 92). In other words, by travelling to a temple outside the limits of a city that is the locus of male power, she ironically gains centrality and importance.

8. In an echo of the situations that had concerned women writers halfway around the world some eight hundred years earlier, another Austen heroine, Anne Eliot, comments that women 'live at home, quiet, confined, and our feelings prey upon us' (*Persuasion*, cited in Gilbert and Gubar, 1979: 60).

CHAPTER 2

SECRETS OF THE FORBIDDEN CHAMBER: BLUEBEARD

Tivadar Gorilovics

The forbidden chamber or door is a familiar element in the world of fairy stories, along with ogres, genies and wicked wizards. The theme of prohibition, which may appear in other combinations in this type of narrative, is here associated with a particular action (entering a room, opening a particular door). While this motif is traditionally present in the literature of folklore, it is also found in modern fiction, for example in the work of the Marquis de Sade[1] or of Oscar Wilde. In *The Portrait of Dorian Gray*, entering the secret room that contains the fatal portrait costs its painter, Basil Hallward, his life. The prohibition may be restricted to a simple test of the incorrigible curiosity of human beings, which is punished for itself, as in the story of 'The Third Calendar' of *The Thousand and One Nights* (1965 I: 175–205). In this story a young prince spends a year being cosseted by forty very beautiful and obliging young women in an enchanted castle. At the end of the year they leave him for forty days, giving him 'the keys to everything, and particularly those of the hundred doors, in which [they tell him] "you will find what you need to satisfy your curiosity and ease your loneliness while we are away"' (1965: 195). There is one door that he is forbidden to open or, rather, strongly warned against opening, and this is the Golden Door. The lucky prince only needs to hold out for forty days, yet the wonders that he finds behind the permitted doors arouse his curiosity to such an extent that he eventually gives in to the temptation to open the Golden Door. He is carried off by a magic horse, which blinds him in the right eye with its tail.[2]

The consequences of transgressing the prohibition are far more serious when the door hides some dreadful secret. In such a case the desire to know leads to a misdeed, the inevitable punishment for which is either death or the threat of death. When the prohibition is uttered by a man or equivalent (for example a wizard, as in the Brothers Grimm's *Fitcher's Bird*) it is generally a woman who gives in to temptation; the reputation of the daughters of Eve in this regard is solidly established in the Judeo-Christian tradition. Bruno Bettelheim has shown that, in such fairy stories, the secrets of the forbidden chamber are explicitly associated with sexuality, for example in relation to marriage; as an illustration he cites *The Enchanted Pig*, in which a book that reveals the secrets is locked away in a room that the three sisters are not allowed to enter (Bettelheim, 1978: 295–303). Similarly, there may be masculine secrets that the woman wants to uncover, despite the formal prohibition guarding them, as in the story of Bluebeard.

Universally known since the first appearance of Charles Perrault's version, the tale of Bluebeard exploits the motif of the forbidden chamber to the maximum, and I shall thus concentrate exclusively on this story and its avatars. However, as Bettelheim also observed, it is not curiosity alone that is at work in such cases: 'Whether it is Bluebeard or the sorcerer in *Fitcher's Bird*, it seems clear that when the male gives the female a key to a room, while at the same time instructing her not to enter, it is a test of her faithfulness to his orders or, in a broader sense, to him' (Bettelheim, 1978: 300). Although, as I shall try to show, this observation does not really apply to the precise example of Bluebeard, it does highlight the absolutely crucial motif of disobedience. It seems likely that it is unconditional obedience that is really at issue in the test that the woman undergoes and to which, in fact, anyone could be subjected, regardless of gender. However, in the story of Bluebeard, the antagonistic relationship between the sexes manifests itself in all its violence. The powerful male, who has 'secrets', appropriates the (inalienable) right to guard them by any means. Proof, if it were needed, is offered by the question of what Bluebeard's *first* wife could have seen in the forbidden room.

The tale of Bluebeard made such an impression that it has since been reworked many times, with the same imaginative and interpretative freedom as has been displayed in the rewriting of the great founding myths of European civilisation. These versions will be compared, both with the original story as developed by Charles Perrault and with each other, to bring out the novelty or degree of originality of the different versions in relation to the original story. Of the very many later versions, only a few have been selected for discussion, for a variety of reasons.[3] These are Grétry's opera, *Raoul, Barbe Bleue* (1789), Ludwig Tieck's *Ritter Blaubart* (1797), Offenbach's comic opera (1866)[4] and works by Anatole France (1908), Maurice Maeterlinck[5] and Béla Bartók.[6]

Charles Perrault's tale of Bluebeard relates:

> Once upon a time there was a man who had fine houses in Town and Country, crockery of gold and silver, gilded furniture and carriages; yet, unfortunately, this man had a blue beard. This made him so ugly and fearsome that there was not a woman or girl who did not run away from him. (1981: 149)

We are thus dealing with a great lord who lives surrounded by opulence, but whose physical ugliness frightens both women, who are assumed to have enough experience of love, and girls, who are presumed to be innocent. The expression of this ugliness (and emblem of virility) is the colour of his beard, which was, according to the usual explanation, a bluish black.[7] When Bluebeard seeks a bride, his neighbour's two daughters are at first reluctant 'because he had already married two women and no one knew what had happened to those women'. However a well-organised party changes the mind of the younger, who 'began to think that the Master of the house no longer had such a blue beard and that he was a very decent man' (1981: 149). Her observation makes us think of the words of cruel La Rochefoucauld: 'Virtues are lost in self-interest as rivers are lost in the sea.' So they are married and a month later Bluebeard goes away 'on important business', leaving his young wife with all the keys of the house (total freedom to amuse herself as she chooses and to spend money as she wishes), with one prohibition:

> the key to the little room at the end of the great gallery in the lower apartment: open everything, go everywhere, but where that little room is concerned, I forbid you to enter it, and I forbid you so strongly that, if you do happen to open it, you can expect no limits to my anger. (1981: 150)

This prohibition, which is given no more justification than those issued by God in the Bible, is accompanied by a threat of punishment in the event of transgression. It is abundantly obvious that the forbidden chamber contains some secret, hence the temptation to curiosity. Indeed the narrator relates that 'the temptation was so strong that she could not overcome it' (1981: 151). While her friends and neighbours are quick to take advantage of the absence of her fearsome husband by exploring the castle, openly expressing their envy at the luxurious surroundings, she hurries to the door of the little room, which, 'trembling', she eventually opens.

We know what happens next: in this room she comes upon the horrible sight of the murdered women's bodies and drops the key, from which she cannot afterwards remove the bloodstains, 'for the key was Fairy' and, when Bluebeard returns, she has to take the consequences of her disobedience, in other words, death.

The narrator, who sides with 'the poor woman', shows her 'at her Husband's feet, weeping and begging his forgiveness, with all the signs of true repentance for not having been obedient', but Bluebeard remains unmoved. The wife is shown as a remorseful woman who displays the quintessential Christian feeling of repentance, while the husband maintains an attitude of deliberate bad faith in which his total lack of mercy, hard-heartedness and refusal to forgive are no more than a sham, since Bluebeard has calculated and foreseen everything. The woman's brothers who come and kill him are thus simply dispensers of justice, whose intervention makes it possible for the story to have a happy ending. We learn that the heroine then manages 'to marry a very decent man, who made her forget the bad time she had spent with Bluebeard' (1981: 154).

Before moving to an examination of the literary (and musical) reworkings of this story, it is worth noting the psychoanalytical reading as proposed by Bruno Bettelheim. Above and beyond its obvious hermeneutic aims, this reading constitutes, in my eyes at least, a kind of rewriting in so far as it seems to stretch the resources of Perrault's text unnecessarily.

Bettelheim sees the prohibition as a test of the wife's conjugal fidelity and honesty. For him the ban is not so much a trap as a test. Such a view can be justified only if Bluebeard is an honest man and his wife has been guilty of infidelity, and this is indeed what Bettelheim thinks. 'It is left to our imagination', he explains, 'what went on between the woman and her guests with Bluebeard away, but the story makes it clear [!]

that everybody had a high time. The blood ...on the key seems to symbolise that [the heroine] had sexual relations. Therefore we can understand her anxious fantasy which depicts corpses of women who had been killed for having been similarly unfaithful' (1978: 301). Although Bettelheim accepts that this is not the only possible interpretation of Perrault's tale[8] and that the story of Blue Beard can also be read as one which shows 'the destructive aspects of sex', he is visibly attached to the motif of 'sexual temptation' (1978: 301).

Since the story of Bluebeard takes place in an *Ancien Régime* setting, it is quite natural that it should have been reworked into a 'revolutionary' version, a liberation story in the genre of Beethoven's *Fidelio*. In Sedaine's scenario, the knight Raoul is a feudal tyrant who holds the beautiful Isaura captive. She is freed by the brave Vergi, who is the true hero of the story. Isaura's liberation is also the triumph of light over darkness, in other words, the triumph of freedom.

In Ludwig Tieck's dramatised tale, Bluebeard (whose name, Hugo von Wolfsbrunn, connotes wolves) is a rich lord and a hardened and brave warrior, who asks for the hand of Agnes von Friedheim, a happy, lively girl who, despite her husband's blue beard, is not afraid of him at all. The first three acts of this play are taken up with a long introduction, involving numerous characters, and Bluebeard does not appear until Act IV. Apart from this, Tieck follows Perrault's tale fairly closely, although he does make an effort to give it a psychological dimension, on the one hand by a lengthy analysis of Agnes's growing curiosity and, on the other, a no less lengthy account of the reasons that have made the husband test his young wife. According to the mistrustful husband, curiosity is the quintessential sin of the daughters of Eve and this misogynist's worst fear is that he will be cuckolded. 'Woe', says he, 'to the deceived man who trusts to the false charms of women, to the innocence of their eyes and their smiles... Deceit is a woman's trade.' Instead of murdering his wives, Tieck's Bluebeard condemns them to death and executes them. Isaura is freed by her two brothers, finds another, less dangerous, suitor and sees her sister Anne married; in other words it all ends happily, as in Perrault's tale.

In contrast, Offenbach's opera was intended as a social satire in which Count Oscar, Chamberlain of King Bobèche, sets out to look for the king's daughter, who has disappeared, while Prince Bluebeard's alchemist, Popolani, goes in search of a self-proclaimed virgin by the name of Boulotte, who is to be his master's sixth wife. When Boulotte arrives at the court, her uncouth manners and use of slang words raise eyebrows. In the meantime we learn that Popolani has hidden the women whom Bluebeard has told him to kill in a cellar. However, nothing is really taken seriously in this play, with its complicated, amusing plot and engagingly cynical Bluebeard, who sings, 'No widower ever was happier than I' – a good-natured Bluebeard with a bohemian lifestyle. In this case the reworking of Perrault's tale takes it in the direction of derision, following the well-established rules of the parodic genre which Second Empire theatre seems to have been so fond of.

It seems possible that Anatole France had at least an unconscious recollection of this parodic version when writing his own, forty years later. His text begins by debunking a 'certain school of comparative mythology', which taught, he says,

> that the seven wives of Bluebeard were the dawns and his two brothers-in-law the dusks of morning and evening... Those who might be tempted to believe this should remember that an erudite bookseller in Agen ... proved, in 1817, in a highly specious manner, that Napoleon had never existed and that the story of this so-called great captain was nothing but a solar myth.

France also rejects the hypothesis identifying Bluebeard as the marshal of France, Gilles de Rais, believing this to be one of the many legends that abound in literature and historiography (France, 1930: 127–29). Although his Bluebeard, called Bernard de Montragoux, is physically highly virile and enjoys an immense fortune, he is in reality an extremely timid man, manipulated and remorselessly exploited by women. This is revealed through his successive marriages. His neighbour, who has two daughters to marry off, is a ruined widow who 'had instantly focused her attention on M. de Montragoux, whom she saw to be simple, easy to deceive, very gentle and quick to fall in love beneath his rough, untamed exterior' (1930: 147). Her daughter Jeanne, who becomes this inoffensive Bluebeard's seventh wife, regularly meets her lover in a little room that resembles Perrault's famous forbidden chamber in name only. The entire story of Bluebeard is thus turned inside-out, stripped of both the motif of the forbidden room and its fantastical element, the bloodstained key that strikes fear into the heart of Perrault's heroine. Here the victim is not the woman but the husband, the archetypal duped husband of classical comedy. The fact that, in France's work, Bluebeard's wife is aided by two brothers who are real villains does not change the fact that the narrator's chief target here is woman, and particularly woman in the context of marriage.

Maeterlinck's version, which in fact predates that of France, is of a quite different nature. Maeterlinck completely changes the basic elements of Perrault's tale. Ariane (whose name brings with it all the prestige of Greek mythology, associated as it is with that of Theseus, killer of the Minotaur) is not the weak, naive, curious and tearful wife of Perrault's tale; she is a woman of character who, though not insensible to Bluebeard's seductiveness and quite aware that rumours are circulating about her, takes him as her husband. Once wed, she stands up to him and refuses to be under his control, like a true militant campaigner for the emancipation of women. It seems she has agreed to marriage only with the firm intention of challenging the institution's long-held principles, including that of the unconditional obedience of the wife, who is expected to accept, with Molière's unforgettable Arnolphe, that all the power lies with the bearded side. As soon as she appears, Maeterlinck's Ariane declares: 'He loves me, I am beautiful and I shall have his secret. The first thing to do is disobey; it is the first duty when the command is threatening and unexplained' (1901: 133).

If Ariane wants to know Bluebeard's secret, it is not out of simple curiosity. Bluebeard himself (whose beard is never mentioned in the text of the play) is no longer the vulgar murderer guided only by the death drive; he is a husband who seems to love his wife, as long as, of course, she accepts her duty of absolute obedience to him and gives up trying to find out his 'secret', which in this case probably means his past. In Maeterlinck's work Bluebeard plays a part formerly attributed to Satan, that of aping god; for, unlike Perrault's character, he is ready to forgive the guilty party once the sin of disobedience has been committed. 'Give up seeking to know', he says to her, 'and I can forgive' (Maeterlinck, 1901: 143). This must also have happened with the wives who preceded Ariane. In Maeterlinck's version, instead of corpses lining the walls there are 'simply' well-trained women, reduced to shadowy lives in an underground chamber in the castle which becomes the forbidden room for each newcomer.

This is where Maeterlinck's Ariane upsets the *status quo*: instead of allowing herself to be turned into the guilty culprit by the Master of secrets, she confronts him with the duty of transparency, which she states is the very condition of his own freedom. In so doing, she takes on the rebel's role and is supported by the peasant crowds, in other words, by a popular revolt. This, given that the play was written in the 1900s, at a time when many workers' protest movements were surfacing, gives the story a highly-charged social dimension that is understandably entirely lacking from Perrault's tale. It is the peasants who save Ariane from Bluebeard rather than her dragoon and musketeer brothers. Ariane is in no way a victim; on the contrary, she is a 'heroine' in the full sense of the word, who plays her part as a solitary rebel to the end. Although she does not succeed in persuading her sisters that they should leave their shadowy existence as wives reduced to nothing, her moral victory is nevertheless complete. When the peasants bring Bluebeard back before her, 'solidly garrotted' and bleeding from his wounds, instead of finishing him off, she cuts the cords that bind him and, giving him one last kiss on the forehead, leaves him to the only wives he deserves, his weak and consenting victims.

Maeterlinck's work returns to the motif of the permitted and forbidden doors, but whereas in Perrault's tale the number of doors is not given, Maeterlinck's text mentions six silver keys for those that may be opened and one golden key for the forbidden door. In Perrault's tale the keys to the permitted doors give access to Bluebeard's riches, which he allows his wife to enjoy in total freedom, without any restrictions. In Maeterlinck's work, each room that can be freely entered contains an enormous pile of precious stones, differing in type from room to room. However, despite appearances, the purpose of these 'treasure-houses of nuptial jewellery' is not to display the Master's wealth, but rather to enable the author to play a subtle game of poetic symbolism, using the various connotations and symbolic values that can be attached to the stones (see Chevalier and Gheerbrant, 1982). From room to room we pass; from the violet amethyst, symbol of temperance and humility, to the blue sapphire, celestial stone of purity and hope which is said to guard against the wrath of lords and to increase courage; from the rare, pure and precious pearl, lunar symbol linked to water and woman, Greek emblem of love and marriage and image of the Kingdom of Heaven in the gospel (Matthew 13: 45–46), to the enigmatic green emerald, stone of secret knowledge, which was so often used as a talisman; from the red ruby, the blood stones which Ariane sees as a sinister presage of threat, to the diamond, the only stone with which Ariane is willing to decorate 'her hair, arms, throat and hands' (Maeterlinck, 1901: 138) as diamonds are at once limpid, hard, luminous and symbolic of perfection and even immortality, stones that drive away wild beasts, phantoms, sorcerers and all the terrors of the night. Ariane says of them,

> Oh, my pale diamonds! I was not looking for you, but I salute you on my road! Immortal, dew of light!... You are pure, tireless and will never die, and what dances in your fires ... is the passion of light that has penetrated everything, does not rest and has nothing left to vanquish but itself! (Maeterlinck, 1901: 138–9)

It is armed with this inner light, which the diamonds merely make visible, that Ariane descends through the forbidden door into the hall of shadows to try to free her captive sisters.

Bluebeard's Castle by Béla Balázs (1884–1949) and Béla Bartók is a 'mystery', much closer to Maeterlinck's play than to Perrault's tale.[9] Here, too, Bluebeard is not the husband of bad faith who wants nothing more than to catch his wife blatantly disobeying him and lying to him in order to kill her. His wife, Judith, does not follow the example of Perrault's younger daughter, but nor does she want to turn Bluebeard into another Holofernes. Béla Balázs's Judith is a woman who has left not only her family – father, mother and brother – to follow Bluebeard, but also her fiancé, which suggests that she has fallen suddenly and madly in love and betrayed those she loved before. The fear inspired by the blue beard of Perrault's great lord has been replaced by the seductiveness of the character, who himself also appears deeply attached to his new wife, although he cannot share the absolute love that she continually demonstrates. For this modern Bluebeard is in fact a torn and secretive man, incapable of letting go because he is irredeemably walled up in his solitude, imprisoned in an incommunicable past. This explains the honest scruples he feels when confronted with the enthusiasm of Judith, whom he tries to warn.

> Do you not hear the bell toll?
> Your mother is dressed in black.
> Your father is putting on his sabre.
> Your brother is saddling his mount.
> Are you still ready to follow me?

To which Judith replies,

> Bluebeard! If you drove me away,
> I would stop on your threshold,
> I would lie down on your threshold.[10]

In Balázs's version all the doors are closed and must remain so, in other words all the doors hide secrets. To Judith's question – 'why are they closed?' – Bluebeard replies: 'So that no one can look in.' However Bluebeard gives no orders, he simply asks his beloved not to seek to know. When they come to the seventh door he says, 'You are the light of my castle,/So kiss me without questioning me.' But Judith absolutely wants to know: 'I don't want you to keep/Doors closed to me.'

Rather than being 'very feminine', or simply 'very human', this attitude reflects the need to know and the desire to save the other. Judith wants the sunlight to flood the cold, dark castle. She therefore goes from door to door and the doors open one after the other on to places that are not always rooms; she discovers in turn a torture chamber, an arms store, Bluebeard's treasure (the only room that recalls Perrault's tale), a secret garden in the shadow of steep, sharp rocks, then the kingdom itself, all of Bluebeard's 'fine lands'. After these the sixth door opens on to 'a quiet, white lake, a motionless, white lake', the lake of tears.

The secrets behind the doors have one characteristic in common: in all of them there is blood everywhere. The man's past is nothing but an uninterrupted series of murders, whether real or symbolic, and total knowledge or confession of these would cast endless night over the lives of the lovers. The unbearable weight of omniscience is not for human beings.

The castle, it is clear, is the very soul of the man who is loved, which the woman who loves and is loved wants both to penetrate, in order to know all its secrets and, at the same time, to free from the shadows in which it struggles. Redeeming love, as Judith sees it, can be linked to the romantic tradition and, in particular, to the way in which the theme was treated in Wagner's *Lohengrin*. By entering the seventh door – behind which lie the bodies of Bluebeard's three wives – Judith agrees to become the guardian of the castle's night (i.e. Bluebeard's secrets) and, therefore, the fourth victim.

It may be that art in literature and music consists simply of the perpetual rewriting of a few great existential, and therefore fundamental, themes. These would include the importance in human life both of secrets, protected by all kinds of prohibitions and threats, and of irresistible curiosity – the powerful attraction exerted by the desire to know and, indeed, to know everything, though the adventure may lead to death itself. Such a view finds one possible illustration in the many versions of the tale of Bluebeard, where a simple story is literally re-invented and re-imagined in ways that reveal more about the secret desires, fears and anxieties of the authors – situated at particular historical and cultural junctures – and their negotiations of these complex issues, than any meaning embedded in the text.

Translated by Trista Selous

Notes

1. The 'separate chamber' into which Saint-Fond takes his victims in *Les Prospérités du vice*. When Juliette shows 'the most extreme curiosity as to the nature of the singular fantasy in which Saint-Fond indulged with the women to whom he made the final pronouncement', Mme de Clairville warns her against 'pursuing her mysterious passion' (Sade, 1969: 185–6).
2. Those who, like Barrès, celebrate human curiosity as the source of knowledge and love, cannot fail to disapprove of the morality of these stories. In 1891 Barrès noted: 'I read with dismay a little book for children in which curiosity was criticised' (Barrès, 1922: 6).
3. Among the historical works inspired by the character of Bluebeard we could also mention Huysmans' 'investigation' of Gilles de Rais in his novel *Là-bas*, but to include this work would be to introduce an entirely different set of questions, which would lead us away from the focus of our discussion.
4. For musical versions of *Bluebeard* that predate Bartók's opera, I have referred to the summaries provided by the Hungarian musicologist György Kroó (1962).
5. Without access to the scenario written by Maeterlinck himself, I have been unable to include the three-act opera by Paul Dukas (1907), which the *Petit Robert* dictionary of proper names resumes as follows:

   > Resolved to deliver the five wives who have fallen victim to Bluebeard, Ariane marries the fearsome monster. However when they are freed, the captive women prove so attached to their chains that Ariane leaves them to their fate.

   In any case Maeterlinck's play, which is much earlier than the opera, was entirely independent of it. According to Laffont-Bompiani's *Dictionnaire des personnages* (Bouquins, 1984), the argument of Dukas's opera seems to be very different from the 'tale in three acts'.
6. The 'mystery' by Béla Balázs (1910–1911), which first appeared in a magazine and was dedicated to Bartók and Kodály, was reworked in 1912 and became the scenario for Bartók's one-act opera (opus 11), which was not staged until 1918. In an article written after the first night of Bartók's opera, Kodály reserved particular praise for the scenarist, 'a true writer', 'a true playwright': 'the particular merit of Béla Balázs is that he was willing to sacrifice one of his finest and most poetic ideas for the benefit of the opera: in this way he contributed to the creation of an admirable work' (see Szabolcsi, 1968: 71–2). The text will be cited in my (literal) translation from the Hungarian edition.
7. See *Le Trésor de la langue française*.
8. Bettelheim expands this idea further with a series of observations on the psychology of the unfaithful woman.

9. Balázs knew Maeterlinck's work and there is no doubt that he was influenced by it, at least partially.
10. N'entends-tu pas sonner le tocsin?
    Ta mère s'est vêtue de noir,
    Ton père ceint son sabre,
    Ton frère selle sa monture,
    Es-tu toujours prête à me suivre?

    Barbe-Bleue! Si tu me chassais,
    Sur ton seuil je m'arrêterais,
    Sur ton seuil je me coucherais.

CHAPTER 3

SECRECY AND MASQUERADE IN STENDHAL

Jean-Jacques Hamm

Henri Beyle, alias Stendhal, alias Dominique, Mr. Myself, M. de Lery, Auguste, Alceste, Tempête, Chapuis, Col. Favier, Fauris Saint-Bard, D. Gruffo Papera, Louis-Alexandre César Bombet, Junius, Banti, Comte Change, Comte de Chablis, Don Flegme, William Crocodile, and all his other nearly two hundred pseudonyms, was a writer of whom Mérimée said, 'He never wrote a letter without signing it under an assumed name... He dated his letters from Abeille instead of C[ivitavecchia]... No one knew exactly whom he was seeing, what books he had written and what travels he had been on' (quoted in Stendhal, 1972: 340). Stendhal, that most secretive of writers, was a veritable Proteus of the patronym.

Of course the climate of postrevolutionary France demanded a certain prudence. Beyle the traveller and diplomat had left the very well-informed Imperial police behind, only to be faced with the police of the Italian states and principalities, where any writing might be seen as suspect. It was a good idea to misdirect their prying eyes, even if this meant making statements destined to leave more than one historian perplexed. Thus, on the first manuscript of Stendhal's memoirs, the *Vie de Henry Brulard*, written in 1835, we read: 'To the gentlemen of the Police. This is a novel in imitation of *The Vicar of Wakefield*. The hero, Henry Brulard, is writing the story of his life at the age of fifty-two, after the death of his wife, the famous Charlotte Corday' (1982: 961). To say that Stendhal enjoyed fabricating secrets is something of an understatement. My discussion here will take a three-pronged approach: firstly, I shall propose a reading of certain figures in which the traces of secrets can be seen, secondly, I shall put forward a hypothesis concerning the psychological emergence of secrets and the textual consequences of this, and thirdly, I shall give a few pointers as to the types of reading indicated by a propensity for secrets.

I shall not deal at length with those times and places where the plot explicitly involves a secret, such as the scene in *Le Rouge et le Noir* when Madame de Rénal has to remove the portrait under the mattress without looking at it before her husband finds it – an incident that enables the heroine to understand feelings for Julien Sorel (jealousy and love) which she had until then hidden from herself. Overall the narration is fairly clear about what is at stake in the story throughout the novel. Stendhal seldom gives us prolonged combats against shadowy forces or masked enemies, and there are few comparisons with the creeping dangers experienced by some of the heroes and readers of Henry James, Franz Kafka or Marcel Proust.

However, the texts contain inscriptions of secrets that we can decode if we are skilful. Most frequently these come to us through the language and its deviations, as in the insertion of English in the following: '*Bien compter avec mes passions. La première, la plus forte, l'unique, this of fame; n'en parler à personne, la satisfaire en silence*' ('Take proper account of my passions. First, strongest, unique, *this of fame*; tell no one about it, satisfy it in silence') (1981: 329). A trilingual reader who knew something of Stendhal would have little difficulty understanding, '*Une vue de Venise dans le deuxième acte du* Roi Théodore*: è in questo bel paese che dovrï andar a fare la μ*' ('A view of Venice in the second Act of *King Theodore:* it was in that country that I was to go and do the *μ*' [*Filosofia nova*] (1981: 67). The following, on the other hand, requires more explanation:

> On the *pantoufle.*
> *Odi profanum vulgum et arceo*
> *Le chant est mon vinaigre* of the four thieves.
> When I am singing *sotto voce* a fine italian aria, *je ne suis pas empoisonné par le profond ignoble qui m'asphyxie de toutes parts à Bourgoin.*
> *L'ignoble ferme le robinet de mon imagination et de ma sensibilité* which makes all my pleasures. (1981: 909)

> *On the* slipper.
> I hate profane vulgarity and keep away from it [the quotation is from Horace (*Odes*, Book III, I)].

> Song is my vinegar *of the four thieves* [a mixture of garlic and camphor that was said to be an antiseptic].
> *When I am singing sotto voce a fine italian aria,* I'm not poisoned by the profound ignoblility which stifles me from all around in Bourgoin.
> Ignobility turns off the tap of my imagination and my sensibility *which makes all my pleasures.*

Stendhal's cryptography would be a gift to any apprentice decipherer. For example, his use of the names Omar, Gliebro, Ruda and Samtho gives us anagrams of Roma, Broglie, Daru and Thomas. Gionreli, one of the many metatheses, is religion; the *jetesuis* ('Ifollowyou') are the Jesuits; the old menttesta is the Old Testament and the Kerepubl is the republic. The most *fripon* (mischievous) of Kings is Stendhal's usual name for King Louis-Philippe. This tower of Babel both hides and reveals texts that censure private biographical elements or political and ideological beliefs. As Gérard Genette suggests, it offers 'an enigmatic transparency' (1969: 192).

Then there are the moments that express absence, leaving us on the threshold of scenes we never enter. In such cases the author's discretion gives rise to suspended scenes. The nuptial chamber is such a place. In Chapter 19 of Book II of *Le Rouge et le Noir,* Julien Sorel comes once more to Mathilde de La Mole's room by means of a ladder:

> 'It's you!" she cried, rushing into his arms... [...]
>
> ....
>
> Who could describe Julien's overflowing happiness? Mathilde's was almost as great. (1952a: 559)

In the same way, at the end of *La Chartreuse de Parme,* a voice in the darkness says: 'Enter here, friend of my heart', followed by a long silence and a long ellipsis of a few years (1952b: 488). Happiness is *atopos,* beyond the scope of the writing, and so is sexuality. Intense moments are expressed by the fading away of the text. Gérard Genette has shown the degree to which 'the elision of powerful moments is one of the characteristic features of Stendhal's narratives' (1969: 181).

There are also figures that prevent us from knowing whether or not we are dealing with the reality we seek. Fabrice del Dongo's time at Waterloo is dominated by paraleipsis, in other words a lack of the information necessary to understand what is at stake in the unfolding of events. In the case of a narrative with internal focalisation, paraleipsis makes it impossible to understand people's private, secret thoughts and the fundamental issues underlying the events described. The most striking example of this is in the novel *Armance*. Octave de Malivert, a young aristocrat who has every reason to be happy, is a strange person who often behaves in an inexplicable way towards his cousin Armance. The two young people are in love, however, and the obstacles to their union gradually lift. Yet Octave de Malivert has a secret that is making him unhappy, which he vows to himself he will tell Armance, but only by letter, after they are married and have spent happy times together. The curious reader remains outside the vital secret that destroys the hero and the two women close to him. Interpretations from outside the text offer keys that in no way solve the mystery but which, because they tend to demand exclusivity for themselves, reduce the heuristic value of the narrative.

So why did Stendhal feel the need to deceive and mislead his readers in this way? I do not propose here to give this question – which the texts continually pose – some psychologising answer involving a causal explanation based on the raw material of Stendhal's life or biography. It seems to me relevant here to return to the oft-expressed idea, which I shall borrow from Jacques Lacan's formulation, to the effect that 'Whenever we speak of cause, on the other hand, there is always something anticonceptional, something indefinite ... there is a hole, and something that oscillates in the interval. In short, there is cause only in something that doesn't work' (Lacan, 1998: 22). The secret concerns only that which no longer exists or indeed does not exist. I shall refer here to the philosopher Clément Rosset's argument in *Le Réel Traité de l'idiotie*:

> Isn't what most psychoanalysts are working on in fact the bringing to light of such illusory secrets and improbable discoveries? Aren't they trying ... to force into speech something which precisely has nothing to tell us... Not that people ultimately have nothing to hide; on the contrary they always have at least one secret they always jealously protect, which is precisely the fact that they have no secrets, nothing to hide. (1977: 27–8)

There is no secret, apart from the place that has no name, the absent place where, they say, something happened whose traces mould the processions, the undertakings of writing, in Stendhal's case both at the fragmentary thematic level and at the level of respiration and punctuation. If there are no origins, we can at least speak of an after-effect (*Nachträglichkeit*), a reinvention rather than a transcription. But first there is a slow approach that must always be started again from the beginning, an aspiration to undertakings that cannot be completed for a very long time.

Stendhal is a writer who never gets to the places he is making for, or will not get there from the outset. We could say that his work is shaped by two projects: the first, after 1801, is the desire to write the story of his life, the other to be a new Molière. This theatrical project, which Stendhal pursued for about forty years, never produced a finished play, although his dramatic fragments amount to around seven hundred printed pages. We find the story of Henri Beyle's life in his journal, in a more or less continuous form until 1817:

> Milan, 28 Germinal Year IX [18 April 1801].
> I'm undertaking to write the story of my life day by day. I don't know if I shall have the strength to carry out this project, which I began in Paris. (1981: 3)

The author's life takes shape in many masks with *Rome, Naples et Florence en 1817*, *De l'Amour* and *Promenades dans Rome*. In *Rome, Naples et Florence*, he presents himself as M. de Stendhal, cavalry officer, presumably Prussian. In *De l'Amour* he attributes the manuscript of his book to 'M. Lisio Visconti, a young man of the highest distinction, who has just died in his home country of Volterra' (1980: 30). At the same time, ever more numerous fragments appear, establishing the chronology of his life and work. In 1820, a *Notice on M. Beyle* (by himself) begins, 'Henri Beyle, born in Grenoble in 1783, has just died at [blank] ([blank] October 1820). After studying mathematics, he spent some time as an officer' (1982: 967). Here he gives some details of his career under Napoleon and his activities since then. The fragment ends with a catalogue of his likes and dislikes:

> He loved Shakespeare and felt an unconquerable disgust for Voltaire and Mme de Staël… He had a deep affection for his sister Pauline and loathed Grenoble, his native city, where he was brought up in an appalling fashion. He had no love for any of his relations. He had been in love with his mother, whom he lost at the age of seven. (1982: 970)

On 20 June 1832, Stendhal began writing his first long autobiographical work, *Souvenirs d'égotisme*, which described the years he spent in Paris between 1821 and 1830. The genre called 'autobiography' had come from England and was starting to come into fashion. In 1834, Stendhal's personal enemy,

Chateaubriand, published a Preface in the form of a testament to his *Mémoires d'Outre-Tombe*. On 23 November 1835, Stendhal began writing the *Vie de Henry Brulard*.

As Béatrice Didier notes, in autobiography 'there are almost always one or two embarrassing confessions to be made' (1983: 17). These are moments that should be left blank in the text, but whose vital traces have to be included, since it is these traces that dictate and justify the necessity of the undertaking. In such confessions autobiographical writing becomes a bull's horn, to borrow an image from Michel Leiris (1946: 12), a threat to a psychological order based on secrecy. Something happened, which was felt to be serious and often continues to be seen as shameful, but must be told to allow the cathartic process that has been set in motion to produce its liberating effect. This something, almost nothing, an indiscreet glance, can be told only in the ellipsis of an allusive clue. Stendhal's text reads:

> But I have for some time been putting off telling a crucial story, one of maybe two or three that will make me fling these memoirs on to the fire.
>
> My mother, Mme Henriette Gagnon, was a charming woman and I was in love with my mother.
>
> I hasten to add that I lost her when I was seven years old... I wanted to cover my mother in kisses and that there should be no clothes. She loved me passionately and would kiss me often; I would return her kisses with such heat that she was often obliged to leave me. I hated my father when he came and interrupted our kisses. I always wanted to kiss her breasts... She was generously proportioned, very fresh and I think her only failing was that she was not tall enough. Her features were perfectly noble and serene; she was very lively, preferring to run and do something herself than to give orders to her three servants and she read Dante's *Divine Comedy* in the original...
>
> She could not take offence at the liberty I'm taking with her by revealing that I loved her; if ever I see her again I will tell her so. Besides she did not share this love... But I was as criminal as could be, I loved her charms with fervour.
>
> One evening, when for some reason I had been put to sleep on a mattress on the floor of her bedroom, this lively woman, light as a doe, leaped over my mattress to get to her own bed more quickly.
>
> Her bedroom was kept locked up for ten years after her death. (1982: 555–56)

Long preparatory sentences and a great many precautions are necessary to allow the confession to burst forth. Yet the aim is to defer it. The leitmotif of burning the manuscript constantly returns like the author's warning to himself. The mother is described with remarkable speed: a silhouette, an air, vivacity. As Béatrice Didier notes, 'we know about Stendhal's reticence in relation to the descriptive genre, and that it is one of the problems he often fears in *Brulard*' (1983: 178). And then, quickly, in the space of one sentence, comes the description of a scene, above the bed on which the child is lying. Yet nothing happened, unless this is a twofold confession, of a relationship of love, which the author stresses, and the quick description of a woman's fleeing movement, presented as though it was just by the by. The scene is accompanied by a drawing, or rather a plan: in the centre of the room, the mattress marked with the letter H; in the top right-hand corner, Henriette's bed crossed with an X, as though forbidden. A fireplace, the 'black dressing-room', a bathroom, three windows and two doors complete the setting.

A 'lively woman, light as a doe', leaps over the mattress from where H, in other words the spectator in a juxtaposition of the points of view of child and narrator, looks. This real or fantasised experience, which is doubtless real in fantasy, produces a vertical representation of the world. Who is looking? Who is looking and being looked at? A child lying on a mattress. What does he see? A dead end? A metaphor? There is nothing to say about what happened: at most a flash, a moving shape, a doe leaping, not even a hunt for happiness. What remains in the look is impossible to capture, except by a suggestive spatialisation of the moment. Something occurred in the verticality of a moment which demands to be replayed, linking subject and object in a place where the look from below and that from above, the eye of God and, almost certainly, the mother's genitals are interminably merged; in which the mother's eye merges with Henry Brulard's, in the only probable and improbable way for the narrator to deal with an experience both evanescent and intolerable, and intolerable because it is evanescent. A moment, a doe's leap and it is all over.

Can this primitive scene be described as determining, and what does it determine? Firstly, a place in which I, the spectator, am captured by the passing flash, the lightning of the moment. On the battlefield Zeus, in other words Napoleon, passes in a flash before Fabrice del Dongo, who is dumbfounded and cannot see. Other unexpected meetings in which the glance seizes a fleeting object include Ernestine and her hunter in the tale of the same name, later Lamiel and the narrator, glimpsed in a Paris street. In these elliptical yet essential meetings, the essential is not articulated, 'I could never speak about what I adored, such talk would have seemed to me blasphemous' (1982: 700).

The nagging question of the effect of such a scene can be answered by drawings when there is no other answer, where there is no longer even a place. It is surprising to note that Stendhal's personal work contains few drawings, leaving aside the *Vie de Henry Brulard*, which is full of them. There are a hundred and seventy-five in all, representing, proportionally speaking, one drawing every two and a half pages, compared to one every eighteen and a half pages in the other personal works. These drawings fall into three categories. The first contains twenty-seven drawings of objects, animals, trees, geometrical shapes, lists of letters and inscriptions. The second consists of twenty-four landscapes or groups of landscapes. It is the third category that is of interest here. What is the purpose of the one hundred and twenty-four plans that break up the text? They could be regarded as a mapping procedure within an autobiographical text. Vertical projections are antidotes to doubt. At the same time they enable the narrator to articulate a presence reduced to a letter, and thus to hide a group of feelings and details. A drawing is discretion itself in its abstract precision, which seems to have no substance.

A letter emerges from this collection of drawings; it is the letter H, in other words Henry's letter, and also that of Henriette, his mother. Mother and son are united in a repetition of drawings, in an indissoluble and yet virtual superimposition, a secret marriage consecrated in the privacy of a letter, a marriage that the memoirs tell in secret, at their beginning and end.

The *Vie de Henry Brulard* begins with a vast panorama of Rome. The narrator, standing on the hill of Janiculum, says he can see 'the Villa Aldobrandini, containing the sublime fresco of Judith by Domenichino' (1982: 529). Scholars have reminded us that the narrator is wrong, that from where he is standing he cannot see the Villa Aldobrandini, which does not contain Domenichino's Judith in any case. This landscape is thus a landscape of desire. In other places the Villa Aldobrandini is synonymous with happiness for Stendhal. Domenichino's Judith is in Rome proper. Yet here we find a number of personal elements together. This picture represents the moment of happiness when Judith reveals the head of the enemy, Holofernes, to the people. The heroine has used love to trick and kill him.

The foreground of the picture shows three little children of different ages, three moments at the start of a human evolution that ends with death in love. Through a mistake that can be described as heuristic, Stendhal's text, in the cataphoretic manner of a signifier-figure in the signified that is to come, draws our attention to the writing of allusion and suggestion. Love leads to death, a fear that Stendhal expresses in many narratives, many novels. And there is more.

Domenichino, a poor artist, simple, incorruptible and noble, whose work is all simplicity and freshness, has a privileged place in Stendhal's writings. Dominique was a pseudonym that Stendhal liked and that he first used in his Diary on 4 September 1806. Dominique comes from Domenico, the first name of Cimarosa, the composer discovered by the narrator on his arrival in Italy: 'At last I was going to the theatre, it was Cimarosa's *Matriomonio Segreto*, the actress playing Caroline was missing one of her front teeth. That's all I remember of divine happiness' (1982: 951). Judith and Dominique, Domenichino's Judith, tales of secret weddings that end in blood, stories of nuptials that the text cannot recount, that it can only articulate by fading away into suspension or ellipsis. Something happened that has no name, to which no name can be applied. Pseudonyms and lists of names and initials are so many attempts, among others, to grasp this ungraspable moment.

How should we read Stendhal? His texts are marked by a constant tension. The movement of the chronicle-narrative follows a syntagmatic organisation. Thus *Le Rouge et le Noir* can be read as the fictional life-story of an exceptional young man destroyed by society. The nineteenth century has given us a great many narratives on this model. But Stendhal's novel is punctuated with a great many paradigmatic, vertical breaks which interrupt the flow with mini-narratives that are sometimes symbolic, sometimes suggestive. A novel like *Armance*, a secretive novel if ever there was one, plays with micro-elements whose series itself eliminates the possibility of establishing stable themes or symbolisation. A two-dimensional structure is thus set up for the reader, in which a contingent verticality destroys the horizontality necessary to the syntagmatic, anacataphoretic axis, rendering it contingent in turn on a necessary verticality. I shall illustrate this by means of three examples.

First I shall return to the question of cryptography. The legend started by Mérimée has it that, out of 'absent-mindedness one day in [Civita-Vecchia] he wrote a coded letter to M. [de

Broglie], and sent him the code in the same envelope' (1982: 340). This incident accords with the logic of Stendhal's cryptography, which tends to be transparent because it is intended for a different game. It is easy to find Rome in Omar, and Roma, but it also contains Amor and *à mort* ('to death') as in the epigraph to Chapter XV of *Le Rouge et le Noir*:

> *Amour en latin faict amor;*
> *Or donc provient d'amour la mort,*
> *Et, par avant, soulcy qui mord,*
> *Deuil, plours, pieges, forfaitz, remords.*
>
> ['Love in Latin gives *amor*;
> So death comes from love,
> And, before that, the worry that devours
> Mourning, tears, traps, crimes, remorse'] (1960: 85)

Thus stress reveals a semantic chain.

Secondly, there is the problem of the emblem that might unleash a set of themes, but cannot do so after the event, as it is part of an open or incomplete micro-structure. This is the case of names in the narrative. We can make a comparison with the name Mme Bovary, used by Flaubert. The story suggests at least two interpretations, of which one has animal connotations, while the other suggests variation: a laughing ox and a Mme Beau who varies. Names such as Armance or Julien Sorel have a semantic field only in a paradigmatic reading that has to involve both rhetorical games and cultural content.

Thirdly, I return to the endless list of pseudonyms. The picturesque or grotesque nature of the suggested names should not make us forget that beyond their playful aspect lies a negative patronymy, in the sense of a negative theology. Henri Beyle could wear any name in the world but his own. Symptomatic of a psychological fiasco and the settling of old scores with his hated father, whose name he certainly mentions in other contexts, it also gives him the boundless privilege of incompleteness, which is perhaps Stendhal's fundamental secret. Not finishing means continually starting again, returning over and over to the wonderful secret – the fundamental *aporia* facing the author and his readers.

Translated by Trista Selous

CHAPTER 4

THRESHOLDS OF DESIRE AND DOMESTIC SPACE IN NINETEENTH-CENTURY FRENCH FICTION

Tony Williams

One of the most important developments that has taken place in the modern period has been the privatisation of family life, which social historians have linked to the growth of machine production from the eighteenth century onwards. Displacing the domestic labour force from the home, machine production led to the separation of place of work and the home, which in turn meant that the domestic sphere came to be more highly regarded and developed as a site of affectivity, the locus of a range of intensified emotional experiences (Cheal, 1991: 81). The increasing differentiation of public and private spheres was reinforced by genderisation: the ideology of separate spheres clearly identified women with the private world of the home and men with the public world of work and politics (Wolff, 1990: 12–13; Pollock, 1988: 67–8). The privatisation of family life did not, then, affect men and women equally. Women generally were confined to a subordinate role in the domestic sphere, whilst men were able to move freely between both public and private spheres. The genderisation of public and private spheres was fundamental to bourgeois culture and worked to the disadvantage of women (Mossman, 1993: 184–5).

With the increasing separation of the spheres, the domestic interior becomes a bastion of privacy, which emerges as a new ideal of bourgeois culture. Eleb-Vidal's study of the evolution of the architecture of private life traces the way in which in the nineteenth century there was a growing attempt to construct buildings in which the intimate life of the family was protected, in line with the dictum of Talleyrand, 'Private life must be walled up' (Eleb-Vidal, 1989: v). Private space was not, however, conceived of in monolithic terms. One fascinating aspect of the opposition between public and private was the way supplementary distinctions within the private sphere were established, even though the private sphere as a whole was seen predominantly as the woman's domain. In the designs for grander apartments and mansions a distinction was made between rooms designed for public or semi-public ceremonies and receptions and those reserved for family life. For instance, in France, the courtyard was the building's public face, whilst the garden was a private area. There were also distinctions between masculine and feminine territory within the private sphere with certain rooms, such as the smoking room, designed for exclusive masculine use and others, such as the boudoir, for feminine use (Apter, 1991: 39).

The bedroom in particular was a key space and underwent a number of changes. At the beginning of the century it still functioned in certain classes as a public space: George Sand's grandmother, for example, received visitors sitting up in her bed. In the eighteenth century in the upper classes the practice was to have separate bedrooms but in the nineteenth there was an increasing tendency for the bourgeois couple to share a single bedroom. As the bedroom becomes less public and more private there is increasing scope for it to be constructed as a secret space within the bourgeois household, with entry into it forbidden to all males apart from the husband.

Social historians have extensively documented the changing perception of domestic space. What is of particular interest for the student of literature is the way the new value-charged domestic sphere is exploited by novelists, and, more specifically, the way in which the topography of adultery changes as a result of the emergence of the domestic sphere as secret site of heightened affectivity. In broad historical terms, notions about what constitutes the proper space for adulterous love undergo a significant change (Miller, 1988: 319). In the first half of the century, one of the effects of the ideology of domesticity was to ring-fence the home as a kind of preserve of conjugal love, setting up invisible barriers to extramarital encounters. The bedroom is viewed as a sanctuary and, precisely because it is viewed as a secret space, it becomes invested with a powerful erotic charge. In later fiction, in contrast, the embargo on the private sphere is lifted, leading to the collapse of the image of the married woman as angel in the house. One of the most striking features of late nineteenth-century fiction is the activation of the private sphere as a locus of adultery. The increasing use of domestic space for erotic purposes has the effect of desacralising the home and scenes of adultery on home ground lose much of their earlier scandalous charge.

Many novelists were preoccupied with adultery in the first half of the century but an embargo on adultery within the domestic sphere appears to be operating, driving illicit love out of the home. In a number of novels written in the first half of the century there is a striking predilection for the carriage as locus of adultery. Enclosed within a semi-private space but paraded in the public sphere, the adulterous transports of the unfaithful wife are safely removed from the sanctity of the home.[1] There are, however, a number of occasions where adulterous activity does invade domestic space, generating an atmosphere of great intensity.

Balzac wrote more extensively than any other novelist did in the nineteenth century about the problematics of marriage. In *Le Lys dans la vallée* (1836) Balzac depicts a pattern which is found in several nineteenth-century French novels involving a young man becoming fixated upon a married woman who, securely installed in her maternal role and domestic setting, remains forever virtuous. On one occasion, her young admirer spends the night on the threshold of her bedroom, listening to her through a 'slit' in the door, weeping with rage, without her ever becoming aware of the way her virtue has been 'alternately destroyed and respected, cursed and revered' (Balzac, 1961: 203). The bedroom remains inviolable, a forbidden place which Félix de Vandenesse can never enter. Secret space is exploited even more dramatically in *La Grande Bretèche*, which was one of several cautionary tales about the dangers of adultery Balzac wrote in the early thirties and later incorporated into a longer work, *Autre Étude de femme* (1842). Dominated by a pattern of thresholds of secret spaces being breached and resealed, the story opens with the main narrator first penetrating the grounds of a ruined and deserted château, which is hermetically sealed and overgrown, like something out of a Gothic novel. Full of curiosity, he attempts to find out more about La Grande Bretèche but has to overcome the reticence of three secondary narrators. From a lawyer he learns about the last will and instructions of the last occupant, Madame de Merret, who has ordered that La Grande Bretèche should be sealed up for fifty years. An innkeeper tells him about the mysterious disappearance of a Spaniard who had lodged with her. Finally Rosalie, the maid, reveals the original drama that had taken place in the now abandoned château. Returning home early Monsieur de Merret hears voices in his wife's bedroom, then the sound of the key in the door of the inner closet in which she keeps her clothes, but when he finally enters finds her alone. She swears on the cross that there is no one in the closet and, deeply suspicious, he immediately proceeds to have it walled up (Balzac, 1952: 260). When he leaves his wife, she tries to get Rosalie to open up a gap in the wall but he returns immediately and stays with her for twenty days to prevent her unblocking the closet (Balzac, 1952: 262). The reader is left in no doubt that Madame de Merret's Spanish lover had been hidden there and had finally died as a result of Monsieur de Merret's sadistic revenge.

The narrative has a suggestive power in excess of the simple story recounted. Talleyrand's dictum, 'Private life should be walled up', is implemented in various ways: walls of various kinds surround the molten core of adultery that lies at the heart of *La Grande Bretèche*, including, as well as the literal wall which seals up the cabinet, the wall of secrecy which surrounds the events. The servants are sworn to secrecy by Monsieur de Merret and of Rosalie it is said 'That girl is like a stone wall' (Balzac, 1952: 255). But more important is the symbolic drama that is enacted. Commenting on Julie's famous repudiation of adultery in Rousseau's *La Nouvelle Héloïse*, Tony Tanner writes:

> No gap is permitted: indeed it is as if marriage is used to preclude the possibility of any gaps and all the problems of fissures and interstices... Thus marriage must be a seamless whole and union – above all the gap caused by adultery is dismissed as effectively unthinkable. (Tanner, 1979: 169)

In the light of this image of adultery as gap, the title of this story, *La Grande Bretèche*, carries a suggestive resonance, for it recalls the word 'la brèche', meaning a breach or gap. Madame Merret's adultery is a gap, which her husband tries – symbolically – to close up. However, Monsieur de Merret's act of walling up the closet is a bit like shutting the stable door after the horse has bolted. The damage has been done, the adulterous breach of marriage's 'seamless whole' has occurred. There is also an attempt to shore up the past but the narrator successfully breaches the walls of silence surrounding the original events, just as many fictions of adultery throughout the century insist on revealing skeletons in family cupboards. The narrator enters therefore into an ambiguous complicity with the adulterous wife and it is perhaps no accident that he uses sexual means to prise the secret about the past out of Rosalie.

George Sand displays a particular sensitivity to the domestic sphere and, perhaps more than any other novelist of the time, succeeded in turning the bedroom into a kind of sanctuary. In her early works the heroine's bedroom is a locus of sublimation, providing a means of focusing the difficulties experienced by both sexes in expressing sexual desire. In George Sand's first novel, *Indiana* (1832), the heroine, married to a petty tyrant, is unable to reciprocate the strong physical desires of her romantic lover, Raymon de Ramière. One of the most memorable scenes in the novel takes place in Indiana's 'circular bedroom' (Sand, 1984: 100), decked with flowers like a religious altar and containing at its centre 'a bed white and chaste like that of a virgin' (Sand, 1984: 101). Noun, Indiana's maid and foster sister, who is Raymon's mistress, dresses up as Indiana and takes Raymon to Indiana's bedroom, hoping to revive his dying passion. In a state of considerable confusion, he looks in the mirror and thinks that the image of Noun reflected in it is that of Indiana: 'He seemed to be grasping, in the last shadowy shape of Noun reflected there, the slender and supple waist of madame Delamare' (Sand, 1984: 104).

At the height of passion he again imagines Noun is Indiana: 'It was her again that he dreamt of on this modest, spotless bed, when, overcome by love and wine, he carried there his dishevelled creole' (Sand, 1984: 105). At the level of Raymon's sensibility a drama of profanation has been enacted in Indiana's bedroom and Indiana herself risks being contaminated by the orgiastic encounter that has taken place in it: 'Have I not opened up your bedroom to the demon of lust? … and won't the senseless ardour which fills this lascivious creole, in turn, … become attached to you and eat away at you' (Sand, 1984: 106).

There is something extremely powerful but also obscure going on in this scene. It has been suggested that the doubling of Indiana and Noun, the one resistant to sexual desire, the other receptive, is bound up with George Sand's inability to imagine a female desiring subject (Rabine, 1976: 10). Indiana is both profaned through Noun and spared profanation, through the displacement of sexual activity onto Noun. The bedroom, then, is the secret space where ideal and reality come into violent conflict, producing a seismic upheaval in the libidinal economy of the novel. It is a kind of impasse in which the heroine is both sexualised and desexualised, leaving all concerned – Indiana, Raymon, Noun, author and reader – in a state of considerable bafflement.

In George Sand's second novel, *Valentine,* also published in 1832, there are two extraordinary bedroom scenes in which the sexual fate of her heroine hangs in the balance. The first takes place on the night of her wedding, when she drugs herself with opium to calm her agitated nerves, all the time surveyed by Bénédict who has smuggled himself into her bedroom with the intention of preventing the consummation of her marriage. In her drugged state, Valentine imagines she has married Bénédict, rather than Lanzac: 'You are the one I was in love with… How have they allowed it?' (Sand, 1988: 134). She then thinks her husband is coming and throws herself into Bénédict's arms for protection. Bénédict is tempted but finds a way of resisting his desire:

> He lifted up the locks of her hair and filled his mouth with them to prevent himself from crying out, amidst his tears of rage and love. Finally, in an instant of unspeakable pain, he bit the round, white shoulder which was revealed to his gaze. (Sand, 1988: 135)

After an enforced separation Bénédict spies on Valentine in the 'oratory', where the struggle to respect her virtue is so great that he faints. His weakened state elicits an energetic response:

> Recovering all her energy as a result of the need to help him, she held him up and dragged him to her bedroom, where she brewed some tea for him… At that moment, the kind-hearted and gentle Valentine became the active, efficient housewife, whose life was devoted to the welfare of others. The terrors of a passionately loving woman subsided to be replaced by the concerns of friendship. She forgot what place she was taking Bénédict to and what was bound to take place within her heart…. (Sand, 1988: 193)

So strange is the look he gives her, however, that she drops the cup and scolds her foot, which he then kisses fetishistically (Schor, 1986: 364). It is at this point that the long-drawn-out affair is finally consummated. In both of these scenes the bedroom is entered by the male lover, who has effectively crossed a threshold into a forbidden realm in which desire, constantly deferred, can finally be expressed. What is significant, however, from the heroine's point of view, is that it can only be expressed in a roundabout way, through a detour first through semi-consciousness, then through maternal solicitude. Sexual activity as such gets confused with sleep on the one hand and mothering on the other.

From the man's point of view, the bedroom is an impossible place, in which contradictory reactions are called for: respect for the virtue of the heroine, somehow more palpable in the bedroom, desire for consummation provoked by her undressed state. Consummation is preceded by a symbolic wounding – the scalding of the foot – followed by instant reparation – the kissing of the foot – both clearly linked to the crossing of that other threshold, the hymen.

These examples suggest that the bedroom is a very special literary space in the first half of the century. As the ideology of domesticity begins to lose its potency, however, the bedroom begins to shed some of its charge. In the middle of the century, however, there is still a reluctance to allow adultery to take place on home ground. In Flaubert's *Madame Bovary* (1857), the definitive novel of adultery, the locus of adultery is variously a forest, a woodcutter's hut, a hired cab and a Rouen hotel room. In one brief scene (Flaubert, 1971: 174) where Emma and Rodolphe meet atypically on home ground, in the consulting room used by her husband, two very different patterns are invoked. Rodolphe finds the situation amusing, makes fun of her husband and says that he would knock him down if he came in. He is already treating adultery as knockabout farce. Emma, on the other hand, expects him to be carrying pistols like a romantic hero. For her adultery is high drama. This conflict of attitudes exemplifies the broader opposition between the ways in which adultery on home ground tended to be treated before Flaubert and the way it came to be treated after him. Although *L'Éducation sentimentale* was published later, as far as attitudes to domestic space are concerned, it reworks motifs which had been exploited by Balzac in *Le Lys dans la vallée*. Much of the drama of adoration is played out in a domestic setting, which constantly enhances Madame Arnoux's maternal charms. Generally speaking, Madame Arnoux is seen in the more public spaces of her homes – the dining room or the living room. There are two occasions, however, when Frédéric imagines her or glimpses her in the more intimate surroundings of the bedroom or the boudoir.

> In spite of himself, he glanced at the bed in the depths of the alcove, imagining her head on the pillow; and he pictured the scene so clearly that he could scarcely refrain from clasping her in his arms. She closed her eyes, soothed, inert. (Flaubert, 1984: 169)

Normally Frédéric sublimates desire in a kind of religious adoration of Madame Arnoux. This is the earliest unequivocal sexual response. Significantly, it occurs on the threshold of the alcove in which the bed is glimpsed. It is as if the sight of the bedroom brings home to him the sexual dimension of the saintly figure he reveres. But his impulse to seize her in his arms is resisted. Later, having become 'the parasite of the household' (Flaubert, 1984: 171), Frédéric's hopes are raised, when he learns that Madame Arnoux is on her own at her husband's pottery factory at Creil. He dashes off to Creil, arrives unannounced, and finally goes into her bedroom:

> Madame Arnoux was alone in front of a wardrobe mirror. Her dressing gown was half-open, with the cord hanging down her hips. The whole of one side of her hair was spread in a black wave over her right shoulder; and she had her arms raised, holding her chignon with one hand while she was thrusting a pin into it with the other. She gave a cry, and vanished. (Flaubert, 1984: 195)

The half-dressed state in which he finds Madame Arnoux elicits another burst of desire, which expresses itself in heavy-handed compliments whose main effect is to frighten Madame Arnoux into self-defensive 'bourgeois maxims' (Flaubert, 1984: 195). As in *Le Lys dans la vallée*, if the bedroom triggers desire, it also still inhibits its active and effective expression.

The bedroom and domestic space generally become desacralised in Zola and other Naturalist writers. In the Naturalist novel, the bedroom, which in earlier fiction is often likened to a religious sanctuary, is the principal locus of adulterous encounters, many of which have a burlesque or farcical quality, particularly when the married woman is caught *in flagrante*.[2] Zola's great comic novel, *Pot-Bouille* (1882), which is set in a modern apartment block, contains a good example of such a scene, when Berthe is discovered by her husband in Octave's bedroom and runs from apartment to apartment in search of a refuge. In order to force entry her husband hammers at the door and tumbles into the apartment when it suddenly gives. What characterises the scene is the loss of dignity of all concerned. The irony is that both Octave and Berthe are distinctly lacking in ardour. Octave has just made love to another woman and regards the pre-planned visit of Berthe as a 'tiresome task' (Zola, 1964: 282) and when Berthe reflects on what has happened, she doubts whether it was worth all the risk (Zola, 1964: 293). What happens in this and similar scenes where the wife is caught *in flagrante* is that a private encounter in the private sphere is turned into a public spectacle, which is equally humiliating for all concerned. The movement of the wife who runs away or the lover who is escorted off the premises marks the spilling over of the private into the public and the bankruptcy of marriage as an institution. The laughter which such scenes invariably provoke stems from repressed uncertainties which are brought out into the open.

The most deliberately bathetic example of the married woman being loved on the premises is that of Marie Pichon. The naive mother in *Pot-Bouille* is scandalised at the very thought of making love in Octave's room (Zola, 1964: 115) but readily submits to him in her own constricted dining room. Zola takes a kind of perverse delight in sabotaging the conventional image of virtuous motherhood. Living on the same floor as Marie, Octave is privy to the intimate details of her life (pram, baby, etc) and roped into the family circle made up by the family unit and her parents, the Vuillaumes. Great play is made with a romantic novel, George Sand's *André*, a copy of which is lent to her by Octave. In the course of their lovemaking, it is knocked to the ground and its binding damaged, symbolically enacting the disintegration of the ideal of romantic love that has just taken place. On her own home ground Marie comically and incongruously seeks to achieve 'the blue realm of ideal love' (Zola, 1964: 75) in a hit-or-miss fashion: 'And, suffocating again at this thought, feeling suddenly faint, she threw out into thin air a clumsy kiss, which brushed the ear of the young man' (Zola, 1964: 75).

The sordid nature of the setting is stressed and with the door open and dishes on the table and Lilitte in her cot, the dining room seems ill chosen, but there is a form of spatial fixation at work because the same scene is later repeated, 'And she yielded in the very same spot, where she had fallen into his arms, the previous year, as an obedient woman' (Zola, 1964: 278). On both occasions heavy emphasis is laid on the atmosphere of domestic intimacy of the dining room:

> She had closed the door and was clearing the table of the glasses, which were still lying around. The cramped room, with

> its blackening lamp, retained the warmth of the little family celebration. (Zola, 1964: 279)

Zola is seeking to undermine the conventional idealisation of the home by transforming it into the site of an extreme form of sexual ineptitude. The repeated references to Berthe's 'icy lips' and the insistence that 'she hadn't even experienced any pleasure' (Zola, 1964: 76) clearly establish that she is a non-desiring subject. The mechanical coupling on the dining room table is the complete antithesis of the ideal of romantic love, the search for which motivates her instant compliance. So great is the disparity between dream and reality that Marie, unlike other married women, seems, to be wildly out of control within her domestic orbit. In particular, she is unable to regulate the passage from the semi-public dining room to the more private bedroom, because she is totally unaware of what is happening to her. Adultery has become just as dysfunctional as marriage, and Marie is in no sense empowered by the way she makes love on the premises. Zola has liquidated both the idealised image of maternity, which is part of the patriarchal imaginary, and any suggestion that romantic love can be viewed as potentially positive. Domestic space has become caricatural: all the trappings are there but the lover has usurped the position of the husband, looking after the children, sitting in the husband's chair, even fathering his children for him! *Pot-Bouille* is an ironic reply to the novel of adoration, with Octave's disengagement and lack of emotional involvement being stressed, contrasting with the drooling wonderment of a Frédéric Moreau.

The changes that take place in the way domestic space is exploited in these novels link up with broader changes in the perception of female adultery. Female adultery, which in the first half of the century is a burning issue, turns into platitude in the second half, at least in certain circles, thereby actualising the famous observation in *Madame Bovary* 'she found in adultery all the platitudes of marriage' (Flaubert, 1971: 296). The fundamental shift in attitude is reflected in a transformation in the fictional exploitation of domestic space. The bedroom is initially perceived as a secret space. It is rare for the lover to be found there and it is rare for the novelist to describe it. When the lover does make his way into the bedroom, it is as if he is trespassing on sacred ground, and this makes for some highly charged scenes in early nineteenth-century fiction. Authorial attitudes seem, on the whole, to endorse the view of the bedroom as a secret space but there is a kind of doubling of the lover's penetration of domestic space and the novelist's exploration of the hidden underside of marriage. Somewhere around the middle of the century, as adultery becomes banalised, the bedroom is desacralised. Characteristically, the bourgeois wife ceases to regard the domestic sphere as a kind of desexualised no-go arena, using it instead for her own erotic purposes. Scenes in which the wife is discovered *in flagrante* take to an extreme the process of making the private public. Whilst there are comparatively few bedroom scenes in novels written in the first half of the century, they proliferate in the second half. In ceasing to be, in fictional terms, a secret space, the bedroom loses much of its charge: if adultery becomes platitude from Flaubert onwards, the bedroom becomes banality.

The growing narrative investment in the private sphere in itself is transgressive. According to Littré, '[I]t is forbidden to seek to know what is going on in the home of a private individual' (Eleb-Vidal, 1989: v) yet this is what the nineteenth-century novelist, following in the lover's footsteps, does increasingly. It might be asked whether there is something unsavoury about 'the narrator-critic intrusively spying on scenes of nineteenth-century domestic ritual and its attendant erotic fixations' (Apter, 1991: xiv). The question is posed most acutely when narrator and reader enter the bedroom. Although the secret spaces which are being spied on are literary, not real, and the acts of adultery imaginary, not literal, the voyeuristic content of much nineteenth-century narrative is difficult to deny. It would seem that once a culture defines certain spaces as secret, the forbidden entry into them, whether imagined or real, falls into the paradigm of the peep-show.

Notes

1. See, for example, Balzac, *La Muse du Département*, Mérimée, *La Double Méprise*, Champfleury, *Les Bourgeois de Molinchart*.
2. See, for example, Huysmans, *En Ménage* and Paul Alexis, *Madame Meuriot*.

Chapter 5

Women's Sanctuaries and Spatial Transgressions in the Novels of Jean Giraudoux

Victoria B. Korzeniowska

'Societies', Shirley Ardener comments in the book *Women and Space*, 'have generated their own rules, culturally determined, for making boundaries on the ground, and have divided the social into spheres, levels and territories with invisible fences and platforms to be scaled by abstract ladders and crossed by intangible bridges with as much trepidation or exultation as on a plank over a raging torrent' (Ardener, 1981: 11–12). The criteria that determine the spatial segregation identified by Ardener are numerous and can include class, wealth, race and gender. These have been amply discussed elsewhere by feminists and social geographers. What I propose to focus on in this essay is the role of gender in spatial segregation, since it is gender which is attributed with the origin of the classic binary division of space into male-dominated public spheres and female-dominated private ones. Men run society, women run the home, men's power and privilege arising out of their domination of access to knowledge and women's disempowerment from their exclusion. Women are permitted into the public sphere, but only into areas where their presence is unlikely to threaten men's power base. To reject these spatial constraints is to transgress, to break an unspoken, yet tacitly accepted code which governs everyone's lives, and to court disapproval from one's peers.

Space in the fictional universe of Jean Giraudoux is similarly segregated according to gender. In both his fiction and drama, Giraudoux's portrayal of women was, and still is, a cause of critical debate, but whereas the men are in offices signing international treaties and preventing wars, the women are meeting their lovers in hotels and restaurants. Men control politics, diplomacy, high finance, business and education – traditional bastions of patriarchal power in the public sphere. Heroines lead the traditionally idle life of women endowed with significant wealth. Their spaces are restaurants, hotels, the theatre, the races and the rich *quartiers* of Paris – public spaces in which their presence is unlikely to subvert male supremacy. The public/private divide does exist, but it is not Giraudoux's main focus, and we rarely see his heroines in the domestic sphere; the exception being Edmée in *Choix des élues* to which I will return later.

Most of Giraudoux's novels are city fictions, and a significant number of them are set in Paris in the 1920s and 1930s. Giraudoux himself was born in Bellac, Limousin in 1882 and died in Paris in 1944. Although his early years were based in small provincial towns such as Pellevoisin, Cérilly and Châteauroux, much of his adult life was spent in Paris where he successfully combined a career in the diplomatic service with his ambitions as a novelist and dramatist. Whereas for some authors such as Simone de Beauvoir and Violette Leduc, Paris is very much gendered as either masculine or feminine (Hughes, 1996: 115–32), Giraudoux's capital is both. It is masculine in scale with its imposing architecture and monuments dedicated to great men; masculine as it is dominated by men in powerful professions who appropriate the knowledge, power and politics from which women are excluded. But it is also feminine as its labyrinthine quality allows women liberation, independence and anonymity and opens up possibilities unavailable in small provincial towns in which no one can have secrets. The following quotation from Giraudoux's political novel *Bella* (1926) exemplifies these advantages.

> We were in the Place des Pyramides. From a taxi which she suddenly stopped, a young woman signalled to a second taxi, quickly got out of the first one, paid without asking for her change, jumped into the second and disappeared. We had just witnessed the evasive action of an agitated soul, of a klepto-

> maniac on the run, of an adulteress under close watch. (Giraudoux, 1990: 900)[1]

Giraudoux's capital is thus a space in which experiences can be gained and multiple identities created within certain boundaries. This image of Paris is not unique to Giraudoux, and Liz Heron in *Streets of Desire* observes that 'city fictions are often narratives of self-discovery, and, by removing women from the family unit, these female *Bildungsromans* ... whose complications are various, seem to insist on the autonomous status of female experience' (1993: 2–3).

Autonomy, however, is not unconditional and Giraudoux's Paris is hierarchically structured into male and female/rich and poor spaces, and to violate (voluntarily or otherwise) these invisible boundaries is to court serious personal consequences. The city can be the area where women escape from, or escape to, and within which they explore, or challenge, the boundaries of female space. It is therefore a paradox, a contradiction, simultaneously offering space both for sanctuary and transgression, for freedom and confinement. Personified as a haven which protects women and gives them their own space, the city can, however, withdraw the special status it confers upon women at any time, something Maléna discovers with the onset of war in *Combat avec l'ange* (1934).

> She was also counting on Paris. She was hoping that this city, which she had lived in and loved for so long was not, after all that, going to demote her to the rank of an outsider. But she was mistaken. The citizenship which she was seeking in her walks throughout Paris was constantly and cruelly refused. Paris was freeing itself of her affections and their former close relationship. All the city's style, statuary and architecture suddenly rejected any relationship with her. (Giraudoux, 1994: 433)

For Juliette, the heroine of *Juliette au pays des hommes* (1924), Paris is the inevitable destination for a brief spell of independence before her marriage to the prosaic Gérard. Only the liberating anonymity of Paris allows such an adventure, concealing the heroine from prying, provincial eyes and permitting the fulfilment of personal fantasies. Juliette's urban initiation and entry into its male bastions of power and knowledge in search of all the potential fiancés whose names she had written in a notebook as a girl confirms the gendered segregation of space in the Giralducian fictional universe. The Paris which she encounters is very masculine, the *pays des hommes* of the novel's title. Men dominate culture, power and knowledge, and occupy all those spaces and buildings which symbolise status and position. Women's space lies elsewhere, on the streets that surround these erections of patriarchy and where women's presence is not subject to control or censure. Juliette is not seeking to challenge this state of affairs, but rather looks to explore the potentialities of female urban space. 'Every day', we learn, 'Juliette's notebook guided her to a different part of Paris. This was not her way of rebelling against the narrow destiny reserved for young women. On the contrary, she intended to investigate all those possibilities which sometimes extend the limits of life's boundaries' (Giraudoux, 1990: 818–19).

Juliette's attitude is characteristic of most Giralducian heroines whose challenge to the prevailing patriarchal order and the role allotted to women is usually a temporary interlude followed by a more lasting conformity. Giraudoux's portrayal of women's role in society is characterised by ambiguity and hesitation since although he supports the need for greater emancipation for women – including spatial emancipation – he simultaneously wishes to preserve traditional family values and women's role within the home. Like many of his contemporaries, Giraudoux advocated a return to order and stability after the upheaval of the First World War. The war had marked the end of an era for France and the nation emerged from the conflict with its population decimated, its morale and self-image severely shaken, its economy in ruins and its geographical borders violated. The need for national regeneration in many areas of French life was therefore widely recognised, although there was no consensus as to how this could be achieved. One approach was to see women as the potential agents of national recovery and much of the discourse of national salvation was therefore simply a restatement of perennial values, imposing a new interpretation on women's traditional role and promoting pre-war gender stability. This view was endorsed by both men and women and also feminists. It is also characteristic of much of Giraudoux's fiction and drama, finding theoretical expression in his series of lectures entitled *La Française et la France* given at the Université des Annales in 1934. It was this latter work with its combination of traditional views and moderate calls for emancipation that led to Giraudoux being seen as a moderate feminist.

Juliette's discovery of and relationship with Paris is thus typical of Giraudoux's work, being a temporary prelude to marriage and conformity. Her urban adventure contrasts with that of other Giralducian heroines, whose association with the city is more permanent. For these protagonists, there is an appropriation of particular areas of the city which merge with their social identity and form the backdrop to their relationships. One of the most striking examples of this is in Giraudoux's novel *Bella* – a political novel and modern *Romeo and Juliet* in which Bella and her lover's dawn meetings confirm the city's status as a private haven:

> The joys reserved for lovers in an already exhausted and saturated city, were ours at an hour when my love and I were the only couple in Paris... Every elm in a square, every lime tree in a courtyard, the Bois de Boulogne, the parc Monceau had, through twelve hours of special inhalation and distillation, prepared for us the purest Parisian air in which two lovers had ever embraced... She came out of the Champs-Elysées metro station which was, at this hour, the most exclusive in Paris, being almost entirely reserved for masons and plasterers... We were the only two humans in Paris spared its troubles, but enriched by its charm. (Giraudoux, 1990: 891–92)

The Giralducian city is thus a sanctuary in which women can pursue erotic relationships away from disapproving eyes. It is, however, more than this. Elizabeth Wilson, in *The Sphinx in the City*, comments that 'urban life created a space in which some women could experiment with new roles' (1991: 65) and Bella, like many of Giraudoux's heroines, hides her true identity at the beginning of her relationship. It is not until later on that the lovers discover that their families are, in fact, political enemies. Such anonymity is only possible in Paris, since the city enables the heroine to abandon one identity in a particular *quartier* and assume another when she moves elsewhere.

Nelly, the heroine of *La Menteuse* (1969), is the supreme exponent of this mutability and she experiments with multiple fictitious identities. For the prosaic Gaston, she is an unexceptional, middle-class woman who has revealed most of her secrets. For the wealthy Reginald, Nelly is unique and ethereal and she therefore prolongs her anonymity as long as possible in order to maintain his illusion. When Reginald does want to know about her past, she creates a mythic existence for herself to satisfy his fantasies. This means re-creating herself geographically to invent a past which is appropriate to his social status.

> When Reginald was absent from Paris, she created new outings for herself; one day she went to Belleville, she spoke with some

> people from Belleville, she went as far as the Pré-Saint-Gervais. A young girl's life could easily be situated there, between this quiet little town and these hills from where you could see the city. All the monuments gave her the framework for a new life. (Giraudoux, 1994: 692)

Inevitably, both men discover the truth and the 'other' Nelly, but the way this truth is expressed is largely in spatial terms as each discovers the other Nelly's Paris. Gaston's visit to the area of the city which Nelly shares with Reginald is an abrupt awakening:

> He surveyed Nelly's *quartier* from the step where, each evening, she went back to boredom, disgust, duty, went back to Gaston. He saw her little realm, whose boundaries were created by the need to buy provisions for dinner. The cake shop where Nelly bought strawberry tarts, he recognised the pastry, one day when Nelly must have been in a hurry to do her shopping, she had bought one, which was so good that he asked where it came from. He had the address now. (Giraudoux, 1994: 750–51)

Reginald's discovery is equally disturbing, as he sees Nelly metamorphose before his very eyes.

> He felt that she had arrived in her neighbourhood. He saw her go into a shop... All this shopping which seemed so dignified when she deigned to devote herself to it in their neighbourhood, here became the activity of an average, organised and dutiful, middle-class housewife. (Giraudoux, 1994: 768)

This freedom Nelly has to change identity confirms the city's status as sanctuary since it enables women to challenge conventional morals and to formulate different identities.

The liberating quality of the city is also a central feature of *Choix des élues* (1939), in which the heroine, Edmée, uses urban space to constantly recreate herself (see Korzeniowska, 1999). *Choix des élues* is unusual in that the novel is set in the United States and is mainly centred inside Edmée's living spaces. The beginning of the novel is particularly claustrophobic and the heroine has no personal space, no 'room of her own'. One day, it all becomes too much and she heads for Washington Park with her daughter Claudie. Here, she tastes her first experience of spatial emancipation:

> A great feeling of serenity came over Edmée. She was not resting after the day's activities: she did not need to, she wasn't tired. She was resting because of severe exhaustion, something

> which she had not suspected, but which had been building up over the years since childhood... There was no doubt about it, she was in the only corner of the earth which truly belonged to her. (Giraudoux, 1994: 512)

As this last line confirms, it is in the urban park that Edmée finally feels that she has some personal space. This discovery is quickly followed by an active search for a room of her own and Edmée and Claudie do not go home, but spend the night in a hotel. 'The hotel', Wilson comments in *The Sphinx in the City*, 'was similar to the department store or the café, for it too was both public and private, and yet neither. Like the department store, it was an intermediate, amoral zone in which appearances – however fictitious – and the ability to pay were all that counted' (1991: 59). Sanctuary, for Edmée, as for other Giralducian heroines, is thus found in the urban environment, in the limbo between the public and private sphere, and the anonymity which Edmée finds in the park and hotel offers other possibilities of being.

Such liberation is, however, problematic, since the autonomy which women enjoy in the urban environment is often viewed by society as engendering disorder and transgression. The city is thus a paradox: simultaneously embodying a secret space in which women can access their true potential and find fulfilment, yet inviting transgression into forbidden places proscribed to women by social convention. According to Wilson, attitudes towards women's presence in the urban environment have often emphasised the dangers. 'The city', she asserts, 'offers untrammelled sexual experience; in the city the forbidden – what is most feared and desired – becomes possible. Woman is present in cities as temptress, as whore, as fallen woman, as lesbian, but also as virtuous womanhood in danger, as heroic womanhood who triumphs over temptation and tribulation' (1991: 5–6). It is this fear of the city as an amoral zone permitting erotic emancipation for women which, Wilson argues, led to attempts at imposing greater spatial restraint on women (1991: 157), while Gerda Wekerle, Rebecca Peterson and David Morley in *New Space for Women*, contend that 'this social stereotyping of people and environments also has the effect of reinforcing the social order, with all its inherent prejudices and discriminatory practices' (1980: 4). The boundaries between what constitute desirable and undesirable spaces for women are thus there as instruments of control and anyone flouting these boundaries is likely to court disapproval.

In the Giralducian fictional universe, the challenging of spatial constraints would also appear to be a necessary part of becoming a woman and of accepting the role allotted to women in French society. Each heroine has her own spatial map which defines her identity and to deviate from this map is to subvert this given identity in search of a new one. However, venturing into the unknown often entails negative consequences and any subversion or transgression thus ultimately promotes tradition and the status quo.

The Giralducian city is as much the scene of spatial transgression as the zone of sanctuary and what one person views as the acquisition of personal space, another may see as a violation of hidden social boundaries. This is particularly obvious in the case of Edmée in *Choix des élues*. When she and Claudie spend the day in Washington Park, followed by a night in a hotel, she sees it as a personal haven away from the constraints of her everyday life, but her husband Pierre views the event very differently and condemns it as a distinct spatial transgression. He is unable to understand the reason for his wife's behaviour, considering residence in a hotel to be commensurate with vagrancy. A man with traditional middle-class values, Pierre regards any violation of the codes which govern social and private space as having the potential to result in chaos and degeneracy. Edmée is part of the prosperous life which he has created for himself and he therefore sees her adventure as an attack on the home concluding that 'the household was no longer pure' (Giraudoux, 1994: 523) and asserting 'if a wife is unfaithful to her husband, it is a matter for them both, but for no one else. If she is unfaithful to her home, the damage has incalculable repercussions' (524).

Disciplined spatial segregation is thus part of the formation of gender according to Pierre, and Edmée has violated the sanctity of women's space by becoming a public woman. Her appropriation of new spaces indicates to Pierre that she is no longer under his control, she is rejecting the limitations of the space allocated to women and he fears this to be symptomatic of an approaching wider rebellion.

His fears prove to be founded as Edmée progressively pushes back the boundaries of feminine space and contests accepted notions of respectability. She first of all obtains economic independence working for a Hollywood studio, but this fails to satisfy her and so she progressively frees herself from familiar people, possessions and spaces. At one stage, she lives alone, but this is not Virginia Woolf's room of her own, since her surroundings are squalid and Edmée has become an opium user. Transgressing the sanctity of traditional bourgeois space and women's space has resulted in degeneracy and vice, not liberation and fulfilment, and the heroine has come to occupy spaces which are considered socially unacceptable for respectable women.

Spatial transgression is also a central feature of *Combat avec l'ange*. Maléna and her lover, Jacques, have an idyllic relationship, an essential element of which is their close association with specific urban spaces. One day, however, whilst out walking alone, they both transgress for no apparent reason and diverge from their usual itinerary. 'My walk', Jacques confesses, 'led me away from everything which would have too obviously reminded me of her, namely the streets in which our restaurants and shops were located... My meeting with her this evening lay in the place from which she was the most absent' (Giraudoux, 1994: 322). Their guilt is accentuated when they find each other *in flagrante delicto* with unfamiliar parts of the city, each thinking about an idealised version of the other person in their absence, and it is the destabilising impact of this double transgression which marks the beginning of problems in their relationship.

Maléna begins to feel unworthy of Jacques and seeks to remedy this by an acquisition of knowledge. The way she does this is to challenge the boundaries of bourgeois women's space and to embark on 'an Alice in Wonderland type adventure through life' (Giraudoux, 1994: 338). 'Her walks', we are told, 'were new. She made José take her out alone to Montsouris, to Ménilmontant, along the Saint-Martin canal, to the areas which, according to Amparo, you just do not visit' (Giraudoux, 1994: 368). Her incursion into such areas is not sympathetically portrayed since much of it is pure voyeurism. Giraudoux's Paris is divided into rich and poor spaces and spatial segregation is presented as desirable since it ensures social harmony. Maléna's intrusion into the poorer parts of Paris has thus destabilised the spatial equilibrium and the unfortunate and needy subsequently diverge from their usual route and seek out Maléna in her own private space, her home: 'the house was under siege. All the associates of misery and suffering have a shark's instinct when it comes to guessing the precise instant when a particular mortal can be their prey... They had a new route through Paris which took them to her street' (Giraudoux, 1994: 357).

On one of Maléna's walks 'in the wrong part of Paris' (Giraudoux, 1994: 423), she becomes aware of how out of place she is and how disruptive her actions are. She saves a child from drowning, but she feels totally ashamed: 'Maléna felt that she was an intruder in this neighbourhood, in this environment, even in this foul water. The incident belonged to these poor people, to poor people in general, not to her' (Giraudoux, 1994: 425).

Nelly's urban strolls in *La Menteuse* are equally transgressive but, unlike Maléna, Nelly has no scruples. She enjoys mixing with the working classes, since she likes to be the centre of attention. The spaces which she occupies with Reginald and Gaston give her the opportunity to experiment with multiple identities but, in both cases, she is also transgressing, since she is violating the trust of the men who occupy these spaces. Ultimately, Nelly's urban incursions do not serve any purpose since she alienates both her lovers and does not find the personal fulfilment which she craves.

Nelly and Edmée's failures confirm the dangers of infringing spatial boundaries, since transgression is not depicted as the source of long-term happiness. Giraudoux's heroines may find sanctuary in the city, in the urban space which in Giraudoux's novels is women's secret space: anonymous, exciting, full of opportunities for independent action, erotic freedom and self-invention, but this is not always a source of lasting fulfilment. It is a multilayered environment in which control over women is less possible than in other spaces and, in this way, can be a zone of emancipation. Some literary heroines, according to Heron, 'interrogate the city for answers to the uncertainties of identity' (1993: 9) and this is certainly true of many of Giraudoux's female protagonists who take advantage of the city to experiment with temporary, alternative existences and for whom the challenge of finding new spaces and new paths through the city can be seen as a metaphor for a woman's passage through life.

Giraudoux's spatial ideology is, however, predominantly one of *laissez-faire* and his heroines' secret spaces rarely lie beyond the barriers imposed by society. A number of heroines do enjoy an urban adventure which gives them a taste of emancipation, but this is usually a prelude to conformity. Such ideas on the relationship between women and the public sphere were not exclusive to Giraudoux since the desire for a return to social stability was a major focus of the interwar years. It goes without saying that social stability did not imply a radical overhaul of traditional gender roles or unrestrained emancipation, but rather a return to the pre-war gender order.

In spatial terms, this implied the division of spaces into masculine and feminine ones as well as subdivisions according to class. As I have already indicated, such traditional views were espoused by men, women and feminists, a fact which confirms the ideological confusion concerning women's role in the interwar years.

Giraudoux's men view urban space differently. For them also, it is a zone of self-discovery, but the spaces available to them are less limited than those of women. Men are shown to dominate culture, power and knowledge – all of those spaces which create status and position. Man's space is pivotal to the functioning of society, woman's is Other/elsewhere. Women are excluded from privileged male areas and can only enter as a pretty distraction or, at best, a secretary. Giraudoux's heroines, for the most part, do not challenge this spatial discrimination, but unquestioningly accept their second-class spatial status.

Those heroines who do question this gendered segregation of space introduce disorder which destabilises the spatial equilibrium. Several resemble *flâneuses*, in their voyeuristic/self-seeking exploration of the urban environment, but as the case of Edmée and Nelly demonstrated, the adventure into these forbidden places does not furnish the satisfaction which they were seeking. It rather generates turmoil in their own and other people's lives. As with so many facets of Giraudoux's work, his conclusions regarding space are ambiguous. On the one hand, he recognises the existence of spatial boundaries and underlines the limitations which these impose on women yet, on the other hand, he also emphasises the dangers of transgression; a dualistic message which characteristically evades resolution.

Notes

1. The English translations are my own.

CHAPTER 6

FORBIDDEN DESIRES: ADOLESCENT SEXUALITY IN JEAN COCTEAU AND ANTAL SZERB

Franciska Skutta

In novels as in life, bedrooms can easily become places of secrets and prohibition. Their natural isolation favours withdrawal, the accumulation of bizarre objects and the pursuit of peculiar occupations; the creation of a little closed world in which the bedroom's inhabitant reigns supreme. However, when the room is occupied by two people, it inevitably becomes a place of hidden conflict or connivance, by turns prison and refuge for its occupants and a disturbing or fascinating place for those kept outside.

A well known literary example of such a room is that shared by Paul and Elisabeth in Jean Cocteau's *Les Enfants terribles*, yet this room is one of many that exert a bewitching power over the characters in a novel and, 'by proxy', over the reader. Some years after the publication of *Les Enfants terribles* in 1929, the same fascination with a room would recur in *The Traveller and the Moonlight*, a Hungarian novel by Antal Szerb, published in 1937, in which, as in Cocteau's novel, a bedroom occupied by two adolescents, again brother and sister, becomes the scene of their extraordinary life and takes on a mythical importance in the eyes of the characters.[1] The similarities between the two rooms and their occupants are striking: an absent mother who has died young; a withdrawn father; a strange intimacy, tinged with innocent eroticism, between the brother and sister, who each have an androgynous beauty and an unusual personality; a contempt for order and various norms (chaotic room, rejection of school and 'honest' work, indifference towards money and concomitant passion for theft); a desire for isolation and enclosure in an imaginary world externalised in theatre, and lastly, a fascination with morbidity and poison, leading in both cases to eventual suicide.

We should not, however, be misled by the publication dates of the two works. Antal Szerb (1901–1945) was a novelist, poet, essayist and author of a literary history (1941) in which he described Cocteau's novel as one of the masterpieces on childhood from the new literature inspired by Freud and Proust (Szerb, 1957: 500). An immensely cultured man with a gift for subtle aesthetic appreciation, his novel is not a pale imitation of Cocteau's work, particularly since the 'terrible children' of the old quarter of the Hungarian capital had already appeared, long before those of the French novelist, in a short story that Szerb wrote (but never published) as a young man in 1919 entitled 'How did Tamás Ulpius die?' It seems that Szerb was so haunted by the idea of childhood secrets that, long after this first sketch in short story form, he reworked the theme and developed it into a novel. His novel thus retains its originality in relation to Cocteau's due to its distant origins in Szerb's own work. In the same way, despite their similarities, the two rooms – in the rue Montmartre and the castle quarter of Buda – represent two independent worlds whose roles in the narrative structure of the two novels are at least partially different.

Curiously, in both cases the first appearance of the room in the text is linked to illness. In the rue Montmartre Paul suffers from a wound caused by an overly hard snowball, then has a relapse following the death of his mother and spends a long time confined to the room he shares with his sister Elisabeth. Similarly the Hungarian hero, Mihály, is a delicate youth who suffers a nervous breakdown from which he is to some extent cured by his friend Tamás Ulpius. It is their complicity, born of sickness, that enables Mihály to pay his first, decisive visit to Tamás and to penetrate the room that the latter shares with his sister Eva. Besides being a premonitory motif, illness thus becomes a pretext for presenting the room as a background element, a place whose enclosed and intimate nature makes it the perfect setting for periods of convalescence and meetings between friends. However, gradually, in both novels, the room ceases to be a neutral space which is simply necessary to the unfolding of the plot, and becomes a kind of active participant, the benevolent or opposing partner of the protagonists throughout the series of events that takes place.

The particular status of the room manifests itself at several levels in both novels, from that of linguistic formulation through to the sense of space in the characters' lives. At the purely linguistic level it is significant that, instead of being primarily a circumstantial spatial complement, the word *room* (and also, by metonymy, *house* in Szerb's novel) often figures as a subject (and sometimes object), enabling it to represent the theme of the sentence or of an entire paragraph. There is of course nothing surprising in this in the descriptive passages, such as the first description of the house of the Ulpius family, in which the narrator Mihály combines physical presentation with an evocation of atmosphere, suggesting the importance of the place from the outset:

> [the house] was only old and dilapidated on the outside; inside it was very beautiful and welcoming, like one of those old Italian hotels. Yet in many ways it was disturbing and, with its large rooms and works of art, looked like a museum. (Szerb, 1992: 27)

On the other hand, in the short spatial notations which are more closely bound to the narration – as often happens in Cocteau's work – this kind of recurrent thematisation of space highlights the strangeness of the room and its profound influence on the characters: 'Elisabeth undressed. There was no embarrassment between brother and sister. The room was a shell under which they lived, washed and dressed like two limbs of the same body' (Cocteau, 1965: 41); or again: 'It was only after this [return from holiday] that the room sailed away. It had put on sail its stowage was more dangerous, its waves were higher' (74).

These metaphorical expressions suggest the complexity of the relationships that become established between place and characters. On the one hand, the strangeness of the place could seem to be a simple reflection of the characters of those who occupy it and who refuse to organise and experience their space as others do: the 'junk room' full of heteroclite objects radiates 'the disconcerting atmosphere of Paul and Elisabeth' (Cocteau, 1965: 31), while the 'museum' in which the Ulpiuses live forms the ideal setting for people who do not feel at home in their own time and, like Tamás, are fascinated by the past. 'For Tamás the old was normal and the new bizarre and strange. He dreamed constantly of Italy, where everything is old, made for him' (Szerb, 1992: 30). Similarly, it is not surprising that Mihály, who comes from a respectable bourgeois family, should be enchanted by this old house, which enables him to escape an everyday reality that intimidates or disgusts him.

On the other hand, however, a phrase like 'the room sailed away' or, in Szerb's work, an oxymoron such as 'The bounds of the Ulpius' house were expanded' (Szerb, 1992: 45) reveal that instead of remaining in the shadow of the characters, the room (or house) takes control of itself; it takes initiatives, constructing itself as an independent world with its own laws. It is in this way that the room reveals and realises its true function, that of responding to its inhabitants' aspirations, for these two brother and sister couples, who are not made to live in the world of positive realities, need to create a space around themselves which is in harmony with their deeper natures. 'Gain time before adulthood' (Szerb, 1992: 50) is Mihály's motto; his friendship with Tamás and Eva produces changes in him that are incomprehensible to his own family, who themselves come to represent another world in relation to the free world of the Ulpiuses that Mihály desires. The room itself perfectly fits this rupture, or opposition, between inside and outside; night and day people in the Ulpius' house reach worlds that are far distant in time and space by improvising often cruel historical scenes,[2] while in the room of Paul and Elisabeth – who have less knowledge of history – ritual scenes designed to combine pleasure with pain, complicity with competition (such as the crayfish scene[3]), require bizarre accessories that would make a 'normal' room impossible to live in. The comforts of the room in Rue Montmartre are certainly 'not of this world' (Cocteau, 1965: 50).

It takes all sorts to make a world they say. If a room is to replace the outside world in the lives of these rebellious young people, it has to take on a wide range of that world's characteristics. Thus, Paul and Elisabeth's room acquires the appearance of a city, in which disorder 'formed streets. These perspectives of boxes, lakes of paper and mountains of dirty washing were the patient's city and setting' (Cocteau, 1965: 51). Moreover this artificial landscape, organised to suit Paul, has its own 'meteorological conditions', a 'storm temperature without which neither of them could have lived' (51), yet ;the air in the room was lighter than air. Vice could not have withstood it, any more than some microbes can resist altitude. Pure, alert air, into which nothing heavy, low or vile could penetrate' (58). In this pure air, the room starts to come alive;

no longer simply a static object, it is like a living organism that moves through different phases of life, 'the room continued' (115), and, later, it 'slid towards its end down a vertiginous slope' (173). Lastly, this living body has a powerful and tyrannical mind, so that when it is on holiday, 'it was a holiday from the room, "from the grind"' (68) and the children 'imagined escaping through the game of having to live in a cell, shackled to the same chain' (68).

The room of these terrible children is an enlivening space during Paul's convalescence, when its creative spirit generates games, a whole theatrical experience every day, and it forms a protected space closed to the outside – into which the occupants do, however, deign to admit two 'chosen people', Gérard and Agathe. Gradually, however, the room becomes a malevolent and indeed destructive force, eliminating first the potential intruder, Elisabeth's fiancé, who represents the rejected outside world, and ultimately killing the very creators of its now suffocating world apart. Towards the end of the novel the room, endowed with an 'occult force' (161), seems to dictate Elisabeth's monstrous acts, for 'the spirit of the room was replacing her' (139), she acts 'out of room spirit' (157) and, 'standing along with the room, she challenged ... the whole world' (172) until her own death. Yet the suicide of the two protagonists is at the same time the death of the room, for when one wall is pulled down by Elisabeth's fall, it turns 'the secret room into a theatre open to the audience' (176) in the outside world. Thus, in one sense, the room has taken its function to the point of perfection; both refuge and prison, it has accompanied Paul and Elisabeth in the supreme rebellion of death, which is inevitable but voluntary. At all times 'the spirit of the room was on guard' (118).

In Szerb's novel voluntary death and a total refusal to integrate into the order of the foreign outside world constitute the glory of Tamás Ulpius alone. Although his room is powerful at the beginning – for the chosen intruders, Mihály and two other curious young men, 'became totally assimilated' (Szerb, 1992: 44) with Tamás and Eva – it disintegrates when 'daily reality became to flood [it] and, with this reality, decomposition' (46). However, if the end of the room, the separation of the chosen ones and the entire development towards this end are represented here in a less tragic tone than in Cocteau's novel, it is because the story of the rebellious adolescents' secret room is told here in a different type of narration, as the distant memory of the protagonist–narrator Mihály, who recounts it nostalgically to his wife on the honeymoon. Cocteau's terrible children and their room are one and the same and the story lasts as long as the room lasts. For Mihály life – and the narrative – continues, but without the room. The positive reality of adulthood has triumphed over the happiness of youth, but at least Mihály still has the painful joy of rediscovering the liberating spirit of the only room in which he has really felt at home.

Both these adolescent couples meet the challenge of 'feeling at home' in a profoundly alien world with natural, unself-conscious courage. The room in which they shut themselves away provides a secret space of absolute freedom from the constraints of the world outside, enabling its inhabitants to live – and die – in accordance with their own laws. Is it really possible to speak of transgression in the lives of these people, who rebel against bourgeois morality, calmly and spontaneously, in the spirit of play? Such a view can certainly be maintained; the very chaos of these rooms would be unacceptable to the inhabitants of the 'normal' world outside, not to mention the young people's attitudes and contempt for society's rules. But if the behaviour of Paul and Elisabeth showed the slightest vulgarity, the narrator would be unable to utter the following fine words, which could equally well apply to the hero of the Hungarian novel, 'Perhaps these uncultivated souls, were obeying some order, carrying out a manoeuvre as disturbing as the one that closes the petals of flowers at night' (Cocteau, 1965: 80).

Translated by Trista Selous

Notes

1. Page numbers refer to the French translation, *Le Voyageur et le clair de lune* (1992).
2. For 'The life led by Eva and Tamás in their house was perpetual theatre' (Szerb, 1992: 30) and, to adapt to his friends, Mihály has to take part in their games, based on Tamás's passion for history. They have a strange preference for 'plays' 'that always culminated in images of violent death' (31) – such as the stories of Judith and Holofernes, the Borgias, or the cruel deeds of Ivan the Terrible – because of the erotic pleasure experienced by the two boys at being the victims of Eva, 'the woman who deceives, betrays and kills men' (38).
3. Around midnight in Paul and Elisabeth's room (with Gérard for an audience), 'the spirit of the room would give three knocks' (Cocteau, 1965: 78), and 'a few minor changes aside, the same play would always begin ... The changes were introduced by Elisabeth. She would create surprises. Once ...

she pulled a cut glass salad bowl from under the bed. This salad bowl contained crayfish. Elisabeth put her lovely bare arms around it, clutching it to her breast, looking greedily from the crayfish to her brother ... The crayfish scene continued until Paul, who could bear it no longer, begged her to give him one. Then she had him at her mercy and punished his greed, which she loathed' (80–81).

CHAPTER 7

QUESTS IN A CUPBOARD

Agnès Cardinal

In 1947 the Argentinian writer Jorge Luís Borges published a short story entitled 'The Aleph'. It stood at the head of his first published collection and is, by any standards, a rather strange tale. Its narrator, who is called Borges, tells us that an Aleph is something indefinable, a point in space which, somehow, magically draws together within itself all other points.

In the story, the narrator, an unsuccessful writer, hears from a colleague about his childhood discovery of an Aleph, hidden in the recesses of the cellar of his home. Despite being told not to, the boy had opened a trap door and gone down the nineteen steps of a steep staircase: 'I descended secretly, went rolling down the forbidden stairs, fell off. When I opened my eyes I saw the Aleph' (Borges, 1972: 119). The narrator is persuaded to descend in turn, and also comes upon the Aleph, which overwhelms him with a multitude of vertiginous vistas. Spellbound, he sees, all at once, every aspect of the Orient and the Occident, of the North and the South; within the tattered labyrinth that is London, he glimpses simultaneously horses with swirling manes running along the beaches of the Caspian Sea; he deciphers the obscene letters which the woman he loves is writing to another man, while at the same time, he finds himself counting all the ants in the world…

In its essence the story represents a revery on the awesome potential of the human imagination. Within its realm, everything becomes possible. As the normal constraints of space and time fall away, so do all the other shackles that keep the human spirit captive within everyday reality. Borges furthermore suggests that the imagination flourishes at its most vigorous, at its most luxuriant, in the realm of the forbidden, in the dark and secret place that is the subterranean private sphere, deep in the 'cellar' of our being.

In 'The Aleph' the narrator emerges from his underground experience invigorated and triumphant as well as defensive and defiant. The Aleph must remain his secret. 'It is all mine! It is all mine!' he feels. To his eager onlooking companion he pretends that, after all, nothing out of the ordinary had happened in the cellar. Yet at the same time he cannot wait to escape from prying eyes to rush home so as to ponder his extraordinary experience in private. Later he will court public interest when he submits the story of the Aleph for publication.

One of the most compelling aspects of Borges's fantasy resides in his recognition of the tension which lies at the heart of the creative process. The imagination flourishes most vigorously and most extravagantly, he suggests, in the jealously guarded recesses of the self, while, at the same time, it is equally driven by the urge to express and thus to externalise its most hidden visions.

The paradox will be familiar to most of us. We recognise it, for instance, in the teenager who cowers furtively and possessively over a diary to which, in furious bursts of writing, the most secret thoughts, frustrations, and fantasies are entrusted. In the hunched figure bent over a page, who writes with one hand and hides what is being written with the other, we witness the contrary forces at work in the creative act. Artists, of course, know of this dilemma. Their need to communicate the splendour and power of a private vision is invariably accompanied by the pain of having to lay bare to the world that which constitutes an innermost treasure. Many overcome this problem and succeed in elegantly bridging, usually by way of metonymic displacement, the chasm that exists between inner authenticity and the public consensus. However, others find this gap impossible to negotiate. These are artists whose creative enterprise simply does not allow for the public gaze. Their vision thus remains unmitigated by compromise or adjustment to social considerations. In the locked cellar of the self, below the trap door, their Aleph empowers them to envisage the imaginative realisation of a uniquely personal world.

One of the most extraordinary creators of such a world is the Swiss artist Adolf Wölfli. Diagnosed a schizophrenic in

1895 at the age of thirty-one, he spent the rest of his life in the psychiatric clinic of the Waldau in Berne. His doctors found that the patient's emotional agitation and outbursts of violence diminished if he was given a regular ration of colour pencils and paper. With these tools Wölfli began an artist's routine with extraordinary stamina and application. Over the thirty years of his stay at the Waldau he produced forty-five large home-made tomes and sixteen notebooks crammed full of the most beautifully executed texts, collages, drawings and musical compositions (Spoerri, 1991; 1997). In endlessly altering variations on a few characteristic themes, these creations bear witness to a life wrapped up in the most amazing adventure of the imagination. Rhythmically recurring patterns of colours and decorative shapes combine to form images which tell of the lifelong odyssey of his *alter ego* 'St Adolf II', who journeys tirelessly through time and space, through this world and others (Figure 7.1).

Frequently we glimpse, at the centre of these drawings, the tiny, masked face of the artist himself: prisoner, superhero and creator all in one. The world that Wölfli fashioned for himself may well be his own inviolable domain. Yet it is also true that the aesthetic appeal and sheer energy emanating from the individual drawing, as well as the compelling cohesiveness and inner logic of the entire oeuvre, ensure that onlookers continue to gaze at Wölfli's world in spellbound fascination.

Recurring forms, dense patterning, and the multiple revisiting of a number of basic tropes may well be typical of the work of confined artists who work secretively, obsessively, and in isolation. Wölfli's drawings, it is obvious, are inimitably his own. At the same time they do share certain superficial characteristics with other artists who may well have nothing at all in common with him, other than an ineluctable compulsion to create alternative worlds. In 1961, for example, hundreds of ink drawings were found in a house in the East End of London, after Madge Gill, the occupant, had died. These drawings amount to endless series of intricate variations upon a basic theme in which a female figure is caught up in a web of textures and patterns (Figure 7.2).

On the surface Madge Gill seems to have been an ordinary housewife who lived in the East End of London in the 1930s, but records suggest that her life was not a particularly easy one. She was born illegitimate in 1884 and spent much of her childhood and teens in children's homes. There followed an unhappy marriage, the birth of three sons, and the death of a

Figure 7.1 Adolf Wölfli, *St Adolf-Fountain-Island-Ring-Giant-Snake*, 1913 Coloured crayon, pencil on paper, 96 × 74.7 cm. By kind permission of the Collection de l'Art brut, Lausanne, Switzerland.

baby girl, after which an illness caused her to go blind in one eye. Late in life she recalled that in her early thirties she began to feel an uncontrollable compulsion to create work of an artistic nature. She began with some experiments in esoteric knitting but found her true idiom when she started to do her ink drawings. She would work at night by candlelight, sitting up in bed with her good eye almost touching her material. To

Figure 7.2 Madge Gill, *Composition with Female Faces,* (undated) Ink on paper, 50.8 × 13 cm. By kind permission of Newham Museum Service, London.

justify her obsession she claimed that a spirit voice, which revealed itself to her as *Myrninerest,* had commanded her to undertake her arduous nocturnal task. In this way she created a multitude of images which she was reluctant to show to anyone and which ended up being stacked up in great mouldering piles in her bedroom.

Many hundreds of her pictures are no bigger than a postcard, while others cover the entire surface of rolled up canvas scrolls up to thirty metres in length. All of them she covered from edge to edge with busy filigrees of lines, swirls, chequered surfaces and lace-like patterns from which peeps out, in multiple variations and postures, always the same woman's face. As with Wölfli, so in Madge Gill's created world the artist reappears time and again as heroine, spectator and creator all in one.[1] Here too we come to understand Madge Gill's oeuvre as a multiply refracted and ongoing autobiographical project.

There exist many more such examples of secret pictorial artistry (see Cardinal, 1972). The mention of these two might shed an interesting light on the textual phenomenon of the so-called 'micrograms' of the novelist Robert Walser. Unlike Wölfli or Madge Gill, who effectively fashioned their artistic worlds far away from the public gaze, Robert Walser began as a young writer with publishing ambitions. He was born in Biel, Switzerland, in 1878 and at an early age resolved to embark on a literary career. He moved to Germany, and in Berlin he met some of the most notable figures of the time such as Frank Wedekind, Bruno Cassirer, Hofmannsthal and Gottfried Benn. In Prague the young Kafka was reading Walser's work with delight and admiration and eagerly searched through back issues of *Die Neue Rundschau* for further texts by this still almost unknown Swiss author. In Berlin, Walser published three novels in quick succession, of which *Jakob von Gunten* of 1909 is probably his best. It is an allegorical novel about a school which educates people to be servants. This enigmatic tale, which amounts to a quirky celebration of failure, not only intrigued contemporary critics but even today has the power to fascinate. It has twice been made into a film, of which the second, *Institute Benjamenta* (1995), has achieved almost cult status in intellectual circles in London and New York (Lilienthal, 1971; Quay, 1995).

After the First World War however, interest in Walser's work faded away. Apart from an occasional flicker of appreciation from such eminent figures as Christian Morgenstern, Franz Blei, Robert Musil, and especially Walter Benjamin, Walser's work failed to make any great impact and the writer was forced to return home, disillusioned and penniless. Back in Switzerland he continued to write his 'miniature prose' – short texts on what he perceived to be miniature topics. They were designed for publication in newspapers, but even these he found increasingly difficult to place. Suffering from loneliness and neglect, Walser became more and more aloof and began to shun all personal or literary contacts. In the retreat of rented rooms in various Swiss towns he started to fashion his micrograms – texts written in a minute and virtually undecipherable script. In 1929 Walser's two landladies sent for his sister because they were concerned for their lodger, who had begun to suffer from insomnia and severe anxiety attacks. Walser was then admitted to the Waldau clinic in Berne. It was during the four years that he spent as a patient there that he began to produce the bulk of his microscopic scripts. Because he wrote them so furtively and hid them from sight, they were for a long time ignored, as they were thought to be cast in an illegible private code. Yet they have now turned out to be simply a scaled-down version of his ordinary handwriting. In all, Walser's micrograms amount to 526 sheets of paper, many of them covered from edge to edge and top to bottom with tiny handwriting (Figure 7.3). They have

Figure 7.3 Robert Walser, *Microgram No 195b*, September/October 1925 Ink on paper, 21.5 x 13 cm. By kind permission of the Carl Seelig-Stiftung, Zürich, Switzerland.

now been deciphered and comprise two complete novels as well as numerous fragments of stories and plays (Walser, 1995–96).

Dominant in all of Walser's writing is the preoccupation with the identity and role of the writer. His musings take the form of multiple instances of ironic self-analysis. In a very short text entitled 'Das Talent' ('The Talented One') for example he writes :

> There was once a talent, who day after day sat in his room, looked out of the window and played at being lazy. The talent knew that he was a talent and this stupid and useless knowledge gave him enough to think about all day. (Walser, 1967: 95)[2]

Here Walser pokes fun at himself for daring to believe that he has any right to be a writer. On a similar subject yet in a different vein, his text 'Für die Katz' ('For Zilch') pillories his own laughable ambition of wanting to make his art matter to the world. He uses the phrase 'für die Katz', literally 'for the cat', which translates as 'for zilch' or 'to no great purpose' and connotes a waste of effort. He writes:

> The piece of prose that apparently wants to come into being here is being written in the dead of night, and I am writing it for Zilch, the cat... Zilch, the cat, is of course frequently misunderstood. People turn up their noses at her and when they give her something ... they say dismissively 'it counts for zilch'. And yet is it not true that all human beings have busied themselves from time immemorial for Zilch? (Walser, 1968: 432–434)

Such quirky and playful observations concerning the futility of life in general and the act of writing in particular, and his own pointless endeavours are among Walser's most characteristic themes. In poignant ironic pirouettes he apologises time and again for the compulsion which drives him to write and thus impose his ideas upon the world. He recognises that his writings amount to nothing more than a wasted yet enormously exhausting, slowly evolving exercise in self-portraiture. He refers to his jottings and scribblings as one great ongoing autobiographical project: 'The novel which I write and continue to write remains always the same and could be understood as the multiply fragmented and torn-apart book that is myself' (Walser, 1968: 323). It is, as Walser says, a portrait that will achieve its true and final shape only upon death.

Not unlike Wölfli's St Adolf who peers at us from within the labyrinth, or the woman whose face returns our gaze from within Madge Gill's patterned backgrounds, Walser creates in these increasingly secretive writings a kind of projected and externalised double, who triumphs in realms unattainable to the person failing in the real world. Walser's ironic stance is further compounded. His simultaneous admiration and disdain of the reading public and in particular of the coteries of the greater German cultural sphere, created within him the contradictory stance of yearning to join the very world which he despised most fervently and which he mitigated ultimately into his 'triumphant failure'. It is a failure that may well prompt a retreat into a defiant alternative.

It is not surprising that Franz Kafka should have felt a sense of affinity with Walser. Kafka's delight and simultaneous diffidence about his writings is well documented, as is his plea that his unpublished writings be destroyed after his death. Much has been written about his difficult relationship with his family, especially his father, and the fact of his being a German-speaking Jew within a Czech community. The sense of not belonging, of being at odds with the real world, could indeed be seen as one of the pivotal themes of his work, in which individual experience and a mysterious universal consensus are continually doing battle.

Such considerations lead me, finally, to think of the many women artists everywhere who still tend to see themselves as misfits. There may well be legions of female creators who, because existing cultural structures are unlikely to welcome their tokens of self-expression, keep their work entirely hidden from sight. Young girls in particular are known to entrust to secret diaries what they know would be unacceptable in public. The publication of the wartime diary of Anne Frank, for example, represents a case of such a diary made public only because of the exceptional circumstances in which it came into being and in which it was found.

A final example of defiant artistic underground activity concerns the poignant case of Verena Stefan and her mother. In 1975 Verena Stefan was a young writer who suddenly scored a phenomenal success with her first book *Häutungen* (*Shedding*). In this book she embarked on a daring quest for authentic feminine expression. *Häutungen* is a semi-autobiographical construct made up of notes, poems, dreams and analyses. It charts a vulnerable heroine's movement away from the patterns of patriarchy towards a celebration of female eroticism. Experimental in both style and content, the book broke new ground in Germany's *écriture féminine*. The novel dared to make public a very private outlook. It was a very personal, outspoken and audacious book to write, and, inevitably, it did rather blight Stefan's subsequent development. For her notoriety made it difficult for her, later on, to pursue a successful literary career within the German establishment.

Indeed Stefan's more recent book *Es ist reich gewesen* ('It was all very rich'), published in 1993, has elicited very little critical notice, and yet it is an exquisite little book. In essence, it is a lament on the death of Stefan's mother, with whom the author had a rather troubled relationship. On her deathbed, Stefan's mother confesses to her daughter that deep in the recesses of her linen chest she has kept a hidden diary. In a series of nondescript notebooks this woman had chronicled in secret, when husband and children were out of the house, the comings and goings of forty years of family life, compiling records of her cooking and cleaning, and, now and then, giving vent to her fury and despair at a life entirely spent as Keeper of the House.

In many ways that secret diary of Stefan's mother can be seen as an emblem for women's writing at large. It is still true that, like all artists *in extremis*, women have not, on the whole, been able to successfully negotiate the tension between the private and the public sphere. To this day, the realm of the female imagination still remains largely a place of guilty secrets which are destined never to see the light of day. And yet one might well want to argue that it is precisely from this sense of not belonging to the mainstream, of being outside, of being elsewhere, that there arises the possibility of authentic expression. The recesses of a linen chest might well be the very point in space in which the artist is able to let rip, give vent to anger, to fantasise, and ultimately to create a world which is truly her own.

Rather than a polemic about women's literature, these observations are part of an attempt to search out the origins and dynamics of artistic authenticity. There can be no denying that one of the most invigorating aspects of the free flight of the human spirit is the freedom that only total secrecy affords. It is in the delinquent darkness of cellars and of cupboards, behind the locked doors of asylum cells and secret hideaways, that private creativity can develop the most delicious expression of its innermost self.

Notes

1. The artistic output of Adolf Wölfli and Madge Gill has been classified as *Art Brut* or Outsider Art, both artists being represented in the *Collection de l'Art brut* in Lausanne, Switzerland. See Cardinal, Rhodes and Thévoz.
2. All translations from Walser are my own.

PART II

POLITICS OF THE FORBIDDEN

Chapter 8

Human Interiority and the French Enlightenment

Xavier Martin

Is the inner life of human beings, 'site' of thought and feeling, really a 'space'? From a materialist perspective the answer would be yes, and this was the prevailing attitude of the French Enlightenment, out of which the French Revolution largely developed. The phenomenon has two aspects.

Firstly, and chiefly, the period was dominated by sensualism, or sensationist empiricism inspired by Locke, which tended to reduce all inner phenomena to a banal biochemistry of sensation. Convinced materialists had no intellectual difficulty in adopting this conception, but neither did some philosophers who were acknowledged as being more spiritually inclined (to varying degrees). Voltaire expressed his total support of Condillac, a prime theoretician of sensationism in France, as did Rousseau, who was clearly influenced by sensationist thinking (Martin, 1994: 55–6, 73–6). It is almost certainly true that the French Enlightenment was united on this major point, so that even those who did not favour materialism tended to argue as though they were materialists, and thus more or less became in some way materialists themselves. It follows, incidentally, that in its materialisation of the inner life, sensationism tended *ipso facto* to 'spatialise' it. It is no coincidence that when Gusdorf was describing this doctrinal current, he was quite spontaneously induced to create the formula 'the space within' (Gusdorf, 1973: 50).

Secondly, the Enlightenment was strongly inclined to give credence to physiognomy, which called itself a science and asserted that character and inclination, and thus thoughts and intentions, could be deduced from the material shape of the face (Lavater's *Physiognomische Fragmente* appeared in 1775–1778). One admirer assessed 'the compartments' in Catherine II's forehead, asserting that 'You could read it like a book, without being a Lavater.'[1] Madame de Charrière, an independent spirit, ridiculed this type of method (1981: 384)[2] but she seems to have been alone. Shortly before the Revolution the philosopher Mercier, a future member of the Convention, set great store by Lavater's theories and, correspondingly it seems, appeared obsessed by the idea of 'penetrating' the thoughts and feelings of those around him (for example 1994a: xxx–xxxi, 974, 1026–1027; 1994b: 507–508, 514, 517, 522, 663, 880–883, 1118–1119).

More broadly, the period seems to have been characterised by an obsession with 'transparency'. The theme returns frequently in relationships between people ('if you could read the depths of my soul', etc.) and from the pens of the great authors. The first information Voltaire gives about his hero in the second sentence of *Candide* is that 'His physiognomy revealed his nature.' Diderot confided, 'I like men who have the physiognomy of their natures' (1962: 101). The 'philosophical' Thérèse of Boyer d'Argens promised to reveal 'all the recesses of her heart since her earliest childhood' (1992: 10). La Mettrie said that his 'only mask [was] a transparent face' (1975: 206). In the case of Rousseau, who had the good or ill fortune to possess – if we are to believe him – a 'heart as transparent as crystal' (1991: 446), it is well known that such themes are crucial in his work. Indeed, in his torment, which lasted nearly a year, he enhanced each of his letters with a rather tame quatrain of his own, including the three lines: 'Heaven, unmask impostors / And force their barbarian hearts / To open to the eyes of men' (1980, 1981).[3] Mercier, cited above, continually asked 'Who will help me to read the human heart through its envelopes?' (1994b: 881) and 'Who will take a scalpel to the mind?' (88).[4]

Taking a scalpel *to the mind,* a suggestive metaphor, evokes the priest and the police spy, those 'anatomists of thought', whom Balzac shows clashing with their eyes under the Directoire (1958: 104). Even more, it reminds us that Maupertuis, who presided over the Academy of Berlin, did not rule out the idea that one day the nature of the articulation 'between mind and body' might be directly elucidated by penetrating 'the brain of a living man' by dissection (1752: 83).[5] Moreover, in 1788, Rivarol said something fairly similar in substance, when he suggested that 'he who understands the secrets of anatomy in depth will be able to understand all the operations of the mind' (1988: 218). A few years later, Maine de Biran in his first phase was in no hurry to challenge Maupertuis' audacity, since he conceded that, in this case, the latter 'was perhaps right to a certain extent' (1957: 18). On the eve, or just before the eve, of the Revolution, human interiority tended to be seen in this way as a space, which was in itself neither secret nor forbidden. It had these two characteristics only provisionally, while waiting to be explored and improved by techniques which, it was thought, simply required a little longer to perfect.

In this respect, the omnipresent sensationism promised much, since it considered the inner life to be quite mechanically conditioned by sensations. Indeed Helvétius baldly wrote, 'We are uniquely that which the objects surrounding us make us' (1988: 539). These words are crucial. Gusdorf rightly stresses the strength of 'outer space' over 'inner space' in this doctrinal context, observing that it ultimately 'established the mechanism in mental space' and, consequently, that it held out the hope of 'an exact psychometry' (1973: 50). He also describes the 'determining of the mind by things' and speaks of the self as a simple 'reverberation of the environment' (1976: 110; 1984: 22). He notes that 'consciousness was no more than a store of data, forming the basis for a precarious order that reflected the interrelation of external realities' (1984: 19), precarious because both interrelation and realities were liable to change. He even goes so far as to use the expression 'an outside without an inside' (1982: 371), the latter being so organically annexed to the former in this logic.

The idea that we are only 'that which the objects surrounding us make us', or little more at most, was a commonplace of the time. D'Holbach was almost entirely convinced of it, 'A European transplanted into Hindustan would gradually become an entirely different man as regards mood, ideas, temperament and character' (1990: 154). As a result of his observations Rousseau believed

> that, continually modified by our senses and organs, we carried unawares, in our ideas, in our feelings and our very actions, the effect of these modifications... Consequently climates, seasons, sounds, colours, darkness, light, the elements, food, noise,

> silence, movement, rest, all act on our machine and our spirit. (1991: 409)

This idea is also clearly expressed by, among others, Maine de Biran in his early writings, 'Everything influences us and we constantly change with what is around us' (1957: 3). Cabanis gave full rein to this opinion with the authority of his medical prestige, noting for example that animals, and above all the human animal, 'are, to some extent, the living image of the place' – we would say the environment. Unequivocally reducing the mental to the physical, he even describes 'the physical analogy of man to the objects that surround him' (1980: 411).

From this it follows that a skilful alteration of the environment should be enough to change character and so rectify behaviour; notably, it should be possible to apply this procedure to oneself in the first instance. This is what d'Holbach is suggesting when he writes that 'each of us can in some way make his own temperament' (1990: 154). It is also precisely the aim of the *Traité de Morale sensitive* ('Treatise on sensory ethics') that Jean-Jacques Rousseau wanted to write and which he intended to subtitle *Le Matérialisme du Sage* ('Materialism of the Sage'). This treatise was to postulate that 'everything offers us thousands of almost certain handles by which to govern, as they originate, the feelings that we allow to dominate us', with the aim of *'forcing the animal economy* to encourage the mental order that it so often troubles' (1991: 409). The materialist d'Holbach and the spiritualist Rousseau, scapegoat and attacker of the 'Holbachic coterie', here share the same principles and the same logic, demonstrating the unity of the Enlightenment on what are clearly fundamental issues.

As the Revolution unfolded, pedagogical ideas became integrated into this logic of acting on the self by mastering the origins of sensations. Thus a philanthropist who wanted the Assembly to accept that 'We are subjected to the perpetual influence of the objects that surround us' claimed that children should be taught an understanding and concrete grasp of everything that surrounded them (Ayoub & Grenon, 1997: 110).[6] When Boulay de la Meurthe advocated what he called the 'instruction of things', in other words 'that given us by the objects before our eyes, which surround us', he was expressly referring to Locke, Helvétius and Condillac.[7] A little later Maine de Biran, who was very interested in the idea behind the *Treatise on sensory ethics* (1955: 124 n 2)[8] (so much so that, as Gouhier wrote, it 'acts as the blueprint law of his thought'

(1970: 76)), and who was, in many ways, reliving Jean-Jacques' inner hesitations and conflicts, espoused the conviction, in his maturity, that 'all our freedom' consists in orientating our processes for producing sensations and ideas 'towards the external causes ... capable of altering us or giving us these sensations and ideas' (1955: 381). He does however clearly balk at accepting fully that one can act on oneself by an act of will (for example, 1955: 199).

But the fact is that, for the Enlightenment, this process was all the more applicable to others, whose feelings and actions were thought to be open to remote control by such a method. Here lie the roots of the profoundly manipulative impulse of the French Revolution. To express the absolute and deceitful control that the master should seek to have over his young pupil's will, Rousseau poses the following question, which he evidently considers elementary and anodyne, 'With regard to him, do you not have at your disposal everything that surrounds him?' (1966: 150). We should recall two things here. First, this propensity for the total, and indeed totalitarian control of the inner life had a powerful influence on the pedagogy of the French Enlightenment, and even gave rise to the use of the word 'totalitarian' by some connoisseurs.[9] Secondly, in this respect there was no clear separation between the political and the pedagogical. Man was knowable and modifiable throughout his life using the techniques of sensationism. 'For', wrote Cabanis, 'surrounded by objects that constantly create new impressions in him, man never leaves off his education for an instant' (1980: 411).

Similarly the hoped-for political progress was bound to involve a bold penetration of the minds of the people by the forces of reform. Rousseau's *Social Contract* (which according to him – but do we know? – was merely 'a kind of appendix' to *Emile* (1969: 282)), expressly implied the drastic reshaping of human nature, and he had written approvingly that 'the most absolute authority is that which penetrates man's interior' (1979: 251). As for Mably, he also had no hesitation in asserting that it was the legislator's clear role to 'descend into the human heart and penetrate all its corners and all its secrets' (1792: 90).

Rousseau and Mably were 'spiritualists'. The advocates of materialism were all the more willing to justify this inordinate examination, which the prevailing scientism of the time seemed both to promise and legitimate. Boosted by Newton's discoveries and Locke's anthropology, Hume wanted to be 'the Newton of the inner space' (Gusdorf, 1984: 20) and to reveal 'the secret springs and principles by which the human mind is actuated in its operation' (1788: 26).

As we know, sensationist empiricism 'gives precedence to elements from the external world' (Gusdorf, 1984: 19); it suggests, and indeed, in all rigour, must imperatively postulate that the laws of interiority are merely an extension, a particular example of the laws of the physical world. As we have seen, this 'established the mechanism in mental space'; in other words, it is 'the laws of external phenomena' which provide 'the key of intelligibility applicable to the inner order' (Gusdorf, 1976: 115). This inner order is not a forbidden place, since ontologically-speaking it has no density: 'Human awareness is simply a machine for recording and combining the signals received from the outside', the human subject did not go beyond 'its reality as a simple support for its sensations' (Gusdorf, 1982: 361–362) and, according to Montesquieu, 'our mind and soul' were reduced to 'a series of ideas' (1941: 22); nor was it essentially a secret place, since the clear thrust of scientism was to elucidate everything, to '"unfold" reality completely and to open it out all on one level, following the principles of regulation in homogeneity' (Gusdorf, 1969: 153), which of course, in the final analysis, would have had the precise effect of abolishing the 'recesses' of consciousness. Indeed Balzac wrote, of a mind that revealed itself, that it 'unfolded' (1931: 218).

In this way the process was legitimated by its own principles, which, by clearing away any element of mystery from the affair, also rendered any associated respect and prudence hypothetically inappropriate. 'Man will always be a mystery to those who insist on seeing him with the biased eyes of theology' observed d'Holbach (1990: 154). This handicap did not affect the enlightened. The same author also believed that medicine would provide 'the key to the human heart', which would make it possible to 'act on men' and to direct the legislature and institutions accordingly (1990: 153). Good intentions gave additional legitimacy to this manipulative enterprise. When Helvétius wrote, 'To guide the movements of the human doll, one must understand the strings that move it' (1989a: 45), he clearly intended the process to be applied to the best of ends:

> The skill of the groom consists in understanding everything that he can make the horse he is schooling carry out: and the skill of the Minister in understanding everything that he can make the peoples he governs carry out. – The science of man is

> part of the science of government ... – So let the philosophers penetrate further and further into the abyss of the human heart: let them seek out every principle of its movement, and let the Minister who profits from their discoveries make *good application* of them, in accordance with time, place and circumstance. [Original Emphasis] (1989a: 46)

Cabanis the doctor and his ideologue friends, 'based' at the house of Helvétius' widow, believed that they could and should be knowledgeable anthropologists on this model, offering Napoleon, who had newly come to power, 'the key to the human heart'.

Some would see this conquering scientism as a demiurgic excess, an obsession with the perspective of what Gusdorf calls 'a unitary geometry of mental space' (1982: 197), which candidly aspired to take over every aspect of the socio-human in the name of a happiness appropriate to the ant heap.

> [The] distant goal of personal and collective education is to reduce both the individual person and humanity as a whole to reason. The matrix of all truth is a presupposition of totality, whose ambition is to make all thoughts, behaviour and phenomena comply with a unitary norm. (Gusdorf, 1984: 21)

Freedom, a priori, has no place in this schema. It is a fact that the Enlightenment's greater and lesser thinkers all denied that human beings are free, seeing them as simple machines, which they entirely assimilated to animals. These conclusions are necessarily implied by sensationist empiricism. Equality suffered from this logic; as the small number who understood, and were empowered to be manipulators of human nature carved out an abyss between themselves and the multitude destined to be moulded. Hyperelitism was the order of the day. Mme du Deffand, who understood (and appreciated) the philosophers better than most and had such a great affinity with Voltaire on fundamental matters, surprised herself by reproaching him, in a letter dated 5 January 1769, 'Your philosophers, or rather self-proclaimed philosophers, are cold characters ..., preaching equality in a spirit of domination' (Voltaire, 1974: 233). None of this was entirely foreign to the underlying logic of the French Revolution (see Martin, 1993/1991/1995/1999).

As the Revolution unfolded, the theme of human interiority proved a rich seam in both quantity and quality. It began with the ideal and illusion of generalised transparency, an apparent return of the primitive times when, according to Rousseau, 'men found their security in the ease of reciprocal penetration' (Rousseau, 1979: 8). Naturally, this illusion did not last, giving way to an ideal that had become overheated and shrivelled by a fear of the impenetrability of human minds. Increasingly the utopian hope was voiced that these minds could be forced open, so that they could be unmasked and reshaped. 'How sweet it would be to live among us', said Jean-Jacques, 'if the countenance was always the image of the heart's dispositions' (Rousseau, 1979: 7). Clearly such sweetness had to be deferred. The aim of political oaths and public scrutiny, which do violence to minds, was arguably to make interiority surface 'in order, it would seem, that all the night birds should be revealed' (*Archives parlementaires*, 1892: 38, 2).[10] Faces were constantly being composed and scrutinised, sometimes as a matter of life and death. Chateaubriand reported that, during these years, 'fearful, downcast eyes would turn away from you, or else bitter eyes would fix on yours to find you out and penetrate you' (1968: 337). In *Le Réquisitionnaire* (1831), a short story set in a small Normandy town in November 1793, Balzac seeks to describe this interweaving of hidden motives and calculations, in which characters subtly spy on each other, secretly investigating physiognomies. Portalis wrote that 'everyone was afraid of looking like himself' (1834: 392).

For Mona Ozouf 'the foundations of Jacobinism' lay in an 'ideal of perfect social and psychological visibility'; she refers to 'a project of absolute visibility' (1984: 83; 1989: 120). Such a project is strikingly illustrated by Simond, a speaker at the Jacobins' club on 27 July 1792, who expressed an aspiration to '*silent sessions* in which each reads in the others' eyes what is to be done' [Original Emphasis] (Aulard, 1892: 149).[11] A provincial Jacobin, considered by a purification committee to be 'of a character difficult to penetrate', worked to have this rather menacing judgement replaced by the more banal note, 'Cold and human character' (Fray-Fournier: 1903: 265). As regards the mass of citizens who were not part of the revolutionary elite, propaganda, openly informed by sensationism and employed notably during national celebrations, was imperiously designed to reorganise their minds, a task that proved only too necessary as the months and years went by. Mona Ozouf stresses that, in this context, 'the heart of hearts was itself criminal'. She also observes that 'Whoever undertakes to create a new man seeks to take over that person's every thought, ... wages war on interiority' (1984: 83; 1989: 120). According to Gusdorf, 'turning in on oneself, lyricism and interiority ... are the beginnings of high treason' (1982: 132). Tocqueville, meanwhile, felt able to write that 'in democratic republics ... tyranny ... leaves the body and goes straight for the soul' (1986a: 246).

After the Terror, which was consequently a moment when the self-compression of interiority was exacerbated, failure is obvious. A witness notes that previous events have 'taught' the Parisians 'to differentiate movements of the physiognomy from those of the heart' (Fontana: 1997: 821). Those who could not resign themselves to this failure expressed their resentment of the mind, whose 'recesses' become, in their rhetoric, 'tortuous'. The experience of the revolution did not create the term ulterior motive (*arrière pensée*), but it gave it new life since it was, it seems, 'rare before 1798' (Dauzat, Dubois and Mitterand, 1973: 550). The word 'interiority' itself made its entrance into psychological language in 1801 (Rey, 1998: 1861) as a symptom of the propensity to reinvent interiority after it had been more or less denied. After the Terror there was a trend towards its rehabilitation as space that was secret and therefore, by rights, forbidden. Abbé Grégoire expressed this at the Assembly in December 1794, saying that 'to seek to command thought is a fanciful undertaking, since it is beyond human powers; it is a tyrannical undertaking, since no one has the right to set limits to my reason' (*Moniteur* 203b: 388, 3). The attempt to manipulate the interiority of individuals persisted nevertheless, and indeed became more pronounced, during the last years of the Revolution (Martin, 1994: 145–147), as of course did the techniques of dissimulation; Tocqueville wrote that at this time still, 'many were afraid to show their fear' (1986b, 1114). However, statements like Grégoire's show that for many the lesson was well learnt.

Perhaps the only people who needed to learn this lesson were the philosophers and scientists, the *savants*. This is illustrated by the following words from future Convention member Gilbert Romme's younger sister in February 1789, which also represent a call to order and give us our conclusion. Dreaming of 'dance' and 'young men' and 'new country dances', yet pretending to her grandmother to be pious, the young woman remarked, 'If she could read my thoughts, she would think me lost. But *thought is a property which is beyond the scope of mothers and tyrants*' [Original Emphasis] (Bouscayrol, 1979: 92).

Translated by Trista Selous

Notes

1. 'The breadth of the forehead indicated the compartments of memory and imagination; one could see that there was room for everything', etc. Other echoes of the fashion for this 'science' can be found in the writings of d'Holbach (1990: 199–200), or the young Chateaubriand (1978: 95 n) and in a fine physiognomist description of Rousseau by Bernardin de Saint-Pierre (see Rousseau 1981, appendix 606: 342).
2. 'Lavater is mad to talk about our ideas as though they were a troupe of dancers who need so much space to stretch out their arms and perform entrechats and pirouettes.' She also called him 'that charlatan' (1981: 384).
3. Ciel, démasque les imposteurs
   Et force leurs barbares coeurs
   A s'ouvrir aux regards des hommes.
   See Rousseau's own analysis (1981: 79).
4. He is talking here about penetrating the special genius of the actor, in comparison to that of other artists.
5. The experiment could be performed on a criminal. 'A man is nothing, compared to the human race: a criminal is even less than nothing' (1752: 84).
6. A draft presented to the National Assembly by A.-J. Dorsch, 'French citizen', on 7 March 1792.
7. In the Council of the Five Hundred, 7 April 1799: *Moniteur* 203a: 826, 3.
8. Where Gouhier identifies the passages evoking Rousseau's *Treatise on sensory ethics* throughout the works of Maine de Biran.
9. See Gusdorf (1984: 27): 'This remodelling proceeding from outside to inside' follows 'the paths and means of a *totalitarian pedagogy*, whose outlines are to be found in the treatises of Helvétius, d'Holbach, Condorcet, Bentham and in revolutionary legislative reform' and M. Grandière (1998: 239), who uses the expression *'pedagogical totalitarianism'*; see also in particular 'manufactured children' and 'total suppression through kindness' (316) and, in the conclusion, 'totalitarian aspects', 'surveillance and shutting in', 'the will to appropriate the child', 'pedagogical demiurges', 'uniformity of thought'(416) and so on.
10. In the words of Merlin de Thionville, who was demanding a public vote in the legislative Assembly, 23 February 1792.
11. The expression is not very rigorous, but its meaning is clear.

Chapter 9

The Hidden World of the Marais

Gordon Phillips

When the Romans settled on the Ile de la Cité and the area to the south, known as Lutèce, the Marais was a marshland. Surrounded by the Seine to the south and an oxbow to the east and north, it constituted a flood plain. At that time the only signs of a settlement were a landing area – roughly on the site of the present Place de l'Hôtel de Ville – and a road running due north, the present day rue du Renard. These then – the Seine, the rue du Renard and the site of the old oxbow – roughly form the borders of the present day Marais. As the population increased, further 'barriers' demarcated the area: in 1190, town walls were constructed under the orders of Philippe Auguste and later, in 1356, a second wall was built by Charles V.

What I will examine here are two juxtaposed groups of streets within the Marais, which are culturally so important to two diverse marginalised groups – more precisely the 'Jewish area' around the rue des Rosiers and the 'gay area' around the rue St. Croix de la Bretonnerie. To consider Jews or gays monolithically is of course problematic in that social class, race, ethnicity and gender will all play a role in shaping their identities, and references to this complexity will be made in the course of this essay. However, I am primarily concerned to show how this part of Paris has become a metaphoric site for what has been happening politically and culturally in France; the life, culture and aesthetics of the area reflect the inhabitants' attitude to the rest of society and the prevailing attitudes within the rest of society towards them. I will consider how in recent years this separate space, previously secretive and unwelcoming to outsiders, has ceased to be a quasi ghetto, becoming instead a more open environment. Finally, I will consider whether such a development is to be welcomed. In order to understand this process, it is first necessary to briefly trace the history of the Marais and establish why the area should attract two such different groups.

During the Merovingian period, from the fifth to the eighth centuries AD, the area comprised several islands and ecclesiastical settlements began to establish themselves there. This was very separate from the rest of Paris, because prospective builders had to negotiate hard with the monks, who were happy to wait for higher prices, and thus it remained otherwise relatively vacant until the 1500s (Ranum, 1968: 83). By the second half of the fourteenth century, the royal family had residences at St. Paul and Tournelles. Later, Henri IV sponsored and directed the construction of the Place Royale, which was completed in 1612, and which is now known as the Place des Vosges. The royal connections, combined with this fashionable square, led several aristocrats to have private *hôtels* built in the area: Diane de France, the Guises, Charles de Valois, Sully, le Duc de Maine to name but a few.

The *hôtels*, served by narrow streets – Haussmann did not create his wide boulevards here – engendered a sense of a hidden world, because the aristocrats sought to provide themselves with a seclusion fitting to their independent wealth and power. Ranum describes the 'ideal' *hôtel* as a dwelling sitting on a rectangular half acre of land, of which from the street all that could be seen were the high walls, high slate roofs and twenty foot doors of the carriage entrance (1968: 151). Unlike the houses in the Place Royale, the *hôtels* were very much designed to keep out the prying eyes of outsiders and windows were rare on the ground floor because the nobles lived upstairs, above the kitchens and rooms used by servants (Ranum: 84). Thus, when the doors were closed, the *hôtel* was impregnable to bandits, police and beggars.

When the king relocated to the Palais de Versailles in 1678, the Marais ceased to be the fashionable place for the aristocracy or the bishops to live, and so they too began to move out of the area, relocating to the west: Place des Victoires, Place Vendôme and Faubourg St. Germain (Ranum, 1968: 284). The 1789 revolution was the *coup de grâce* as religious communities and aristocrats were expelled and the grand mansions were gradually subdivided into smaller dwellings and sold, in the first instance, to the bourgeoisie.

This process of subdividing both horizontally and vertically continued – smaller flats meant cheaper rents – and the population density increased enormously thanks to an influx of people of more limited means. Accommodation was particularly cheap here because the improvements made elsewhere by Haussmann – better sewerage, better water supply, wider roads, slum clearance and building projects – inevitably meant an increase in rents (Christiansen, 1994: 105). Consequently the Marais drew in refugees from this 'gentrification' and a cosmopolitan population began to establish itself there, most notably Jewish migrants (Winchester, 1993: 211). To quote Berg: 'Amongst the places of significance to Jews, the oldest and the most famous is without doubt the eastern part of the fourth arrondissement' (1997: 295).

A Jewish presence in the area was not new; we know that Jewish families lived on the nearby Ile de la Cité as early as the sixth century and that from the twelfth century they settled in the Marais itself, on the banks of the Seine around St. Gervais. This small community gradually moved north to the present-day Jewish area around the rue des Rosiers, where records show that Jewish weavers practised their trade as early as the thirteenth century.

The Jews were expelled from Paris in 1394 because, according to Roger Kohn, pillaging of their property by non-Jews left them too poor to contribute to the royal coffers (Berg, 1997: 66). After this period it is difficult to talk of a Jewish community: some were allowed to remain by virtue of converting to Christianity, some survived clandestinely and others, especially from the mid fifteenth century, were given permission to return and practise their trade, but had to renew this authority every two to three months (Berg, 1997: 70).

In 1791, Jews were given French citizenship and Napoleon opened up certain professions to them. Prejudice continued, but the capital, and more particularly the Marais, offered a sense of security within a Jewish community. The earliest settlers were from the provinces, especially Alsace and towns such as Bayonne and Bordeaux. Further arrivals came from eastern France with the cession of Alsace and the northern half of Lorraine to Germany in 1871. Philippe describes them as '*israélites*' who were first and foremost French, but nevertheless, according to Weinberg, such a high concentration of Jews in the Marais reinforced natural ties of religion and ethnic tradition which underlay the cohesiveness of the community, a community which must have been all the more close-knit because of the physical closeness of the dwellings and the fact that the industries were so small scale (Philippe, 1992: 26; Weinberg, 1977: 6).

Keen to leave an area which reminded them of hard beginnings, many more affluent Jews began to move away from the network of small narrow streets around the St. Paul *métro* station for Montmartre, Belleville and Ménilmontant (Berg, 1997: 196). In the latter part of the nineteenth century and early part of the twentieth, they were replaced by Jews from central and eastern Europe, attracted to the French capital by economic growth and legislation which offered them relative freedom, and to the Marais in particular, because of the availability of cheaper accommodation. Berg claims that by the end of the nineteenth century 80 per cent of all Jews leaving central or eastern Europe chose to settle in Paris (1997: 194). This process – east European Jews settling in the Marais, while second generation Jews moved out – had a number of effects.

Firstly, the appearance and atmosphere of this part of the Marais completely changed: oratories opened in which Yiddish, rather than Judéo-Alsatian, was spoken; kosher shops opened and shop windows began to display Polish and Russian foodstuffs. More than half of the Russian Jews chose to set up in the clothing industry and the *pletzl* of the Marais became renowned for their Jewish tailors. In fact, fur coats, common in their country of origin, became fashionable and affordable here as well (Berg, 1997: 194–196). The aesthetic decline of the area accelerated as workshops and lean-to sheds filled the courtyards of the *hôtels* in order to support small-scale intensive industries such as jewellery, leather-working, clothing and spectacle making (Winchester, 1993: 211). A common stereotype of the time, that Jews were primarily involved in usury, was far from true and based purely on prejudice (Philippe, 1992: 31).

Secondly, there was increasing hostility between the native and immigrant Ashkenazic Jews. This was not merely an effect of the wide social and economic gap between the two, but also of a fundamentally different approach to living in France. While 'native' Jews generally feared the creation of ghettos and the visibility that might increase the incidences of anti-Semitism, 'immigrant' Jews often disapproved of the former's readiness to assimilate (Weinberg, 1977: 6).

Thirdly, the area around the rue des Rosiers became very much a ghetto by the 1930s, as the least assimilated and poorest elements of the immigrant Jewish population had settled there (Weinberg, 1977: 5). These were often immigrants who, with no ready capital, were desperate for money to pay back their transportation to Paris or to pay for the rest of the family to join them. They were, however, cruelly exploited as cheap labour in the clothing and textile trades, this being particularly true of those who had a very poor command of French, especially if they had entered the country illegally, thus risking arrest and expulsion. Weinberg claims that, in the 1930s, 50,000 immigrant Jews worked in the textile trade, either in the ateliers or as home labourers (1977: 14, 15). The Laval government of 1935 had put quotas on the number of foreign workers in any firm, but employers risked only a small fine, and could save a fortune by employing them at very low rates of pay.

Living conditions were poor and cramped. Indeed, a study revealed that in 1930 it was not uncommon for an immigrant family of 6–8 people to live in a single room (Weinberg, 1977: 21). This must have been a factor in the spread of tuberculosis, from which 7 per cent of the inhabitants of the *pletzl* were suffering in 1935 (Weinberg, 1977: 9). Life for these people then was incredibly hard; one observer comparing their plight to that of a man 'bicycling on butter' (Weinberg, 1977: 16).

One cannot imagine the despair felt by this Jewish community when the creation of the Blum government in 1936 led the fascist *Action Française* to cover the walls of Paris with posters pertaining to 'Jewish domination' and 'the Jewish empire' (Berg, 1997: 252). Rumours were soon beginning to spread amongst Parisians that Jews were trying to stir up hatred and fear of Germany, and, as war became ever more likely, so the hostility towards them increased. After the *Anschluss*, there was a noticeable upsurge in anti-Semitism, which caused leading figures in the community to advocate discretion (Weinberg, 1977: 175). Weinberg quotes Lambert, writing in *L'Univers Israélite*, 27 May 1938: 'Immigrants should practice moderation: they should not speak in public lest someone should hear their foreign accent' (1977: 205). The Stalin-Hitler pact could only have added to their feelings of hopelessness.

Capitulation, occupation by the Nazis and the ensuing *statuts des Juifs* meant that they were forbidden certain professions, were forced to wear a yellow star and were subjected to the most humiliating loss of rights: they could not move house, own a radio, telephone from a post office or café or travel in any but the last carriage in the métro (Berg, 1997: 277).

Of the 80,000 deported Jews, 2,500 survived the war and returned to Paris, usually to the nineteenth arrondissement (Berg, 1997: 291, 349). This made a total population of 50,000 – the biggest Jewish community in any European city. The community however was transformed especially between 1956 and 1960 with the arrival of Sephardic Jews from North Africa – 110,000 from Algeria and 140,000 from Morocco and Tunisia (Berg, 1997: 325).

The area around the rue des Rosiers was thus transformed as the 'new' Jews adopted a much more strident and assertive approach to their Jewishness. Berg describes this as discretion giving way to a Mediterranean exuberance (1997: 346). This has shown itself in the ceremonies of the '*Simhat Torah*' and the 'Rejoicing of the Law', as well as in the celebration of marriages, when noisy processions lead the couple to or from synagogues.

The exuberant and cosmopolitan nature of the Marais was probably a prime factor in attracting another group, the gay community, from the end of the 1970s. Other areas of Paris had been associated with male homosexual acts – in particular the Jardin des Tuileries during the nineteenth century – but this was an anonymous, covert world. The Marais represented the beginning of a commercialised gay scene and although gay establishments now exist in other parts of Paris, this area remains of prime importance. I should signal however that the gay scene in Paris was slow to establish itself – the first gay bar did not open until 1979 – and never really gained the intensity of certain districts in cities in the USA or the UK (*Spartacus International Gay Guide*, 1997/98: 211). This may appear ironic in a country where homosexuality (both male and female) has not been illegal since the days of the *Ancien Régime*, when sodomites were burnt at the stake, but the reasons are probably twofold. Firstly, this was a society that had been profoundly Roman Catholic with a strong sense of the family unit, and therefore public opinion has tended to be hostile. In his book *Sexual Moralities in France 1780–1980*, Antony Copley claims that 'public opinion was just as, even more oppressive, a force in France than the overtly repressive legislation in England' (1992: 232).

Even students involved in the events of May '68 tore down posters with a gay theme because they were scared of giving the revolution a bad name (Martel, 1996: 22). Secondly, prior to the creation of the *Comité d'Urgence Anti-Répression Homosexuelle* (CUARH) in the late seventies, the very nature of French homosexual pressure groups meant they were doomed to failure. In the first instance their invisibility rendered them ineffectual and later their revolutionary stance meant they were so marginalised as to have little or no impact on the decision-makers in government. In order to understand this, it is necessary to trace the history of these groups from the Second World War, after the introduction of anti-homosexual legislation under the Vichy regime.

The only organised homosexual group in the 1950s and 60s, *Arcadie*, had always tried to project a strong, silent image, seeking not to disturb heterosexual society, even to the point of removing the sexual connotation of the label and so calling themselves 'homophiles' rather than 'homosexuals'. They chose to live discreetly apart from the rest of society – to quote their president, André Baudry: 'If we want to live happily, let's remain hidden' (Martel, 1996: 70).

In the early seventies the lesbian led *Front Homosexuel d'Action Révolutionnaire* (FHAR) continued with its separatist stance, but was much more strident, seeking fundamental changes to the organisation of society. As Françoise d'Eaubonne said: 'You say that society must integrate homosexuals, but I say that homosexuals must disintegrate society... Revolution is not only about class struggle but also the overthrow of traditional values and ways of life' (Martel, 1996: 25).

During this period however, an increasing number of lesbian activists directed their energies towards issues other than gay rights – the availability of abortion, rape legislation and anti-pornography campaigns (Martel, 1996: 94). By the late 70s, it was the CUARH that had emerged as the key organiser of symbolic gestures and demonstrations, though these were relatively small-scale; the largest, which occurred in April 1981, numbered some 10,000 people (Bach, 1982: 84). The CUARH was more pragmatic than the FHAR and concerned itself primarily with realisable, short-term goals and in engaging in dialogue with the *Parti Socialiste* (PS). This strategy proved fruitful as, following the elections of 1981, they had an administration sympathetic to their demands. This change of government heralded a gamut of changes, in particular the age of consent which, set at eighteen in 1974, was brought in line with the heterosexual age of fifteen. In fact, within the first year of a socialist government, France no longer accepted the World Health Organisation's definition of homosexuality as a mental disease, censorship on films and books was lifted, public sector workers could be more open about their homosexuality, police raids on gay establishments were stopped and police files on homosexuals were supposedly destroyed (Martel, 1996: 158).

It is not surprising that there gradually emerged a new mood of confidence, which, combined with the influence of a more assertive gay presence in Anglo-Saxon cultures, heralded the start of a more vibrant and diverse culture. As advances in the legal position of gays were made, however, many now felt the battle was won and so a certain complacency set in, the emphasis now tending toward providing the requisites of a hedonistic lifestyle, rather than on protest or political campaigning (Martel, 1996: 174; Baillie and Salmon, 1993: 39). In his book *Le Rose et le Noir*, Martel refers to this period – the early 1980s – as one of segregation to which gays readily agreed (1996: 200). This can be seen first of all in the buildings themselves: within an area of narrow streets and many high walls, the new bars represented a closed, forbidden world. Shutters and opaque windows discouraged unwanted attention and closed doors with a spy hole ensured no intruders could gain access (Martel, 1996: 198). Inside the lighting was subtle, the music loud. This was very much a male-dominated universe where the emphasis was on places to meet sexual partners (Martel, 1996: 176). Lesbians meanwhile kept a lower profile and few women-only bars and discotheques were established; they tended to meet partners through work or existing networks of friends (Martel 1996: 205).

Gay male fashion also played its part in creating a sense of separateness. Mermaids clutching parasols and asking their way to the beach may have featured prominently in the demonstrations of the early 1970s, but by 1980 one was more likely to meet a more so-called 'masculine look' – short cropped hair and denim (Martel, 1997: 34/190).

In the 1990s this separate world changed and still continues to change in four different ways. Firstly, around the junction of the rue Saint Croix de la Bretonnerie and the rue Vieille du Temple a plethora of bars, clubs, restaurants and shops aimed at a gay market have developed. This proliferation is a clear indication of how commercialism has taken over – the power of the 'pink franc' has quickly been spotted and exploited by entrepreneurs.

Secondly, the anti-gay reaction to the Aids epidemic in the 1980s, with increased censorship of films with gay themes and calls in the *Sénat* for the raising of the homosexual age of consent, has given way to more tolerant attitudes: 'Two thirds of the French, according to opinion polls, now reckon homosexuals should have the same rights as married couples; more than half say they would "accept" a homosexual son or daughter' (*The Economist*, 5 July 1997: 36).

Society has changed and, in the capital at least, is more accepting of difference, and so gays have to some extent lost their sense of Other. Young gays have less of a sense of experiencing the forbidden and so a less secretive culture has emerged; spy holes have been removed from doors, shutters taken down, rainbow flags flown in a prominent position, and dimly lit bars have started to give way to open airy ones. The philosopher Michel Foucault died early in this process, in 1984, but he is reputed to have actually missed the covertness and danger of the old days (Merrick and Ragan, 1996: 232).

Thirdly, although a 'gay look' as a political statement can still be seen, it is increasingly rare. Gays and lesbians on the scene, with its emphasis on partying and attracting others, may well be conscious of fashion, but probably no more or less so than their young heterosexual counterparts. Indeed, one cannot help but gain the impression that clothes worn in the Marais are more conventional, more in line with the mainstream, than is the case in London's Soho.

Fourthly, the very separateness these spaces afforded is also being eroded, as an increasing number of heterosexuals, in particular heterosexual women, go to gay venues either to enjoy the allegedly hedonistic atmosphere or to escape for an evening, away from the gaze of predatory males. Indeed, although no reference is made as to how the figure was arrived at, it has been claimed that of the 300,000 or so marchers on the 1997 gay pride march, a quarter were heterosexual (*The Economist*, 5 July 1997: 36). The phenomenon of straight people enjoying the gay scene has increased in London as well – a development which led the journalist Andrew Tuck to coin a new term for such people: 'strays' (*Independent on Sunday*, 29 June 1997: 16). Attitudes to them differ of course; for some they represent a group of unwelcome intruders, for others they are part of a process of breaking down barriers, but for most they are just people having fun!

It is therefore clear that these two adjoining areas of the Marais are not a hermetically sealed environment, but very much a living and lived-in part of Paris. The social and ethnographical make-up of the people living, working or socialising there is constantly evolving, and, as I have shown, the Marais constitutes a metaphor for developments in present-day society. This area may have lost an element of the 'secret' or 'forbidden', but it still represents an area of enormous importance to both cultures.

Society has indeed changed a great deal since the Marais community of the 1930s, which can be summed up in a sentence by Chomsky: 'Immigrants go to shul, mingle with fellow Jews, pray for a better year, and feel at home away from the worries of the outside world' (Weinberg, 1977: 180). Witness reactions to the bomb attack on 10 August 1982 at the *Restaurant Goldenberg* in the rue des Rosiers, which killed six people and injured twenty-two more (Berg, 1997: 343–344). The arrival of President Mitterrand as Head of State that very evening, as well as his return the following year in the company of one of his ministers, Jacques Attali, is of enormous symbolic importance and shows Jewish integration within a multicultural society.

This sense of integration need not mean the end of difference. Jews are anxious to retain and celebrate their culture, traditions and Jewish history and we have seen the creation of the Commission française des archives juives in 1963, the purpose of which is to stimulate the study of the history of Jews in France and, more recently, the opening of the Musée d'Art et d'histoire du judaïsme in the rue du Temple in 1997 (Berg, 1997: 349). Meanwhile several private Jewish schools have appeared in Paris, including one in the fourth arrondissement itself.

In this we can draw comparisons with gay culture. As gays progress along the road to equality, the need to distinguish between sexual orientations diminishes – a process which has been referred to as the 'degaying of society' – and with it the danger of a loss of identity. Peter Tatchell points out the paradox of this situation: 'The ultimate queer emancipation is the abolition of homosexuality and the eradication of the homosexual' (Simpson, 1996: 35). In other words, the more successful gays are politically – fighting for equality in the law – the sooner their demise. So is the party over? Are gays doomed to lose what Martel calls 'happiness in the ghetto' (1996: 179)?

Certainly, if we look elsewhere in Europe, the granting of rights in Scandinavia has led to an impoverished gay community and the *frisson* of being separate from the mainstream has been lost. Anecdotal evidence is supplied by Anna Palmer of Stonewall:

> I was in Denmark recently and they have everything, except the right to marry, so you'd expect there to be a really vibrant culture, but there isn't. There is still homophobia, but no-one

> does anything about it. Here, we may not have all those rights, but the gay culture is incredible. (Tuck, *Independent on Sunday*, 29 June 1997, 16.)

It is essential that 'degaying' or the deconstruction of homosexuality does not lead to the death of gay culture here too. Or is it? We talk so easily about gay identity and the gay community, but what is the gay culture we seek to protect? It is difficult to read *Anti-Gay* and not recognise the negative aspects of gay culture and feel a certain unease at the lack of self-criticism. Indeed one may feel some sympathy with the despair of activists, who see that for many 'gay' has become a ready-made lifestyle, which dictates everything, from the clothes one should wear to the music one likes. However, to blindly follow fashion and prevailing attitudes is surely not the preserve of the homosexual. Gay culture is precisely that – a fashion. It is almost impossible to define because everything, from relationship patterns to lesbian fashion, is constantly changing.

As the number of out gays increases, it also becomes more evident that gay culture is polymorphous, not the monolith it is often presented as. With a group of people coming from all sectors of society, there is bound to be a plurality of gay cultures. In order to be gay, one need not conform to certain clichéd stereotypes or even be wedded to a gay identity. One can be eclectic and choose from a plurality of gay – and heterosexual – cultures, within the worlds of fashion, music, literature, film or venues for socialising.

In conclusion, the Marais has been a site of major importance within Paris for a number of Jewish and gay cultures and it embodies attitudinal developments in society towards them. The move away from marginalisation within a quasi ghetto is, I feel, a welcome development. However, as attitudes towards ethnicity, sexuality and Other change, and previously marginalised communities lose their sense of the secret and the forbidden, we run the risk of cultural homogeneity. The challenge is how to retain a separate space such as the Marais with all the possibilities that it yields. Daniel Guerin may have been talking in terms of voicing political grievances, but his underlining of the need for both integration and a separate space for blacks in America is just as apposite here:

> Black Americans must be able to unite with whites in unions etc., and at the same time it's a specific struggle which justifies a certain separatism. For homosexuals it's the same thing: it is essential they have a place with people like them, where they

> can talk about the oppression they are experiencing, but at the same time they have to participate in a general movement. (Bach, 1982:102)

The Marais currently offers such a space to various groupings. It is both the site of difference for Jewish and gay communities, and a site of assimilation where sameness and difference, whether through sexuality, religion and/or ethnicity, is continuously and visibly negotiated.

Chapter 10

Making Ideal Histories: The Film Censorship Board in Postwar France

Suzanne Langlois

Film censorship has existed as an institution in France since the First World War, and since then the State has never surrendered the power to control the images seen by French audiences, and the images from France shown abroad. Although economic pressure and a more liberal classification according to age groups may have replaced direct intervention, the principal concerns of the State have remained the same: national interest, public order, morality, and violence. Each of these categories defines a vision of French society.

In this essay, my specific concern is French history during the Second World War and its representation in postwar films. My analysis focuses upon the choices made during the twenty-five years following the end of the war, and the way in which the French Film Commission can guide us through the authorised and the forbidden images of France's wartime collaboration and resistance.[1]

Film Censorship: the *Commission de contrôle des films cinématographiques*

Even before the Second World War, France had a system of mandatory visas intended for both internal and export markets: the *visa d'exploitation* (release visa), which allowed a film to open in France, and the *visa d'exportation* (export visa), which allowed the film to open on foreign markets. Importantly, the right to open in France did not necessarily confer the right to open on export markets. Through the years film censorship was placed under the authority of different ministries – an indirect indication of the complex history of the status of film. It moved from the Ministry of the Interior to the Ministry of Education and Fine Arts, and ultimately, in the autumn of 1939, to the Ministry of Information.

Although the liberation of France occurred in 1944, the war was not yet over. The series of decrees applied immediately following the Allies' landing in Normandy (June 1944) remained in effect during the winter of 1944–1945. All films distributed and shown in France, whether new or old, were first examined by a board of censors under military authority. Besides ensuring military security, the military censors had the political aim of controlling filmic content. The Film Service was but one of many of the War Ministry's sections for the control of information. Despite the fact that a *Direction générale du cinéma* had been established by the French Provisional Government in September 1944, the Army continued to control film censorship until the end of the war. The extent of its prerogative went well beyond strict military questions, as had already been the case in Algiers, the seat of the Provisional Government prior to the liberation of France.

The Film Section of the Military censorship held daily screenings to examine fiction and documentaries, ranging from feature-length films to trailers. Captain Lhéritier chaired the section with an officer from military security, representatives from the Ministries of the Interior, Justice, and Public Health, and individual officers to represent the Allies and the French *Service cinématographique des armées* (Film Corps). Each week the chair sent a report of the decisions and visas granted to the *Direction générale du cinéma.* This system of military censorship lasted until 3 July 1945, when a new law re-established civilian authority over film censorship and created a *Commission de contrôle des films cinématographiques* (film censorship board). This was divided into two groups of nine members each, one to represent the Administration and the other representing film professionals (Order no. 45–1464 and Decree no. 45–1472, 3 July 1945).[2] The role of the Commission was to examine all scripts and to put forward a provisional opinion. The Ministry of Information delivered the visas; the official request could be made only when the film was entirely finished, and a print of the exact and integral version had to be submitted, as well as the definitive cut and dialogue.

The Army continued to be represented on this new Commission and, more significantly, succeeded in establishing and creating its own interpretation of the war. Consequently, the military struggle took precedence over the ideological conflicts of the Second World War and only two clearly defined enemies – France and Germany – were present on screen in this restricted and Manichean vision of the war. Such an interpretation, shared by the government, prevented an ideological interpretation of the war that would focus attention on the internal divisions France had experienced during the Occupation, and rekindle heated debates.

It should be remembered that the French film industry was reorganised in 1945 and production began immediately. The first films about the war, documentaries, fiction, or montage films, arrived in the cinemas before any historical scholarship about the Second World War began. Therefore, in the immediate postwar period, films, radio programmes, newspapers, and booklets were the essential tools of knowledge about the war, and a significant part of that information was based on oral and written testimonies.

The Interpretation of French History

As they formed their coherent, if incomplete, vision of wartime French history, the censors were concerned with two main themes: the situation in France during the Occupation, and the role of the military forces. Both subjects were closely linked to French prestige, and both included, at some point, a perception of the Germans and of Germany. Crucially, the various ministries could intervene at any point and pressure the Commission to request changes or to prevent an authorisation, even if the Commission had recommended that the release and export visas be granted.

The representation on film of the situation within France during the Occupation presented problems. Films that exalted the Resistance, such as René Clément's *La Bataille du rail* (1945–1946) about the resistance of railway workers, were supported for export.[3] However, films that depicted negative images of the French population during the war, such as collaboration with the occupiers, denunciations, and black market activities, were not to reach foreign audiences. France was particularly sensitive and forbade export to German-speaking areas now occupied by the French army. Great care was taken to present only an irreproachable version of French history as a country completely overrun and occupied by a hostile foreign army. This is where the two visa system was valuable. Some films received their release visa and could open in France, despite their not so glorious vision of history, but they were refused the export visa for certain markets. For example, *Les Portes de la nuit* by Marcel Carné opened in France in December 1946 but was denied an export visa for the Sarre region, Germany, and Austria (Figure 10.1). When Pathé-

Figure 10.1 *Les Portes de la nuit,* France, Marcel Carné, 1946. Poster from the photographic library, Bibliothèque de l'Image – Filmothèque, Paris. A003/78 René Peron. Rights reserved.

Cinéma made a new request in 1950, it was again denied despite the fact that the Commission had given its permission. A note from the Ministry of Foreign Affairs stopped the procedure by mentioning that the objections made in 1946 were still valid in 1950: this description of collaboration was, to say the least, inappropriate in French-occupied territories.[4]

A late 1940s film, *Retour à la vie* (1949), presented five sketches that dealt with the return of the soldiers at the end of the war. The Commission agreed – six to one – to authorise the film but reminded the producer that the subject's treatment must not provoke any incidents with prisoners' associations and representatives of foreign armies.[5] The only opposing vote, from the Ministry of Population, did not prevent the granting of the authorisation, but the film was forbidden in the Sarre region. When *Retour à la vie* was publicly released, film critics responded negatively to its pessimistic tone and the sense of bitterness and derision it encapsulated.

In the 1940s, French soldiers were not common characters in fiction films. The French military forces were most often depicted in documentaries and montage films, and most of these were made by the *Service cinématographique des armées*, and thus presented the army's perspective. However, later in the decade there was one feature film that aimed to be the '*récit cinématographique*' (filmic narrative) of events in Algiers in November 1942: *Le Grand Rendez-vous* (1949–1950) by Jean Dréville (Figure 10.2).[6] Its subject matter was very sensitive as it dealt with the role of the French armed forces in North Africa when the Allies landed there in 1942 – a turning point in the war and a decisive moment for the Vichy regime of Marshal Pétain and for France. Despite the presence of some patriotic officers, the film glossed over several embarrassing and confusing events that happened in Algiers because the Vichy government had formally ordered all-out military resistance to the landing.

The film was carefully examined by the Commission. Rumours abounded that the military had asked for changes to the script, and an examination of the censorship files confirms this assertion. As a result, the army was not depicted as betraying the country; the role of the officers who welcomed the allied landing was embellished by a voice-over commentary, and only Admiral Darlan – a high-ranking officer loyal to the Vichy authorities – was not rehabilitated. No one on the Commission objected to him being called '*une ordure*' (a bastard). The note from the military censor, Commandant Célérier,

Figure 10.2 *Le Grand Rendez-vous,* France, Jean Dréville, 1949–50. Poster from the photographic library, Bibliothèque de l'Image – Filmothèque, Paris. A097/29 no author. Rights reserved.

states that the script must be altered where it was not in accordance with the historical truth, and it details the action of the patriotic officers. In a letter dated 23 February 1949, the president of the Commission, Georges Huisman, asked the *Centre national de la cinématographie* (CNC) to deliver a provisional authorisation to begin the shooting of the film, since it was understood that the script writers would rapidly modify the dialogue according to the remarks of Commandant Célérier.[7] Furthermore, comments about the ill-treatment endured by political prisoners who, after 1940 and the establishment of official collaboration with Nazi Germany, were forced to work on the construction of the Trans-Saharian rail line, were withdrawn from the script following comments about this passage from a member of the Commission, Mr. Santoni. The subject was not raised at all in the film.

The prestige of France continued to be a major concern during the 1950s, particularly because of the war in Algeria. A short scene in *Nuit et brouillard* (*Night and Fog*) – a documentary film about deportation made by Alain Resnais between 1955 and 1956 – became a bone of contention because it showed the *képi* of a French *gendarme* guarding an internment camp in France during the Second World War. State collaboration was still taboo in French films, and the infamous *képi* had to be camouflaged to eliminate the visual link between the French police and internment camps. But the matter did not stop there. Another twist was added when Germany, the old enemy now turned ally in the Europe of the Cold War, requested and succeeded in having the film removed from the programme of the Cannes Film Festival. This developed into the 'affaire *Nuit et brouillard*'. The film was nevertheless a triumph both for the public and the critics, winning several prizes and having a successful international run.

This was not Germany's first attempt to prevent a film from opening. The year before, in 1955, it had succeeded in having a co-production by Yugoslavia and Norway, *La Route sanglante*, also a film about deportation during the Second World War, removed from the programme. The Commission also recommended that Luis Saslavsky's *La Neige était sale*, a feature film made in the mid-1950s that depicted increased criminalty in the civilian population during the Second World War, move its action's location from Alsace to an unidentified area of Eastern Europe (see Lindeperg, 1993: 472). Film censorship was further tightened in the early 1960s. On 18 January 1961 a new decree (Décret 61–62) replaced the July 1945 legislation and reorganised the *Commission de contrôle des films cinématographiques*. It introduced a compulsory authorisation, based on the script, prior to the shooting of the film. Officially called *avis préalable* (prior notice), it was often referred to as *précensure* (precensorship). This decree remained in place for thirty years until it was replaced in February 1990. Meanwhile, film categories introduced in 1945 that allowed general admission or restricted entry to people over sixteen years of age were replaced in 1961 by new categories: general admission, a 'thirteen' certificate and an 'eighteen' certificate. At this point there were now three groups of eight members sitting on the Commission. As was the case in 1945 the first group represented the Administration, the second group represented the film professionals, and a third group was added to represent certain sections of the public. Some came from groups and associations, while others shared some form of social commitment through their professions such as teachers, doctors, or psychologists (Soudet 1979: 59).

Principally because of the war in Algeria from 1954 until 1962, the tightening of censorship went much further than the film industry and was also applied to the written press, book publishing, and television. The prime example was *Les Honneurs de la guerre* (Jean Dewever, 1960–1962), which premiered in Berlin in February 1962. The film was caught in the censorship web because it made use of an episode from the Liberation of France in 1944 to discuss the current situation in Algeria. In 1961, Jean Dewever declared that the soldiers in his film were German but, in his mind, they could just as well be French; however, if that were the case, the film would have been banned (*Image et son*, October 1961: 8). For several reasons, he felt that he could not directly address the issue of the war in Algeria despite the fact that France had been at war for the past twenty years (*Les Lettres françaises*, 13 July 1961). Documents from the Commission extensively detail the obstacles which Jean Dewever overcame before his film could open in France in 1962.[8] Besides several changes motivated by political and military concerns, the censors added the threat of an 'eighteen' certificate because of violent scenes. Knowing that most film audiences are less than twenty-four years old, and that in 1960 theatrical films attracted close to 330 million spectators each year, the economic consequences of such a restriction are clear.

The Commission had two major concerns: the image of the army and the image of Germany. Immediately after the end of the Second World War, there were no good Germans. In April 1945, the producer of *Double crime sur la ligne Maginot* (Félix Gandera, 1937), a spy thriller adapted from a novel by Pierre Nord, was told to censor the text where a French counter-intelligence officer complimented the German intelligence service. The censor added that this was a general edict which applied to any film which mentioned a 'good German'.[9] No positive portrayal of the enemy was possible. The wording of the request was also significant: the French were involved in counter-intelligence work (*renseignements*), which is part of self defence, while the Germans were spying (*espionnage*), which is a destabilising offensive strategy.

Another controversy erupted when the 1937 film by Jean Renoir, *La Grande Illusion*, reopened in 1946. The new release had at first been banned in 1945, then authorised after cuts were made to the film (Lindeperg, 1997: 209–19). Only rare German individuals could be portrayed as good Germans, for example, the German priest in *Jéricho* (Henri Calef, 1945–1946) or the francophile German officer in *Le Silence de la mer* (Jean-Pierre Melville, 1947–1949). Germany was a bad place and the members of the Gestapo (State Secret Police) were always despicable; the only nuance was that the SS – an independent organisation within the Nazi Party that exerted power in all fields of activity within Nazi Germany – was worse than the *Wehrmacht* (regular army). The situation remained stable until the late 1950s when external factors, such as the Cold War and the construction of the European Community, contributed to changing the perception of Germany. Between 1958 and 1963 relations between France and Germany improved steadily. A good relationship between French President Charles de Gaulle and German Chancellor Konrad Adenauer also helped the matter, and a formal agreement between the two countries was signed in January 1963.

Interestingly, while this détente was taking place, other films were opening in France that had something to say about French history during the Second World War. In the late 1950s a process began to demonstrate the nature of the Vichy regime, a process which did not attract much attention at the time. The war in Algeria (1954–1962) consumed France and her historical perspective. Looking at film production during that period and the reinforcement of censorship laws that affected large segments of film and television productions as well as the press, it is clear that the lens through which films were then, and have since been, analysed, was and is that of the Algerian War. Each film production about the Second World War was closely scrutinised to uncover implicit references to the international situation and condemnation of the French perspective, or allusions to topics such as discipline in the army, torture, and the rights of conscientious objectors. It was the case for Jean Dewever's *Les Honneurs de la guerre*, and also for Claude Autant-Lara's *Tu ne tueras point* (1960–1963) –

the initial title was *L'Objecteur* – which the filmmaker shot in Yugoslavia after numerous difficulties had delayed the project. Finished in 1961, it premiered in France in 1963. The Algerian War had ended the year before, in 1962.

Yet during that period of the late 1950s to the early 1960s, several French filmmakers returned to the historical period of the Second World War – not to discuss the war in Algeria, but to say something about the nature of the Vichy regime and the Second World War itself. The defining characteristics of the Vichy regime being presented to French audiences at the time included anti-Semitism, the inequity of the judicial system, eugenics, violence, and persecution. Contrary to earlier films that left the Vichy regime in a convenient shadowland, films like *Marie-Octobre* (Julien Duvivier, 1959), *Normandie-Niémen* (Jean Dréville, 1959–1960), and *Un taxi pour Tobrouk* (Denys de la Patellière, 1961) showed Vichy as a political reality, even if its dangers were not forcefully presented.

Three other feature films of the period would further establish Vichy's status as the enemy and depict the violent ideological content of the regime: *Léon Morin, prêtre* (Jean Pierre Melville, 1961), *La Planque* (Raoul André, 1961–1962), and *Le Jour et l'heure* (René Clément, 1962–1963). Following this cinematic exposition, questions about human rights and the persecutions could be posed. *Léon Morin, prêtre* condemns the anti-Semitism of the population and the indifference of the French people to the deportation of the Jews. In *Le Jour et l'heure*, the triptych Vichy/Fascism/Police – the regime, its essence, and its instrument of power – is clearly put into place. The filmic representation of the situation in France during the war took second place to the image of the army, which became the primary concern during the Algerian War. The image of Germany was not a significant issue because, using a new perspective, these films focused on ideological questions and did not limit themselves to a 'good versus evil' national interpretation of the war. This change of perspective coincided with the ongoing movement towards a better relationship between the two countries.

While France and Germany were reshaping their relations as European partners, a different perception of Germany could appear on screen. André Cayatte's feature film, *Le Passage du Rhin* (1960), is the story of a French prisoner of war who decides to return to Germany after his release; and Henri Champetier's *Allemagne, l'aigle ressuscité* and *Allemagne, carrefour de l'Europe*, two short documentary films produced by Pathé-Cinéma in

1960, depict the spectacular economic recovery of West Germany under the leadership of Konrad Adenauer.

A similar evolution was taking place in television programmes. In 1959, *Cinq colonnes à la une* presented a documentary, *Anciens prisonniers restés en Allemagne*, about French prisoners of war who had decided to stay in Germany at the end of the war, insisting on their perfect integration into their new surroundings. This broadcast took place within the timeframe of 1958–1963, a period when relations between France and Germany were characterised by reconciliation and rapprochement in order to facilitate the global project of the European Community (Manigand and Veyrat-Masson, 1982: 111–25). Later in the 1960s, films returned to the more traditional national parameters of two countries at war.

New Light

By studying the censorship files relating to twenty-five years of postwar film production about the Second World War, it is possible to identify the historical events and the permissible elements defined as fitting representations of France's involvement in the war, together with the internal, and external factors that contribute to the transformation. The representation of history as a constructed subject makes possible the integration of all the sources that contribute to sustaining a vision of the past. By defining the limits of the forbidden, the *Commission de contrôle des films cinématographiques* became the historian of an ideal France, and the image of France at war it created endured until the end of the 1960s. However, an examination of the definition of Vichy that appeared in films at the beginning of the 1960s, at a moment when the Commission was meticulous about the content and tone of films on the Second World War, prompts the realisation that the focus was no longer on the dark side of the Occupation of France in 1940–1944, it was targeted on the contemporary situation in Algeria. How was this possible?

It is generally accepted that the watershed in the cinematographic representation of the French internal situation during the Occupation occurred at the beginning of the 1970s, but an examination of the censorship files confirms that a fracture already existed in the early 1960s when the first substantiated definition of Vichy was making its way on to French screens uncensored. This leads to a deeper level of understanding about the definition of an ideal France pursued by the Commission. The ideal France corresponded with the inner core of the nation and the foundations of French postwar political, psychological, and moral reconstruction. The ideal France existed within the boundaries of the Republic, its universal principles, and the ideals of the Resistance. The French Army was included within this sphere because it was an army of conscripts/citizens – the army of the Republic, inherited from the French Revolution. Its links with the Republic had another significant historical dimension as British historian Robert Gildea has explained: 'Not until its defeat of Germany in 1918 was the Republic able effectively to lay claim to great-power status' (1994: 119).

The filmic images of Germany and the Germans, the dark side of French history during the Second World War, the extent of collaboration, and the definition of Vichy as a political reality – all of these elements did not challenge or contradict the universal principles and the foundations of the Republic. Vichy could be treated in films because it was considered to be a development that did not belong in the Republican history of France, so the crimes committed by Vichy did not contradict the universal principles of the Republic.

When a contradiction occurred, as it did in Algeria where the French Army, acting in the name of the Republic, was guilty of crimes which violated the principles of the Nation, crisis erupted (see Nicolaïdis, 1994). The difficulties faced by Jean Dewever and his film *Les Honneurs de la guerre* in which the filmmaker used an episode of the Liberation of France in 1944 to denounce the war France was waging in Algeria, are located in this contradiction. By questioning the role of the army and the usefulness of some Resistance actions of 1944, Dewever challenged the honour of the Republic and went to the heart of the issue. In contrast, the brutality of the police under Vichy, as depicted in René Clément's film *Le Jour et l'heure*, was not otherwise censored, precisely because Vichy was not considered to be part of the Republic.

This perception endured. All postwar French governments took care to completely dissociate the Republic from the Vichy regime and to deny any continuity between the two, up until 1997 when President Chirac recognised that French history included Vichy. With increased historical knowledge and the coming of age of a new generation, who introduced a more complex and qualified interpretation of the Second World War, images of the dark side of French history slowly slipped from the forbidden space into the open.

However, light shed on one area of the past leads us to the edge of another shadow. Thus the forbidden spheres interconnect and, as new spaces are illuminated, the hidden secrets emerge. Only a temporary equilibrium can be achieved which, in time, will be challenged. It is the continuum of history.

Notes

1. The sources for this paper come from French film and paper archives (films, scripts, and correspondence). The censorship documents from before July 1945 are located in the Archives nationales (Paris) in the Military Censorship documents (F42 131), and in the archives of the *Commission de contrôle des films cinématographiques* for the post-July 1945 film censorship administration. These files are located in the Centre national de la cinématographie, and they are classified according to film titles. Scripts and other documents, such as correspondence about the production, are located in the archival collections of the Cinémathèque française now housed at the Bibliothèque de l'image – Filmothèque in Paris. The author wishes to thank the Bibliothèque de l'image – Filmothèque in Paris for items from its photographic library.
2. *Journal Officiel*, 4 July 1945. Ordonnance 45–1464 and Décret 45–1472, 3 July 1945. See also the legal texts pertaining to film censorship adopted in France between July 1945 and May 1989 (Théry, 1990).
3. Centre national de la cinématographie, Commission de contrôle des films cinématographiques (hereafter CNC, CCFC), censorship dossier *La Bataille du rail*, session's report, 11 January 1946.
4. CNC, CCFC, censorship dossier *Les Portes de la nuit*. Note from G. Aguesse, delegate of the Ministry for the German and Austrian sectors, to the director of the CNC. In a letter dated 5 August 1950, the director then informed Pathé-Cinéma that the objection of the Ministry was upheld.
5. CNC, CCFC, censorship dossier, *Retour à la vie*. Note from Georges Huisman (president of the Commission) to Michel Fourré-Cormeray (director of the CNC), 20 July 1948. Fourré-Cormeray sent this message to the producer, Jacques Roitfeld, on 24 July 1948.
6. A 35 mm copy exists in the archives of the Centre national de la cinématographie in Bois d'Arcy.
7. CNC, CCFC, censorship dossier, *Le Grand Rendez-vous*, notice from Commandant Célérier, 17 February 1949, and letter from Georges Huisman, 23 February 1949.
8. CNC, CCFC, censorship dossier, *Les Honneurs de la guerre*, session's report 30 March 1960. Several changes were requested by the representative of the Ministry of Information, Mr. Vingtain.
9. AN F42 131, Censure militaire, session's report 19 April 1945. The particular film dealt with in this report was *Double crime sur la ligne Maginot* (Félix Gandera, 1937) adapted from a novel by Pierre Nord. The producer, Sirius, had asked for a new release visa in 1945 and was presented with this request: 'Censurer le texte relatif à l'hommage rendu par les services de renseignements français au service d'espionnage allemand. C'est une mesure générale qui touche tout ce qui accrédite la thèse du "bon Allemand".'

CHAPTER 11

FORBIDDEN REALITY: THE LANGUAGE AND FUNCTIONS OF PROPAGANDA

Magda Stroińska

Language is powerful; language is power.
Robin Lakoff, *Talking Power*

The route to the mind lies along a highway paved with words.
John W. Young, *Totalitarian Language*

The title phrase, *forbidden reality*, may appear awkward at first sight – it seems hardly possible to extend the scope of what is forbidden in order to deal with reality as a whole. We usually deal with fragments of life, such as death or sex, that become taboos for a variety of reasons. However, millions of people in Germany have claimed not to know the reality of the Nazi police state and the concentration camps during Hitler's reign; even more people throughout the world alleged that they were unaware of the reality of Stalin's system of oppression. It is clear that virtual reality is not an invention of the computer era.

I want to demonstrate how language can create a fictitious social reality and what the outcome is when the dominant group is powerful enough to eliminate even the mention of the existing *forbidden reality*. Through an analysis of the novel *Przechowalnia* ('Depot') by the Polish contemporary writer Kazimierz Orłoś, I shall discuss whether it is possible to use *newspeak*[1] to reveal and, consequently, demolish the façade erected by a totalitarian system.

Two Realities and two Languages

In a totalitarian system that claims to have transformed the world, any reality that resists transformation becomes an obstacle and has to be replaced by a fictitious one. People's actual experience is denied, and a new social reality is created by means of language which exists almost exclusively through the media of newspapers, radio, film, television, art and literature (see Stroińska, 1994). It is interesting that different, and often mutually hostile, totalitarian systems manage to produce very uniform art[2] and use similar language in order to construct their respective social fictions.

Many politicians promise to change the world. The more idealistic they sound, the more suspicious we become. But in those places where the Communists reached a monopoly of power, they discovered that it was much easier to proclaim that the world had been changed than to actually change it. They simply claimed their success and staged monumental shows to persuade other countries and their own citizens that life had been ideally transformed. Paradoxically, the worse things were, the more rosy the pictures, like the joyful art from the Soviet Union during the time of the great man-made famine in the Ukraine in the 1930s. The optimism portrayed by the artists could not have been derived from the miserable present. Instead, it

> was injected into totalitarian art from the mythical future. As the present day grew more terrible, as the struggle grew harsher and victory drew nearer, as hunger and terror put an end to more and more millions of lives, so the imaginary heaps of food on kolkhoz tables grew vaster and the smiles on the faces of workers more radiant. (Golomstock, 1990: 191)

Disguised as (socialist) realism, the art in totalitarian regimes reflected not reality but

> ideology and myth in the guise of reality. And it reflected this ideology only too faithfully. From a method of perceiving the world – like nineteenth-century realism – it had been transformed into a method of instilling into the world a particular kind of perception, and as such it was endowed with a dynamic charge. (Golomstock,1990: 98)

Totalitarian art, like totalitarian language, could indeed be seen as what Sapir called 'a symbolic guide to culture' (1949: 162) and a (somewhat distorted) mirror of social reality.

In totalitarian systems, the reality of people's daily lives is denied; it becomes the *forbidden reality*. People may discuss it in private, but it must not be talked about in the official media, nor represented in the arts. As long as the regime can use terror to enforce its policies, there can be no gap between the pseudo-reality of the official propaganda and the forbidden reality: one replaces the other in the official media.

This idea of controlling people's perception of reality through language manipulation was masterfully developed in Orwell's *Nineteen Eighty-Four*[3], where a new language, *Newspeak*, was invented:

> The purpose of Newspeak was not only to provide a medium of expression for the world-view and mental habits proper to the devotees of Ingsoc, but to make all other modes of thought impossible. It was intended that when Newspeak had been adopted once and for all and Oldspeak forgotten, a heretical thought – that is a thought diverging from the principles of Ingsoc – should be literally unthinkable, at least so far as thought is dependent on words. Its vocabulary was so constructed as to give exact and often very subtle expression to every meaning that a Party member could properly wish to express, while excluding all other meanings and so also the possibility of arriving at them by indirect methods. This was done partly by the invention of new words and by stripping such words as remained of unorthodox meanings, and so far as possible of all secondary meanings whatever. (Appendix: The Principles of Newspeak: 312–313)

The forbidden reality still exists, but is banned from public communication (represented by the official media): there are no tools for talking about it as the only language allowed is the totalitarian *newspeak*. The use of any other kind of language is considered a deviation from the Party line and may even be seen as a crime.

The *oldspeak*, to borrow Orwell's terminology, is obviously still in everyday use. Michał Głowiński, a Polish theoretician of linguistic means of propaganda, notes that totalitarian regimes produce a kind of *diglossia* (1990: 146–149) where a large number of people develop proficiency in two functional varieties of language, i.e. in both ordinary language and the *newspeak*, or the language of the group that holds the power. Their use is mutually exclusive: it is hard to imagine a Party official using *newspeak* to discuss domestic problems with his wife (though that was seen as the ultimate goal of the new language development in Orwell's novel), while using ordinary language to discuss official matters would have been made impossible through political repression.

Living in the World of Fiction

One of the goals of propaganda is to make people believe that the world resembles the propagandist image. As a child in postwar communist Poland, I watched numerous films in which the characters built and lived in bright new cities, with modern houses, wide open streets and squares. Young, strong, clean-shaven, smiling men and happy women inhabited those cities, and parks were full of playing children. Life looked like a festival.

I believed that the films showed reality, and I was sad that my part of town was not bright and clean, as it should have been, but grey and partly ruined. Although I never had the chance to be in those parts of the city that looked like those in the films, I assumed that what I saw on the screen was reality, and that I lived in a degraded version. It did not take long to realise that the films were fiction. And although the reality around kept changing, the gap between media images and everyday life remained.

In communist propaganda (or its socialist version in Poland[4]), the relationship between reality and the pseudo-reality created through language was arbitrary – a fact that did not particularly disturb its creators. The pseudo-reality was a utopian goal and it was hoped, in vain, that one day it would be born out of the Old World. In his book *The Soviet Syndrome*, Besançon writes that the scientific utopia of the Soviet system 'has not even begun to be born' and the communist ideology remained only 'a ghost in search of a body… The construction of socialism amounted to the construction of fiction' (1976: 93).

The Creative Power of Language

What we see is often what we have learned to see or what we have been told to see: our view of the world is shaped by our culture, which in turn has been shaped by history and tradition. In some societies, reality is constructed by social agreement or accepted convention; in others, the right to create or shape the social reality becomes the privilege of a chosen group.

One of the most important tools in building new worlds, whether amicably or through violence, is language, and political systems often differ only in the degree to which linguistic creations are enforced by terror. The creative or magical aspect of the language used for propaganda purposes has long been recognised by several authors, including Orwell (1946), Klemperer (1947), Besançon (1976), Bralczyk (1987), Głowiński (1990) and Bogusławski (1994).

Michał Głowiński stresses that by either promoting or excluding certain words, the language can give or deny existence to persons, things and phenomena. In the Soviet Union, books were rewritten and official pictures repainted if they happened to refer to a person or event that became an object of disapproval. Through the power of language, the picture of reality in the minds of those who are subjected to the total propaganda machine can be distorted, and the difference between the given and desired state of affairs blurred (Głowiński, 1990: 8–9; see also Stroińska, 1994: 59).

The Case of Kazimierz Orłoś: Realism in Literature

The fictitious or forbidden realities of totalitarian regimes have been described by writers who published their works either in exile or through the underground press. A prime example is *The Gulag Archipelago*, in which Aleksandr Solzhenitsyn shows how, occasionally and by mistake, fragments of information from the forbidden reality surface in the official media. In the Preface he recalls how, in 1949, he came upon 'a noteworthy news item' in the magazine of the Soviet Academy of Sciences, *Nature*.

> It reported in tiny type that in the course of excavations on the Kolyma River a subterranean ice lens had been discovered which was actually a frozen stream – and in it were found frozen specimens of prehistoric fauna some tens of thousands of years old. Whether fish or salamander, these were preserved in so fresh a state, the scientific correspondent reported, that those present immediately broke open the ice encasing the specimens and devoured them *with relish* on the spot. [Original Emphasis] (Solzhenitsyn, 1973a: ix)

Only readers who had experienced the Soviet labour camps – and Kolyma was a famous detention region – were able to decipher the genuine meaning of this report and picture the entire scene: 'how those present broke up the ice in frenzied haste; how, flouting the higher claims of ichthyology and elbowing each other to be first, they tore off chunks of the prehistoric flesh and hauled them over to the bonfire to thaw them out and bolt them down' (Solzhenitsyn, 1973a: ix). They understood it because they too 'were the same kind of people as *those present* at that event. [They] too, were from that powerful tribe of *zeks* [prisoners], unique on the face of the earth, the only people who could devour prehistoric salamander *with relish*' (Solzhenitsyn, 1973a: ix).[5]

One literary experiment, which shows how the deceptive character of the pseudo-reality could be revealed using no other tool but the language of propaganda itself, is Kazimierz Orłoś's novel of 1985, *Przechowalnia*, which roughly translates as 'Depot'.[6]

The then forty-eight year old Polish writer had been banned from the literary scene for over ten years for publishing *Cudowna melina* ('Marvellous hide-out', a novel that deals with large-scale corruption in a small town), in the Polish Literary Institute in Paris in 1973. He began writing *Przechowalnia* in the 1970s in reaction to the ubiquitous use of Party *newspeak* and its absurdities. When the independent trade union Solidarność was created in August 1980, with one its prime objectives being to reveal the mechanisms of language manipulation, Orłoś interrupted the writing of the book seeing no reason to continue. But the Solidarność movement was crushed in a military coup in December 1981. The authorities returned to the discredited *newspeak*, which after more than a year of political freedom seemed even more absurd than before, and Orłoś resumed his work. After *Przechowalnia* was published in 1985 in London, not even the author's name was allowed to appear in print in Poland. He became nonexistent, his voice silenced, because he tried to describe the reality.

We need to remember that what the Communists used to call *socialist realism* did not represent the world as it was (which was the obvious mistake of *naturalism*, branded as wrong), but tried to extract from it what was typical and what was desired. The objective of an artist was, as Gorky put it, 'to extract from the sum of the given its fundamental meaning and then embody this in an image – this gives realism' (quoted in Golomstock 1990: 182). There was nothing individual about the represented reality. People become a crowd, a faceless mass, used simply as a background for the only individual being, *the great leader*, the *Führer* or *Duce*.[7] Even class enemies had no individual faces but were portrayed as caricatures of human beings, designed as objects of hatred or contempt.

What Orłoś does in his book is, among other things, to give individual faces to some of those who were never portrayed by propaganda. He tells the story of a group of people from the margins of the socialist society, most of them alcoholics, who decide to stage a protest action against the detoxification unit that they, almost tenderly, call *przechowalnia* (thus the title), and where they are regularly beaten and robbed by the personnel.

Their form of protest? To stop drinking. A subtle form of blackmail, as the state monopoly in the production and sale of alcohol was one of the most lucrative areas of the Polish economy.

Demolition of the Pseudo-reality

In a country that denied the existence of alcoholism, unemployment, poverty, prostitution, drug use and AIDS, the topic itself would be enough to prevent publication. But more than that, the book was written in the very language – *newspeak* – that created the pseudo-reality the novel seeks to expose; the vocabulary and rhetoric taken straight from the communist newspapers and television newsreels. The words are empty because they were used by the media not to describe the reality but to postulate something that did not exist. They cannot function as a means of description even though they are used to refer to objects and actions that are familiar to the reader.

Describing the detoxification unit, Orłoś writes: [8]

> 'Depot' – a modern pavilion at the intersection of Prusa and Zeromskiego – is a well-known detoxification centre. A modern composition of concrete, bars and glass – as if it were from the era of 'glass houses'– says Kamieniak laughing.[9] Behind the pavilion is a river. On the other side is the red neon sign of the motel 'On the road'. At night the water glimmers with lights. Officially, people call the 'depot' – 'Detoxification Centre' or 'Detoxification Chamber'. On the blue sign at the door one can read its formal name 'Rehabilitation Centre for Disorders of the c.n.s' [central nervous system].
>
> 'Comrade Marks – that's the end of the journey', the functionary Smolarek said allegedly (everyone here knows the magister). When he left the van, they grabbed him under the arms again.
>
> From the hands of Smolarek, the delivered passenger was taken over by the shift caretaker Nicpoń ['good-for-nothing'], a

> 25 year-old law graduate, temporarily employed in the detoxification centre (after a traffic accident, for which he was facing a 5 year prison term, though his father, a friend of Mizera [the local Party secretary], prevented the sentencing of the son and had secured for him a position in our Centre). In a white uniform and wooden clogs worn with bare feet and with eyes red as those of a rabbit (as a result of conjunctivitis), Gene Nicpoń received Kamieniak with open arms:
>
> 'Welcome, Mr. Magister!', he widely opened the door through which the Centre personnel could check who had been delivered. They walked along a corridor lit with fluorescent lights. The thin white pipes made a humming noise. Some of them blinked from time to time. At the end of the corridor was an ornamentation with a slogan 'Peace, Friendship, Socialism!' and a portrait of the leader of the revolution within a wreath made of cardboard doves. Over the door was a stretched piece of red fabric. (Orłoś, 1990: 8–9)

The description of people and things uses stock phrases from the official *newspeak*. The director of the detoxification centre, Mieczysław Seta (*seta* is a slang word for a 100 millilitre shot of vodka) is described as:

> a meritorious socio-political activist and a highly valued citizen (although he had only arrived in our town three years ago). It was thanks to his efforts that the centre, right from the beginning, was profitable to the State and fulfilled a positive role on the front of the struggle against alcoholism at the time of declining consumption of the products of the State Alcohol Monopoly (17).

Events show that this well-respected citizen was involved in beatings, stealing money from drunken people and a rape cover-up. In *Przechowalnia* even the pig that an elderly female teacher keeps in her cellar is regularly referred to as 'a representative of the pigsty frock', as this was the phrase used in the media to refer to hogs.

The peculiar stylistic effect is partly the result of choosing a narrator who is identified only through his use of language. Using *newspeak* shows that he is part of the town's communist establishment: a low-ranking police officer, perhaps, or the local newspaper editor. He speaks with a lot of reverence about local Party bosses and frequently uses the possessive pronoun *our*, as in 'our Party' or 'our town'. This is reminiscent of the style of the leading articles from Party controlled papers, written or dictated by officials and pretending to represent popular views, amongst other things, by using the First Person Plural.

The narration, however, is unemotional and external. People's words are reported without pretending to discern their feelings and motives. Sometimes alternative versions are given for what other characters might have said or done. Within the Polish communist system of the time, the narrator seems to be an insider – a linguistic device similar in effect to that in the Appendix of Orwell's *Nineteen Eighty-Four*.

The narration is mostly based on *newspeak* with occasional colloquialisms, producing a new subvariety of the Party rhetoric. Orłoś never uses obscene language, replacing vulgarisms with acceptable words used to suggest, for instance. by frequent repetition, vulgar meanings. A conversation between the deputy director of the Centre, Edward Ful (and note that Ful is a nickname for beer), and his fellow caretakers, contains a bizarre mixture of Party talk and colloquialisms:

> Edward Ful, short, bald, with gaps in dentition (upper left front tooth missing) was explaining loudly.
>
> 'Listen, Marks, they say here that the consumption [of alcohol] in the country is growing. And I will prove to you that it is declining!'
>
> 'Come on, people are switching to their own production', disagreed Kot. 'This tells you something, doesn't it?'
>
> 'So what? Take such phenomena as newspaper or book readership; they are growing, aren't they? Take education – growing. And crime, alcoholism, traffic accidents?'
>
> 'They are declining,' Cmielewski was laughing. 'There are less and less accidents!'
>
> 'That's it. We live in an era of declining consumption! Am I right, Magister?' he turned to Kamieniak. (11)

Using *newspeak* to talk about the gloomy reality of 'our town', the narrator crosses the boundary between public and private discourse. The topic is not suitable for public discourse and the form is not suitable for private discourse. Although highly unlikely, this mixture is not impossible.[10]

In the Poland of the 1970s, however, the level of political oppression was, fortunately, not high enough to warrant this kind of cross over between private and public discourse: the terror then was just a shadow of its old self from the times of Stalin. Nevertheless, language-based thought manipulation was active, and learning how to defend oneself against propaganda was, and remains a very important task for any society. Noam Chomsky warns that there is not enough interest and inquiry into these matters, particularly in democratic societies

(1989). A course in intellectual self-defence would be useful for anyone who wishes to stay safe from media manipulation. With the rapid development of digital technologies, dangers of thought manipulation take new, more sophisticated forms but are most certainly growing. The first step toward this self-defence is to learn about the mechanisms of manipulation.

'There is not one truth...'

In the current discussions about the communist past in Eastern Europe, it is often said that there is not one single truth about the 1944–1989 period but rather many different truths, depending on the speaker's position in the system. The word 'truth' is here used more or less synonymously with 'reality' – a multitude of truths being perhaps more palatable than a multitude of realities – but what it really describes is only *points of view*.

In a world in which reality becomes relative, various philosophies offer value systems that can withstand change. One way is to find one's own 'irony tower' (Solomon, 1991), a cognitive distance from events in the real world. This attitude, also called *internal exile*, however, suggests staying, more or less passively, outside the stream of history.

Another interesting answer can be found in Solzhenitsyn's Nobel lecture (1973b: 559), where the author recalls the words of Dostoevsky in *The Idiot*: 'beauty will save the world...' He then continues: 'in the struggle with lies art has always triumphed and shall always triumph! Visibly, irrefutably for all! Lies can prevail against much in this world, but never against art' (1973b: 575).

The same motive can be found in 'The power of taste' by the Polish poet Zbigniew Herbert (1924 –1998), where great importance is attributed to the ability to make aesthetic judgements. Communism, says Herbert, has not produced any beauty and so it could not be perceived as attractive by those who were led by the *power of taste*. It was a time when

> a home-brewed Mephisto in a Lenin-jacket
> sent Aurora's grandchildren out into the field
> boys with potato faces
> very ugly girls with red hands

The communist rhetoric, says Herbert, consisted of 'chains of tautologies', used 'dialectics of slaughterers' and had 'syntax deprived of beauty of the subjunctive'. The study of beauty must not be neglected, concludes the poet, as it is the power of taste that tells us to 'proudly choose exile' (quoted in Michnik, 1991: 166; translated from the Polish by John and Bogdana Carpenter).

These basic concepts should also remain as basic values, 'unambiguous and indivisible' (Orłoś: 1998). The price that has to be paid for making reality relative, and creating multiple truths, is not just the creation of new forbidden territories. It is also the consent to lies, and the history of the twentieth century has shown that it may mean a sacrifice of millions of lives. We should try not to forget this truth in the third millennium.

Notes

1. The term *newspeak*, introduced by Orwell in *Nineteen Eighty-Four*, has often been used to refer to the language of propaganda for the purpose of thought manipulation. Herman (1992) uses the term *doublespeak*, also derived from Orwell. The Polish equivalent term is *nowomowa*, used, among others, by Głowiński.
2. This can be witnessed when comparing paintings from Nazi Germany, the Soviet Union, fascist Italy or communist China, e.g. at the exibition at the Hayward Gallery in London in 1996 (see *Art and Power*, Hayward Gallery, 1995).
3. A similar idea was developed in Stanisław Lem's *Futurological Congress*, where the author says that whatever cannot be named does not exist, and whatever can be named will eventually come into being.
4. Poland never considered itself a communist country. Party slogans kept repeating that Poland was in the process of 'building socialism'.
5. More recently, the wartime diaries of Victor Klemperer, a German philologist of Jewish background, became best-sellers in Germany. Klemperer describes everyday life in the Third Reich, paying attention to the details of Nazi propaganda and analysing how it affected the ways ordinary Germans thought and behaved (1947; 1995). As such, Klemperer's diaries, particularly *Lingua Tertii Imperii*, first published in the late 1940s, offer a rare insight into the mechanisms of a totalitarian state.
6. In Polish, the word *przechowalnia* may be used to refer to a storage place or warehouse. It is also used at railway stations to refer to the 'left-luggage' section. Unlike some close synonyms, e.g. *magazyn* ('warehouse'), *przechowalnia* suggests that what is being stored is of some value. In the book, the word is used by local alcoholics to refer to the place where they were detained ('stored') until sober.
7. This type of representation can be seen on posters designed by Soviet artists, such as Klucis, Rodchenko and Lissitzky. A similar concept was used in Mussolini's Italy and Hitler's Germany. The artists used photographs of 'crowds composed of hundreds of thousands of faceless human units' to produce 'a heroic image of the State in the grip of revolutionary enthusiasm' (Golomstock, 1990: 49).

8. The English translation may, at times, sound awkward. Trying to stay close to the Polish original results in expressions that sound absurd to the English speaker. In fact, they are equally absurd in Polish, the only difference being that they have been used with such frequency that people became indifferent to their absurdity. One such example is the phrase *aktywny działacz partii*. The noun phrase *działacz partii* translates as 'party activist'. It was usually used with the adjective *aktywny* ('active'), which produces in English an 'active party activist'. One could translate the Polish expression as a 'card-carrying party member' or an 'active party member', but this would conceal the linguistic absurdity of their Polish counterpart, which is the focus of this essay.
9. Kamieniak, the main character, is a former communist, now an alcoholic; as a Marxist and a university graduate, he is addressed as either Marks or *magister*, i.e. someone with an MA degree. In writing of the era of 'glass houses', Orłoś makes a reference to the term used by Stefan Żeromski, a Polish positivist writer, to symbolise technical and social progress in the future.
10. Klemperer, an expert on the propaganda manipulation of language in Nazi Germany, repeatedly points out that when control is total and everybody speaks the same language in public, it becomes impossible not to conform (1947).

Chapter 12

Walking a Tightrope Over Forbidden Territory: East German Cinema and Evelyn Schmidt's Film *The Bicycle*

Andrea Rinke

Ironically, though perhaps predictably, the GDR is more attractive now that it has vanished than when it existed. As the American film scholar Barton Byg commented:

> To the extent that the GDR stands for an archaic and repressed part of the German character and now for part of the German past, it shares much of the mythical force of popular culture found in representations of transgression, otherness, the lost mythical past. (1991: 70)

And indeed, since the demise of the GDR in 1990, numerous conferences related to cultural, social or political aspects of the former east German state have been organised nationally and internationally , reflecting a fascination with a world into which access had been restricted for outsiders for forty years, and which is now gone.

During the existence of the two German states, the west German media often tended to stigmatise GDR cinema as a mere part of the regime's propaganda machine, as illustrations of political programmes or idealistic evocations of the 'new socialist *mensch*' (human being), and it is true to say that film production in the GDR was financed and controlled by the state and was thus affected by the Party's cultural policies. However, the extent to which individual filmmakers actually followed ideological directives, and the extent to which specific film projects were subjected to censorship, varied considerably during the life span of the GDR, according to the political climate and to the individual officials in power at any given time.

During the 1970s and 1980s, the arts, especially literature and cinema, increasingly became an alternative public forum to the press and television, which were little more than mouthpieces of Party propaganda. Consequently, those writers and filmmakers who expressed thoughts, attitudes and feelings which deviated, even if only slightly, from the officially proclaimed socialist values, walked a thin tightrope over forbidden territory. At the same time, they often managed to create secret spaces of internal liberty by establishing a 'conspiratorial understanding' with their audiences who had grown to appreciate cinema addressing controversial or even taboo issues in a covertly subversive way.

A typical example of such a cinematic rebellion is the film that I am going to examine in this essay. Entitled *The Bicycle* (*Das Fahrrad*, 1982), it was directed by Evelyn Schmidt, one of the few women filmmakers in the GDR.

During the late 1970s and early 1980s, criticism of GDR society, such as that tacitly implied in *The Bicycle*, was often voiced through adolescents or young women on screen. Despite women being fully integrated into the workforce by that time, they were simultaneously predominantly responsible for looking after the home and the children, for meeting their family's emotional needs. As the 'natural' inhabitant of the domestic sphere, a permitted private space of intimacy beyond public control, the feminine was often used by filmmakers to represent the mildly subversive. East German film critic Oksana Bulgakowa wryly calls the portrayal of the domestic yet restless and personally frustrated woman on screen a '*Koch-Nische für versteckte soziale Probleme*' (cooking niche for hidden social problems) which was tolerated by those in power, as it did not appear to threaten the established order (1991: 98). Rebellious adolescents and female misfits were thus used as vehicles of indirect social criticism and to express more general feelings of disaffection with everyday life under socialism ('*real existierender Sozialismus*'). Young women at the margins of society, such as the heroine of *The Bicycle*, would inevitably look at mainstream society from the outside, challenging blinkered views and established ways of life. This film, as I hope to show, transgressed the officially proclaimed norms and expectations of a 'good' socialist film on various levels.

The Misfit as Model: A View from the Margin

First, the portrayal of the female protagonist presents the 'wrong' kind of heroine according to the criteria of the '*sozialistisches Menschenbild*' (socialist image of the new man). The so-called 'positive model hero or heroine' was intended to combine both the characteristics of a realistic and credible person with the potential for an ideal personality of the future. For instance, in several films produced up to the late 1970s, the filmmakers tended to portray model heroes or, more frequently heroines, who were well educated, professionally qualified and politically conscious, who knew exactly what they wanted, and who were able to address and solve their problems. Examples of these included films about married women and mothers who held down prestigious jobs, such as the heart surgeon in *Das siebente Jahr* (*The Seventh Year*, Frank Vogel, 1969), or the director of a Physics research project in *Liebeserklärung an G.T.* (*To G.T. With All My Love*, Horst Seemann, 1971). In those earlier years, the preference for female protagonists by predominantly male film directors may have been due to the fact that strong screen heroines, who were portrayed as men's equals in their new roles in the work place, could best be used to illustrate the emancipation of women under socialism which was essential to the GDR's self-perception as the 'better' Germany: as a society of true equals, morally superior to the west.

In GDR cinema of the late 1970s and early 1980s, however, there emerged a new kind of female protagonist. These heroines tended to be loners and misfits struggling to survive at the margins of society, thus expressing views and attitudes which clearly deviated from those held to be worthy of a socialist hero. They called into question – albeit in an undercover way – the established values and officially proclaimed truths of the regime.

Susanne, an unskilled factory worker and single mother is struggling to make ends meet. One day she cannot take her monotonous job at a metal cutting machine any longer and walks out. It proves harder than she expected to find other employment, especially since the responsibility for her child rules out night shifts, work at weekends and trips abroad. The child becomes ill, the child's father refuses to advance money to tide her over the crisis, all of which lead to her following her friend Mary's advice: to report her bicycle as stolen and claim the insurance money. Meanwhile she has fallen in love with Thomas, a successful engineer whom she met at her local youth club disco, and he persuades her to move in with him and he gets her a job at his workplace. When her insurance fraud is discovered and she is faced with a court case, she confesses all to Thomas. He is worried that her 'shameful conduct' will reflect on him at work, but in the end decides to help her. However, his initial reaction has hurt and alienated Susanne to such an extent that she leaves him, returning to her old flat. The film ends on a positive note, showing that Susanne is determined to continue the pursuit of happiness in her own way thus preserving her own liberty and independence.

The crime rate in the GDR was very low compared to the West, and therefore petty crimes, such as theft and fraud would be considered serious offences. However, in *The Bicycle*, the desperate situation experienced by one of the weaker members of society, her poverty and loneliness, are depicted in such graphic detail that her descent into delinquency is justified by making it understandable.

This view challenges the concept of a socialist society where nobody is left to struggle on their own, where there is always the work collective standing by to help, and this perspective was promptly condemned as wrong by a GDR critic: 'Neither the heroine nor we [the viewers] are sent through the purgatory of fear and redemption. And consequently, the support offered by society does not receive the appreciation it deserves' (Voss 1982: 14). However, I would argue that quite the reverse is true. Very subtly, and more often through visual imagery than through verbal discourse, this film implies that it is society which is shown to fail someone like Susanne rather than the other way around. It is quite clear to the viewer observing the heroine's body language and facial expressions, which show very strong feelings of fear, shame and guilt, that she is not a cold-blooded habitual delinquent. In fact, throughout the film the heroine is portrayed as someone who is not naturally surreptitious, underhand or devious, but rather is an individual, forced into cautious reticence, withdrawal and secrecy by a repressive and controlling environment.

This portrait of a screen heroine was found unacceptable, and understandably met with scathing comments by most GDR critics, one of whom, at the time, characterised Susanne as 'a screwed-up misfit, suspicious towards everybody except her obscure drinking mates in the disco-cellar' and dismissed the film as a 'lame expression of grumpy discomfort with society' (Holland-Moritz, 1982: 19).

Paradoxically however, in the course of the film, this apparent 'loser' is shown to be worthy of our sympathy and respect, being portrayed in a positive light and inevitably drawing sympathy and a sense of identification from the viewers. In an interview conducted after the demise of the GDR, Evelyn Schmidt summarised the comments made by viewers who had seen the film in local repertory cinemas: 'Those discussions revealed how many people dreamt of holding on to an internal liberty the way Susanne does' (Schieber 1994: 270).

Work as a Dead-end Struggle

The second area in which this film indirectly criticises contemporary GDR society relates to the heroine's workplace: the heroine's negative attitude to her various jobs and the lack of support offered by the work collective.

As an unqualified menial labourer, Susanne can get only monotonous and badly paid factory jobs. Consequently she sees work as a draining dead-end situation, the misery of which she needs to escape from in her leisure time at night. Equally, the daily life of a single mother at the lowest end of the job scale is depicted as an uphill struggle. For instance, in one sequence Susanne is told off for being behind with the Kindergarten payments. In another scene, she misses a job opportunity because her child is ill. By showing, in images of almost documentary realism, the hardships of Susanne's ordinary everyday life, the film effectively challenges two officially proclaimed truths in the GDR. Firstly, the assumption that working women, including single mothers, were enabled through a state-run comprehensive childcare scheme to happily reconcile motherhood with full-time, life-long employment. Secondly, the claim, that work per se was the essential prerequisite for everyone to find happiness and self-fulfilment. The film not only shows these truths to be invalid in a case such as Susanne's, it also seems to call into question a concept of emancipation which is solely based on a woman's right to work, without taking into account personal needs and circumstances of the individual.

It is hardly surprising that some GDR critics found the heroine's attitude to her work and her daily life disturbing, suspecting that it set a bad example to the viewer:

> One ought to consider the means used in this film to depict the 'hardships of daily life': a pot of boiling laundry already turns into a catastrophe, the metal cutting machine at the factory into an intolerable trap. It is normal work, after all, which triggers off the heroine's outbursts of desperation. How many viewers will be led to believe, through this kind of depiction, that everyday life is an intolerable burden? (Voss, 1982: 14)

Susanne' s various work environments in the film are depicted as cold and hostile, as are those people in positions of power – be it the personnel manager at the factory where Susanne first applies for a job, the Party Secretary at Thomas' factory where she works eventually, the members of the 'conflict committee' at that factory, or even Thomas himself in his capacity as head of a women's brigade. It seems that none of these representatives of authority in GDR society are particularly understanding, helpful or tolerant towards those who do not fit in with the norm, leaving someone like Susanne feeling lonely and alienated. One sequence, in particular, shows the members of the 'conflict committee' – nominated workers who are to reprimand individual workers' misbehaviour, such as lateness or drinking, in order to ensure a smooth run of production – as being judgmental and impatient and more concerned with Susanne causing problems at the workplace than with finding out about her difficult personal circumstances.

The heroine is repeatedly seen to seek refuge from her oppressive work environment in the nocturnal privacy of her own four walls or in the subterranean enclosure of a small youth club disco in the town's *Kulturhaus*. During Susanne's visits to the basement disco, getting away from the controlling powers prevailing in the public sphere, she reveals a different, hidden side of her personality, which is lively, spontaneous and fun loving.

In a scene showing two girlfriends bonding and getting drunk together, Susanne confides in her friend Mary about her financial problems, her job situation and her general feeling of despair, to which Mary suggests the insurance fraud. The subterranean meeting place of an alternative youth culture thus serves to represent both the supportive environment of a 'charmed circle' of friends as well as a breeding ground for subversive ideas and illicit activities.

Gender Oppositions – the Class Divide

A third way in which *The Bicycle* deviates from accepted representations of contemporary GDR is that it posits the existence of a social divide in an allegedly classless society. This is done, to a large extent, by constructing binary oppositions of gender identities, in which the masculine represents the ruling class and the feminine stands for those who are dependent on them.

Susanne's secret, private world – portrayed in images of darkness and confined spaces, such as the basement of the *Kulturhaus* – is contrasted with images representing the public sphere, such as the brightly neon-lit wide open space on the floor above where Thomas celebrates his promotion among his colleagues. The two floors in the *Kulturhaus* physically represent the social divide: those 'at the top', people in positions of power, with Thomas, as the well-adapted performer, going through the formal initiation rites for achievers. And those 'at the bottom', the inhabitants of Susanne's 'underworld', a mix of would be drop-outs, dreamers and drifters from all walks of life, sharing both joys and sorrows. The fact that the heroine is inferior to her lover in education, status, profession and self-confidence, points to contradictions in a society which officially proclaimed that women's emancipation had been successfully achieved through their integration into the workforce. Deliberately drawing attention to these unresolved contradictions which the authorities tended to gloss over, Evelyn Schmidt insisted:

> I think one mustn't deny the existence of different social positions, of different chances and abilities for self-development. Although both [S. and T.] belong to the same generation, one shouldn't overlook ... that, whereas some people manage to build up and develop their personality, others lack the challenge or the opportunity to do so, or they are just unable to make the best of these. (1982: 8)

Thomas' position at the top appears to have been bought at the price of humane qualities such as the ability to empathise, to understand and tolerate those who are different from himself, especially those who do not follow the same rigid set of rules. For instance, when one of the female workers in his brigade hesitates to leave her husband (who drinks and habitually beats her) because she is worried about the prospect of being a single working mother of three, Thomas cynically dismisses Susanne's words of pity, sneering: 'With all the state support she'll get, why that's almost a profitable business!'

In contrast, Susanne seems to have benefited from the positive side effects of staying at the grass-roots level of society, in that she has not had to sacrifice some of her humane qualities in order to rise in the world. This is evident in scenes which show how she relates to people who need her help, such as an elderly neighbour, the battered wife at work and particularly her own little daughter. In these relationships Susanne shows a strong sense of solidarity and responsibility and is portrayed as a warm-hearted, spontaneous and giving person.

The unfavourable depiction of traditional masculine gender attributes, such as careerism, opportunism, self-righteousness or lack of the ability to empathise, is thus used to express an indirect criticism of the patriarchal order in the GDR. For instance, when Susanne's fraud is discovered and she confides in Thomas, hoping to get his support in a time of need, he fails her. In a situation where she shows herself to be vulnerable, laying bare her soul – the shame, guilt and fear that have been haunting her in a nightmare – he reacts with irritated selfishness at the prospect of being seen as an accomplice. Far from establishing a conspiratorial 'them and us' mood of a couple in love defying the rest of the world, he takes the official side of those in power, showing an attitude of disapproval and condemnation: 'Did you have to do that!'

However, Thomas' self-righteous belief in his own infallibility is shaken when his superiors reject his rationalisation plans for the factory. Suddenly, he feels betrayed and victimised by those in power: 'They've cheated me deliberately, used me, made a fool of me!' Ironically, he now expects Susanne to take his side against 'them up there' with unquestioning loyalty and compassion for his situation, a stance which he, in her case, was unwilling to take. It becomes clear during their argument that, due to a sense of superiority which makes him assume that his problem is of much greater importance than hers, he does not want to share his feelings of vulnerability with her nor is he interested in her opinion on the matter:

Susanne: 'Of course, you are always right and the others are always to blame. Just like with us...'

Thomas: What's that got to do with anything! You were up to your neck in trouble when we first met and if I hadn't got you out, you'd still be there! I think I have the right to ask you to be on my side now!

Gender relations as constructed in this dialogue mirror the relationship of the patriarchal regime in the GDR to its people, the two sides of an omnipotent '*Vater Staat*' (Father State): comprehensive care and all-pervasive control. As the benevolent provider, Thomas feels entitled to demand gratitude and obedience from 'his woman' in return. In his view, the dependency of the woman on him, as *his* creature, justifies his claim of ownership over her.

However, Thomas oversteps the mark during this scene in a crucial area by questioning Susanne's ability to raise her daughter properly: 'So, what have you ever achieved, then? Tell me!' he barks. And when she calmly replies, 'I have raised Jenny', he sneers, 'Yeah, who's going to turn to crime one day!' At this unfair attack, the camera shows Susanne's stony face in a long close up, shutting her eyes, swallowing and replying in a calm voice which sounds final, 'That's enough.' He has attacked a vital part of her identity, that of a responsible and caring mother whose loving relationship with her daughter is the only stable factor in her life. She leaves Thomas and the comforts of his modern flat and car, returning to her old, run-down but friendly neighbourhood and bicycle, preferring to go through life under her own steam rather than taking the passenger seat. The confrontation with Thomas has enabled Susanne to reflect upon her own values and to assert herself as an independent individual with the right to live life her own way, even if things do not always work out. As Evelyn Schmidt commented: 'The development of self-confidence is an important issue for me, especially for my generation and for women in particular' (1982: 8).

In this context the central, yet ambivalent metaphor for Susanne's development throughout the whole film is her bicycle: from characteristing her as a vulnerable young woman, exposed to the hostile elements while struggling to get past heavy traffic in the pouring rain, to being the hidden evidence of Susanne's descent into crime, until finally becoming a metaphor of liberation, autonomy and empowerment. In the film's closing sequence, one of the very few shot in bright sunlight, the bicycle has come to express the bond between mother and daughter; Susanne is finally succeeding in teaching her small child to ride the bicycle on her own, encouraging her first rather wobbly circles around a market place fountain with little cries of delight. She is no longer suppressing her capacity for spontaneous *joie-de-vivre* and is passing on her newly gained sense of independence and liberty.

In effect, therefore, Evelyn Schmidt's film *The Bicycle* implied criticism of contemporary GDR society in various ways, by sympathetically taking the perspective of a misfit heroine who violates the laws of that society; by questioning socialist values, such as work being the sole source of individual fulfilment; and by positing a social divide in a society which officially claimed equality of all its members to be an accomplished fact. This leaves us with the intriguing question of how a film such as this got past the hurdles of censorship – or did it?

Initially, the DEFA (*Deutsche Film Aktiengesellschaft*) film officials dismissed the indirect subversiveness expressed through the heroine of *The Bicycle* as a rather harmless 'natural' growing process of erring young females, not to be taken too seriously. Such a benevolent fatherly attitude towards one of the few young female directors of the DEFA seems to have been the stance temporarily taken by the managing director of the DEFA when he first submitted the film to the Party's Head of Culture for state approval. In a confidential letter he asks for permission to release the film (which was standard procedure for DEFA films) summarising it as follows:

> In a difficult personal situation, a young woman violates the laws of our society but, in a process full of conflicts, she finds her place in a factory collective. The films warns of a casual attitude towards the principles of socialist lawfulness and order and stresses the responsibility that every individual has as well as the opportunities which exist in our society for everyone to consciously shape their own lives. [2]

This statement is a major misconstruction of the film's message, choosing – for whatever reason – to ignore the fact that the illegal activities of a clandestine misfit are portrayed in a blatantly sympathetic light and from a perspective which is biased towards the struggling under-dog rather than the law-abiding high-flyer. Throughout the film, the official view regarding the relationship between the individual and society in the GDR is questioned, i.e. that the state provides all necessary opportunities for self-development and fulfilment, and that it is therefore the individual's responsibility entirely whether they fail or succeed. Moreover, in a subtle reversal of that view, the film seems to criticise society's attitude, especially the lack of tolerance and understanding, towards those individuals who do not fit in and who transgress the boundaries of the socially acceptable.

It was possibly this hidden message that eventually made the DEFA studio director Mäde retreat from his earlier lenient position towards *The Bicycle*. In an interview conducted after the demise of the GDR, Evelyn Schmidt herself suggested that the authorities later attempted to redeem their misinterpretation of the film by going to the other extreme:

> Maybe the officials responsible for the release had simply made a mistake and got worried when they realised that it had slipped through the net. Perhaps the consequences for me were so devastating, precisely because they couldn't forgive themselves for not having toed the Party line with more vigilance.[3]

The film was, however, in effect indirectly censored by limiting its release to a few performances in minor cinemas only and without any prior advertisements whilst at the same time having it dismissed as a flop in scathing film reviews in the official papers.[4] *The Bicycle* prompted the fall from grace of the promising young director Evelyn Schmidt (she had set out as a privileged student in a master class by Konrad Wolf) by nipping her career in the bud. Subsequent submissions of her own film projects were rejected; she was ostracised, and eventually demoted to assistant director.

Ironically her film is one of the few DEFA films to be sold abroad (to eleven countries, no less) and it was shown on West German national television (ZDF) in 1985. This is how mass audiences in the GDR, preferring the television channels of the class enemy to their own, became aware of it for the first time. Images of the forbidden in the East broadcast from the forbidden territory of the West.

Notes

1. Those related to East German cinema include *50 years of DEFA – a Retrospective*, Reading University, Britain, April 1996; a conference and anniversary celebration in Babelsberg, Germany, May 1996 and *East German Cinema – the View from America*, Amherst, Massachussets, October 1997.
2. DEFA studio director at the time, Erich Mäde, describing films to be released during the first half of 1982 in a seven page confidential letter to the Head of the Department of Culture in the Central Committee of the SED, Ursula Ragwitz, 12 January 1982, p.4. Part of an unpublished archive file entitled *Spielfilm, Künstlerische Filmproduktion 1980–84*, holding documents of the Central Party Archive of the SED.
3. Evelyn Schmidt in an interview with Dieter Hochmuth, entitled: 'Ich habe einfach keine Lust mehr, höflich zu sein!' In Dietmar Hochmuth (ed.), 1993: 132.

4. This way of indirectly censoring controversial film projects that had somehow 'slipped through the net' or where the evaluation of them had changed during their production period, was common practice. See the confidential letter by the Party's Head of Culture, Ursula Ragwitz, 12 May 1981 to the Ministry of Culture, HV Film, in *Spielfilm, künstlerische Produktion*, 1980–84, p.12.

Chapter 13

Naming and Exclusion: the Politics of Language in Contemporary France

Clarissa Wilks and Noëlle Brick

This essay sets out to explore questions of identification and exclusion from a sociolinguistic perspective. It will examine the current linguistic practice of certain major channels of communication in France, political parties and the press, with regard to the naming of traditionally excluded groups such as women, homosexuals and ethnic minorities.

These issues cut across the notion of the forbidden in two senses. Firstly, we are working with the concept of the French language itself as a sacred artefact, a forbidden preserve untouchable by all but an elusive, normative elite. Secondly, we are dealing with the way in which the excluded groups we have identified are represented in the language and with how these representations influence the identification and self-identification of the group. How does the use or the rejection of 'discriminatory language' inform the version of social reality that the press and political parties are seeking to reflect or impose? What mechanisms are operating in the active reclamation of spaces when conventionally excluded groups seek to reestablish their differential identity through the reappropriation of pejorative terms?

Therefore, this essay will discuss notions of linguistic purity and the norm which have a particular resonance in the French context. It will also look at the different levels of awareness of the question of discriminatory language and at the way in which changing linguistic practice affects perceptions of inclusion and exclusion.

Linguistic Purism and the Norm

Notions of the 'purity' and conversely the 'corruption' of language have a particular psychological reality in France. Any process of linguistic standardisation, to include selection, codification, elaboration and diffusion, by which one variety emerges as a prestige norm, will inevitably exclude speakers of the remaining 'non-standard varieties'. While recognising the extreme complexity of the notion of 'norm', for the purposes of this essay we will follow those scholars who distinguish three aspects: firstly, an 'objective norm' which refers to the language that speakers actually produce; secondly, a 'prescriptive norm', that is, the institutionally prescribed standard to be found in dictionaries and grammar books and traditionally promoted through the education system; and, thirdly, a 'subjective norm' which refers to individual value judgements about language (Guenier, 1983: 773). These judgements may vary in the respect they accord to the prescriptive norm but nevertheless implicitly recognise its prestige.

As Bourhis points out, in France the emergence of a standard 'demonstrates that the prestige attained by a standard form of a language may not be just the product of a cultural accident favouring its use but the result of centuries of systematic efforts to impose one variety' (1982: 34). These 'systematic efforts', the well-documented processes of conscious manipulation and control of the French language by the state, began in the sixteenth century. In 1539 the *Edit de Villers-Cotterêts*, seen as the first major instance of language planning by the state, decreed that the *Francien* dialect, later to become standard French, should be used in all administrative documents to the exclusion of other dialects or Latin. The formal process of codification began a century later with the establishment of the *Académie Française* whose principal function was to give rules to the French language. Clearly, those involved in this flurry of linguistic activity around the notion of '*le Bon Usage*' (correct usage) were a self-perpetuating elite group: scholars and grammarians and those in attendance at the centre of power, the court of Louis XIV. By definition, then, those excluded from and by the prestige norm were, in the context of the social structure of the seventeenth century, the bulk of the 'powerless' population.

The legacy of this systematic intervention, which continues, sometimes brutally – witness the attempted eradication of regional languages – until the present day has been summarised neatly by Lodge. It consists, firstly, of the notion that 'the best French is best because it is spoken by the best people', and, secondly, that 'the best French is the best because it is the language of reason and clarity'; a belief most vividly exemplified in the notional ideal of classical seventeenth-century French (Lodge, 1993: 165). The deliberate diffusion of such notions via the education system results in the complementary phenomena of linguistic intolerance and linguistic insecurity. Once such strong ideas of a prescriptive, subjective, value-laden norm have been collectively internalised, any unsanctioned attempt to change language may be experienced by self-styled 'purists' as an attack; language is a forbidden place which must be defended from the incursions of 'outsiders'. This belief in the sacred, monolithic status of the French language is an extremely potent one, giving rise to impassioned resistance to linguistic change on avowedly 'pure' aesthetic grounds. In reality, of course, as suggested by Holmes, attitudes to language are never simple or apolitical, 'Ultimately attitudes to language reflect attitudes to the users and uses of language' (1992: 344).

The degree of linguistic intolerance may vary according to what is perceived to be at stake. Just who is allowed to trespass on the forbidden ground may depend on the threat they appear to pose to established social structures or hierarchies. This can be illustrated by the question of the acceptability or unacceptability of certain feminised professional terms, which appears to depend on the degree of prestige attached to particular functions. Thus, *Le Monde,* although by its own account 'not fundamentalist in linguistic matters' has no difficulty in using *'la Présidente'* to refer to the chairwoman of an association but could in no circumstances countenance *'la Présidente de la République'* (interview with Jean-Pierre Colignon, chief reader at *Le Monde*).

In the same way the notion of the linguistic 'insider' or 'outsider' may be a fluid one. Whilst the initiative for the setting up of the *Commission Roudy* for the feminisation of professional terms in 1984 came from the government via a priministerial circular, the response of the *Académie* and other linguistic reactionaries to the mere establishment of this body demonstrates that state sponsorship is not enough to guarantee 'insider' status. The reactions to the *Commission* illustrate the gender-focused nature of the objections. Houdebine quotes various 1984 press articles referring to *'ces dames de la Commission'* (the ladies of the Commission) as a gathering of *'précieuses ridicules pomponnées'* (dolled up Salon Précieuses) who meet to take tea and to *'enjuponner le vocabulaire'* (adorn vocabulary with frills) (Houdebine, 1987: 21). Women clearly remain 'outsiders' hence this outrage at their audacity in trespassing on the forbidden space of the French language. Years later, reactions appear to be no less impassioned and intolerant. The recent circular emanating from Jospin, the French prime minister, which revived the call for feminised terms to be used for female post-holders, made waves not only in France but even in the press abroad (see the circular published in the *Journal Officiel,* 8 March 1998). The London *Times* published a strongly worded attack on the move in an editorial entitled 'Gender benders' (*The Times,* 10 March 1998).

Awareness of Discriminatory Language

The question of language itself as forbidden territory leads to the issue of language use, and specifically the naming practices of these major channels of communication. At this point we find that the 'insider/outsider' distinction mentioned earlier also has interesting implications. For the 'insider' the use of, or refusal to use, certain labels can be seen as a way of preserving an elite space. For the 'outsider' this space from which she or he is excluded thus becomes forbidden territory. The theoretical position that informs this construct is one shared by many researchers in the field who claim that the use of discriminatory or exclusive language is an active form of discrimination in itself. Its elimination will not, of course, guarantee equal rights for excluded groups, but will nevertheless, as Cameron says: 'change the repertoire of social meanings and choices available to social actors' (1997: 64).

In the context of this research, 'insiders' can refer to the press and political parties who are influential in shaping generalised linguistic practice. 'Outsiders' are those often at the receiving end of discriminatory naming practices: women, homosexuals and ethnic minorities. Therefore, in order to investigate levels of sensitivity regarding discriminatory language amongst these linguistic 'leaders d'opinion', we conducted semi-structured interviews with the chief readers of two major daily newspapers (*Libération* and *Le Monde*) and also with party workers responsible for various publications within a number of political parties including *Le Parti Socialiste, Le RPR, Les Verts,* and *Le Front National* (the Socialist Party, the Gaullist Republican Union, the Green Party and the National Front).

What emerges from the research is that the various institutions may be broadly categorised into two groups: those who recognise the concept of discriminatory language and those who do not.[1] As we shall see, such a broad categorisation in fact disguises some complex nuances in approach to language change. Of our sample, those institutions that did articulate some level of conscious awareness of discriminatory language were the two newspapers together with *Le Parti Socialiste* and *Les Verts*. In all four cases this awareness was focused almost exclusively on women as a potentially excluded group and centred upon the question of the feminisation of professional terms. Both *Le Monde* and *Libération* are still developing their policies on feminisation but are united in recognising the need to codify their response to the issue and are preparing specially dedicated sections in their recent style guides. Jean-Pierre Colignon, chief reader at *Le Monde*, reveals that the newspaper is very sensitive to, and divided on, the issue of feminisation, though few changes actually appear in print. *Le Monde* accepts feminised forms designating what it sees as unimportant functions such as *la conseillère, la députée* or *l'adjointe au maire* (a woman town councillor, member of parliament or deputy mayor) but will not, as indicated earlier, feminise any more prestigious functions: *la sénateure/la sénatrice/la sénateuse* (a woman member of the Upper House) are all rejected.

Libération has recently produced a *Marche Maison* (style book) which does include the recommendations of the *Commission Roudy* but is reluctant to dictate to journalists. According to Hervé Alliet, the chief reader: 'On ne peut pas imposer en matière de langue' (As far as language is concerned, it is difficult to impose rules). In terms of concrete changes the paper has gone only so far as insisting on a small number of terms which already have a certain currency such as *une députée* or *une ministre* (a woman member of Parliament or a woman minister).[2]

In a telephone interview, the newsletter editor of the *Parti Socialiste* claimed that 'il fallait faire entrer la féminisation dans les moeurs', in other words, make feminisation part of linguistic and cultural practice, non-feminised professional terms referring to women are thus rejected. However, recognition of the exclusive impact of the generic masculine appears to be little more than cosmetic. In a text which opens promisingly with *'chères camarades, chers camarades'* (women comrades, comrades), we read that the Socialist Party is committed to the construction of 'une société centrée sur l'homme' (a society centred on man).

In contrast, according to the *Vert Contact* editorial team, *Les Verts* are wholeheartedly committed to the principle of feminisation, which for them has acquired the status of an 'unwritten rule' (although they admit that, like all unwritten rules, it can be overlooked). They are also prepared to go further than the mainstream press in striving to eliminate the generic masculine in their publication *Vert Contact*. However, their attempt to use inclusive language is beset by a number of practical problems – currently they are torn between brackets and hyphens as illustrated in these examples:

les adhérent(e)s/ les adhérent-e-s
les élu(e)s vert(e)s / les élu-e-s vert-e-s.
(women party members and elected representatives)

As suggested earlier, for *Les Verts* most debate on the practical application of nondiscriminatory language has centred on women. Whilst some interesting lexical choices can be observed in their naming practice regarding other excluded groups, they are clearly more tentative here. As regards ethnic minorities, the editorial team expresses a preference for the term *'résidents étrangers'* (foreign residents) as opposed to the more marked term *'immigrés'* (immigrants). Interestingly, they propose the paraphrase *'enfant français de parents étrangers'* (youth with French nationality born of foreign parentage) as a substitute for the *'beur/beurette'* (second generation immigrant youth from North Africa) which they deem to be colloquial. However, it is possible that the preoccupation with register in this case masks uncertainty about the status of this term, which was once a clear badge of ethnic pride and solidarity but is now more controversial. The same suggestion of indecisiveness is evident in the choices regarding the designation of homosexuals where *'les homosexuel(le)s'*, *'les gays'* and *'les lesbiennes'* are all used indiscriminately and monolithically.

Among those institutions in our sample which, in response to a direct question, did not recognise the concept of discriminatory language (the *RPR* and the *Front National*), we also found interesting differences in levels of sensitivity to the question between the two parties, as well as between the public and private discourse within particular organisations. The chief reader at the *RPR* observes that discriminatory language is not a reality for the party and is happy to refer to the language used by the *RPR* to describe, for instance, members of ethnic minority groups as 'very neutral'. This claim may appear ironic given that her preferred alternative to '*beur/beurette*' – a term totally alien to the *RPR* – turns upside down any notion of ethnic identity it might encapsulate. She proposes instead '*jeunes qui veulent s'intégrer*' (youths who wish to be integrated into French society) since those who reject the idea of integration 'n'existent pas pour nous' (as far as we are concerned do not exist). Despite her refusal of the notion of discriminatory language, a covert sensitivity to the relationship between language and discrimination does appear when discussing linguistic practice in the naming of women. Indeed, the chief reader states that 'language can exclude, or rather, language betrays attitudes'.

As regards the designation of women, she claims to speak for the female grass roots of the party when she advocates the feminisation of professional terms. In this desire to be progressive, however, she knows that she is knocking on a closed door and describes the attitude of the party hierarchy, who control the publicly distributed *Lettre de la Nation*, as '*très verrouillé*' (very firmly locked). Even a very modest attempt to get the feminine '*députée*' accepted met with a categorical refusal from her editors. What we are observing here, then, is a discrepancy between the public and the private linguistic face of the *RPR*.

Representatives of the editorial team for the *Front National* publication *Français d'abord* also state that the abstract notion of 'discriminatory language' is not recognised by the party. The nature of this nonrecognition is, of course, different for the *Front National* than for, say, the *RPR*, since public accusations of racism have forced them to acknowledge that a relationship between language and discrimination is perceived to exist in some parts of society and can be used against them. They have in fact been compelled to make changes to their linguistic practice in order to avoid further legal convictions for racist behaviour. However, these changes are made only under duress and represent for the *Front National* team a sort of 'intellectual terrorism' and a form of exclusion. In terms of the metaphor of the forbidden, this is an extraordinary reversal of roles: the *Front National*, a high profile public 'insider' whose mission seems to have been to ensure that France remains an exclusive preserve, is now presenting itself as an 'outsider' denied access to the forbidden domain of 'dangerous' vocabulary. One such notable switch in linguistic practice has been the appropriation of the term '*jeune*' (youth) which the editorial team claims is now used specifically by the *Front National* and its sympathisers to designate young Arabs. The unmarked term for a young white person, according to our interviewees, would be '*jeune adolescent*' (teenager).

This establishment of certain 'secret' terms, transparent only to the initiates of the *Front National*, bespeaks a 'bunker mentality' which is expressed even in the physical space they occupy – the semi-underground, practically windowless building with its stringent security at St Cloud in the affluent western suburbs of Paris.

What we are witnessing in the case of the *Front National* is a sort of 'mirror game' encapsulated in linguistic practice whereby perceptions of acceptance and rejection, the 'insider' and 'outsider' status, are in constant flux. Significantly, a similar mirror game seems to be in operation amongst some conventionally excluded groups themselves. This was apparent in further interviews that we conducted at the *Centre Gai et Lesbien* (Gay and Lesbian Centre) in Paris, a pressure group dedicated to defending the rights of gay men and lesbians and to publicising issues of particular interest to them. The responses of their representative revealed that there appears to be a movement towards reasserting a differential, 'nonintegrated', identity through language, at least for gay men. The 'official' designation for this minority group is recognised as being '*homosexuel*' – a neutral term which does not carry any of the clinical connotations that it has assumed in the United States and the United Kingdom. It is used in France principally to indicate sexuality. The term '*gai*' (always given its French spelling), now also widespread, is seen as a consistently 'sympathetic' appellation and refers to the overall lifestyle of the individual. However, in addition to this more 'mainstream' vocabulary, attempts are being made to reclaim derogatory terms that were used by heterosexual society to condemn the forbidden practices of gay men. For example, the formerly highly pejorative term '*pédé* (poof), is now frequently used in the Centre's publication with positive connotations and as a mark of pride and solidarity. The term is most often written 'PD' (pronounced *pédé*) which may serve to distance it from its original etymology with its implications of paedophilia. We should note, however, that this revalorised term has not yet gained universal currency in

France and continues to be perceived as homophobic outside the capital. Interestingly, there has been no parallel reappropriation of the socially marked term '*gouine*' (dyke) to refer to lesbians. One might speculate that a certain threshold of general social acceptance (afforded to gay men, but not to lesbians) is necessary before this kind of reclamation of language becomes desirable to minority groups.

Conclusion

In conclusion, we can see that the French language is still as much of a battleground as it ever was. The project for the '*défense de la langue*' (defence of the language) sets language up as an untouchable expression of French cultural heritage. The very nature of this mission must then exclude those who perceive themselves as lacking positive representation in the language and whose moves for linguistic change are decried or rejected. The refusal to countenance inclusive language preserves a *status quo* whereby language helps to reproduce a social order in which minority groups are unwelcome in the forbidden territory of 'mainstream' French society.

Conversely, the area of lexical evolution we have examined shows that perceptions of inclusion and exclusion are constantly being renegotiated through language. As we have seen, in some cases, alongside the search for acceptance and integration, naming may also be used to reclaim and reassert social difference. The revalorisation of '*la langue du mépris*' (the language of contempt) (Yaguello, 1978: 150) may thus enable minorities to reestablish positive spaces, against and through the forbidden, which will allow differential social identities to flourish.

Notes

1. For a full analysis of the data see Brick, Noëlle and Wilks, Clarissa, 'Langue et exclusion', forthcoming in the *Journal of French Language Studies*.
2. For a full discussion of this question as regards differences between *Le Monde* and *Libération* see Wilks, Clarissa and Brick, Noëlle (1997).

Chapter 14

Cobwebby States, Chilled Vaults? The Nation State in Contemporary Irish Feminist Poetry

Anu Hirsiaho

I wind up in the ghost place
the language rocks me to,
A cobwebby state, chilled vault
littered with our totems

Paula Meehan, *Don't Speak to Me of Martyrs*

There are ghosts, cobwebs and totems in Paula Meehan's poem *Don't Speak to Me of Martyrs* (1990).[1] When reading it for the first time some years ago, the metaphorical place Meehan calls 'a cobwebby state, chilled vault' awakened my interest. I wanted to ask why Meehan distances herself from the Irish past full of martyrs, not only as a gender-neutral citizen but also as a woman, and at a more general level I wished to explore the possible ways in which a female citizen may question her relationship to 'national' places of male domination. Why is Meehan's 'ghost place' before all else a place in language? Of what kinds of elements does this linguistic national space, 'littered with our totems', consist?

The poem is an example of the complexity of an individual's political memory. In this essay, I shall examine the idea of the nation state in this and two other poems by Irish feminist writers.[2] The writers deal with national identity, but simultaneously problematise the concept because of its totalising tendencies. My concern is not to define the poets' national identities *de facto*, but to investigate the differing meanings that surround the ideas of nation. The idea of *nation-ness* suits my context here: a combination of place and of a sense of belonging, it is more a compilation of atmospheres and meanings in language than one, homogenising, common-to-all national identity.

I shall consider the nation state, or the aforementioned sense of *nation-ness*, in the works of Eavan Boland, Máighréad Medbh, and Paula Meehan. These women have been active in the Irish women's movement and have strongly criticised the gender ideologies embedded in nationalism both through their writing and their actions.

The poems focus on embodied spaces in which there are no gender-neutral citizens but women and men. Their subjects are women for whom the nation state is either a secret space, in which the nostalgic past comes to haunt them, or an antiseptic space that erases history. They deal with the politics of memory, collective consciousness and institutionalised silence in today's Ireland. It is this interplay between nostalgia and amnesia that I am referring to when I use the phrase 'political memory'.

This essay was first written in the spring of 1998 when both Northern Ireland and the Republic of Ireland prepared a referendum on the peace treaty and the revival of a Northern Ireland assembly after twenty-six years of Westminster rule. These processes were of particular interest in my native Finland because the negotiations were led by a Finnish conservative politician, Harri Holkeri. In addition to seeing the iconic image of the smiling Gerry Adams and Martin McGuinness, we also read and heard opinions about peace expressed by the people of Belfast. Few reporters were interested in the acceptance of the peace treaty in Southern Ireland because it was seen as secondary information to the outside world. The outcome of the referendum only proved what was already known about attitudes in the Irish Republic to the conflicts of the North: only 56.5 per cent of the population in the South bothered to vote, and nearly 95 per cent of those voted for the peace treaty, thus sealing the legitimacy of the present border. The referendum results proved that the dream of an all-Ireland Free State is fading away even among the Northern Catholic minority. The 'No' votes in May 1998 were reported to have come from the Protestant loyalists afraid of stronger ties to the Republic. In other words, the Northern Catholic minority supported the peace treaty despite the fact that it enforced the legitimacy of the existing border; autonomy was preferred to Westminster-based government.

Significantly, the three writers whose work I am considering – Boland (b.1944), Medbh (b.1959) and Meehan (b.1955) – were born in the Republic of Ireland and raised as Roman Catholics. Place of birth and religion are particularly important identity 'tags' in the Irish context because they often influence the writer's relationship to geopolitical realities. The younger generation in the Irish Republic are often accused of ignorance about the problems of the North unless they have relatives on the Northern side or move across the border themselves. Notably, only one of the poems discussed here deals with the border, and in an interestingly ambivalent way. Máighréad Medbh,[3] the author, lived for a few years in Belfast and states:

> this illegal border will always be/
> unless we get up off our bended knee
> the priests run my schools and my history
> there's no free state in the Catholic See
>
> (Medbh, 1993: 59)

Regarding the border as illegal, Medbh puts forward different arguments from those of many Catholic nationalists. She attacks the ideology of the Catholic Free State, the Catholic school system and a history dictated by the clergy, whereas for many supporters of *Sinn Féin*, the Catholic Church and school have been important centres of political consciousness; signs of resistance and difference. Medbh's ideal Ireland would be united and secular, not united and Catholic. It is a Southern majority group member's argument as she can 'afford' to distance herself from Catholicism; it may be more difficult for a Northern Catholic writer to deny a religion so strongly identified with political resistance.

The Womb, the Border and Waiting Women

For the women poets of the Republic the real issues are the conservative nationalist forces, and their control of women's bodies and sexuality – not the Northern border. These pro-life and pro-family forces seem to be a rhetorical continuum of the views of long-term *taoiseach* (prime minister) Eamon de Valera (1882–1975), whose radio speeches emphasised a communitarian, family-centred rural idyll: one, united Ireland as a haven from foreign, secularised influences (see Lee, 198: 334). This rhetoric so affected public opinion that as recently as the 1990s condoms still had to be imported from Northern Ireland. The rights of the foetus were added to the Constitution in 1983, and until 1995 divorce was banned. Such a vision is the Northern Irish Protestants' nightmare: Roman rule, Catholic tyranny, in which a vague common good always outweighs the good of the individual.

Ever since the beginning of the Irish Women's Liberation Movement, Irish feminists have had loyalty conflicts between the womb and the border (Nell McCafferty, 1986: 350–351). In particular for Southern feminists, the womb has been the most important symbolic fighting space for bodily self-determination, whereas in the North, many women activists have given priority to the attainment of permanent peace.

Feminist researchers of nationalism, for example Cynthia Enloe (1989: 62–63), spot a strategy of denying women's specific needs, 'the mythical later', in the histories of most newly independent nation states. Instead of participating in the definition of the national interest alongside their men, women are advised to wait until the country gets rid of violence, the economy is in balance and political institutions operate properly. In the Irish Republic passive waiting lasted for half a decade, after which women realised that the state could not even guarantee them a secure position as housewives, let alone satisfy their more individualistic needs in opposing Catholic communitarianism.[4] The new women's movement, launched in the Republic in 1970, was inspired by its Anglo-American pioneers; its secularised theses consisted of those elements that the Church and *Fianna Fáil* had been opposed to while women waited.

Embodied Locations in a Nation State

The selected poems are exercises in the politics of location, a concept borrowed from the American poet Adrienne Rich who approaches time and space from the viewpoint of feminist theory (1986: 210–231). Rich criticises the intellectual laziness of academic, white middle-class feminists. They have for too long explained the oppression of women in 'global', ahistorical terms, as if the same mechanisms of exclusion worked everywhere in the world.

The politics of location includes the recognition that no one just 'happens' to be a member of a certain community, but has predetermined world views that cannot be thrown away overnight. It is more honest to specify one's location in the world than to speak for the good of the world's women. The most immediate location for Rich is the body. She looks beyond the possibility of a stable identity, seeing that one body has many identities, carrying conscious memories and unconscious fragments of where it has been.

Rich encourages women to locate themselves geographically, to mark all the places where the body has been and also the places from where it has been excluded. This kind of mapping is also a political act. A global viewpoint to any political question is impossible; every viewpoint is a place on the map. By writing a text as one's own world map, universal or global assumptions lose their credibility. Drawing on Rich's critique, I am interested in the strategies of the politics of location that Irish feminist writers use when writing about the nation state. Would mapping one's own historical background be a way of overcoming the nationalists' generalisations of 'Irish womanhood'?

Celtic Mists

Home and family are the metaphors for nation, their common mythical axis characterised by looking backwards. A family wants to trace its famous ancestors; a nation needs its heroic past, its story of the defenders of national integrity. In Ireland, one of the most powerful ways to claim the integrity of the nation has been to revive Celtic mythology.

This Celtic revival may have been a defence mechanism against British influences: Celtic-ness became the essence and source of national self-esteem. The fact that the Celts also inhabited parts of present-day Wales, Scotland, England, France, Germany, Hungary and Italy makes these patriotic imaginings somewhat anachronistic, and the Irish have not been able to prove the purity of their Celtic genes. Archaeological traces of other groups cohabiting the island with the Celts have also been found (Green, 1995: 11–14).

Nevertheless, towards the end of the nineteenth century, there were flourishing and often competing societies for Celtic culture in Irish cities. The revival was, from today's perspective, a subculture that included, in addition to poetry recitals, vegetarianism, protection of animals, anthroposophy and feminism. Among its most famous participants were W.B.Yeats and Maud Gonne, who spent much of their time in the hills of Donegal, lying on the grass and philosophising. Yeats believed that he could find strength to liberate Ireland from the depths of Mother Earth, whereas the more pragmatic Gonne channelled her energies into social activism, such as soup kitchens for peasants (Coxhead, 1965: 36). Why did these Celtic societies have such great symbolic meaning for nationalists?

The reason why the Irish Celtic period is easier to 'remember' than in other countries invaded by the Celts (from *circa* 600 BC to AD 500) is the early Christianisation of the island. Many parts of Europe boast of their Celtic heritage but it is Irish literature in particular that bears witness to the Celts' existence, and literacy flourished with the arrival of Christianity. In order to make the Celtic population more open to its message, priests and monks transcribed the bardic folklore and, consequently, many Irish legends include Christian themes, which seem to be reinterpretations of the pagan folk tales (Green, 1995: 11–13).

The Celts had an intensive bond with places. The stories were always 'located' and the locations populated with goddesses, water spirits, hero-gods, shape-changing creatures. Thus, Celtic mythology can be called storytelling of places (de Paor, 1986: 47). The poet was respected and feared as the messenger between the community in this world and the gods and goddesses of the Otherworld (Johnson, 1989: 122).

The goddesses, considered to be closer to earth than gods, protected the most central powers, like sovereignty, war and fertility. The most well-known triple goddesses were Eriu, Banbha and Fódla, who were believed to run the island when the Celts arrived. After initial suspicion they let the tribe come ashore on the condition that the island would be named after one goddess. One of the three, the goddess of sovereignty Eriu, made the newcomers drink a cup of red wine and so the land was named after her (Green, 1995: 73, 81–2).

Woman-as-land became almost an obsession in Irish nationalist writing and in the arts at the turn of the century. Lia Mills calls this tradition the iconic feminine (1995: 69): Ireland becomes a lamenting old mother, whose children have left her for material good, a coy maiden, whose virginity is threatened by a cruel landowner, or an angelic figure as the fairy godmother of nationalist forces. Land could also be portrayed as a cottage, a symbol of 'rooted' femininity, the cradle of the race. The icons condense the core symbols of the idea of nation, and the ideal Irish womanhood that fulfils the nation's needs of bearers of the next generation of the Celtic race (see also Nash, 1993; Innes, 1993).

Embodied Space

Máighréad Medbh's poem *Easter 1991* (1993) is a parody of a poem written by Patrick Pearse, *Mise Éire*, in which an old mother, deserted and sold to Britain, laments her loneliness. Both Pearse and Medbh locate Ireland in a woman's body, the fate of whom has been determined by her sons, male citizens. Medbh wrote the poem on the seventy-fifth anniversary of the Easter Rising in Dublin, after which Pearse and fifteen other agitators were executed by the British army in May 1916.

Medbh radicalises the prototypical nationalist poem. While Pearse's Ireland waits for help from her sons in the hands of the oppressive 'Brits', Medbh's Ireland attacks these sons, the builders of the nation state, and takes control of her own fate. After seventy-five years, Ireland is still conceptualised as a woman, but now she uses rap as a mode of expression. The *body politic* in the poem is sick:

> I am Ireland and I'm sick
> sick in the womb/ sick in the head
> and I'm sick of dying in this sickbed
> and if the medical men don't stop operating/
> I'll die
>
> (Medbh, 1993: 58)

Ireland, an ordinary woman with a womb, has no rights of bodily self-determination. The metaphorical womb refers to the Irish legislation on abortion, which clearly sets the rights of the foetus before the rights of the mother. Pregnancy can be terminated only in a case of absolute emergency, and if the 'medical men' interpret the Constitution too dogmatically, women in risk groups may die from complications (see also Smyth, 1992).

I read Medbh's poem on two levels: both as a subversion of the nationalist iconography and as an incisive analysis of women's lives in the Ireland of the 1990s. Medbh underlines the gendering of national identities. If a country is treated metaphorically as a passive, waiting woman, it is also easy to treat women's sexuality as a national priority, not as individual choices. The Irish pro-life forces argue that allowing Irish women abortion rights would take Ireland conspicuously closer to secular, corrupted Britain and break up the communities based on neighbourhood and good will, the forces that keep society from falling apart (see Smyth, 1992). Irish political scientists (Chubb, 1992: 12–13; Connolly, 1992: 108) refer to this trend as conservative communalism, which reflects the programme of the country's biggest party, *Fianna Fáil.*

Nostalgic Space

Eavan Boland's *Mise Éire* continues the theme of women leaving the land and living in the past tense. *Éire* portrays itself as an idyll, and 'the songs/that bandage up the history' make people's political memories vague and selective, so that the women of the poem know that by singing them they will only betray themselves. Their vision for a nation is now 'displaced into old dactyls' – a nostalgic, secret space in language, a container for the essence of Irishness (Boland, 1994: 375).

To learn again a lost language can be a political act, an expression of loyalty to an imagined Celtic community. Boland has never written poetry in Irish, because she spent her childhood and youth out of the country and missed her Irish lessons altogether. She specifies the relations of place and language as 'mingling the immigrant/guttural with the vowels/of homesickness' (Boland, 1994: 376). Leaving the land means adopting a new language, 'a passable imitation of what went before'. If she remains silent, her Irishness may go unnoticed. This is the Irish experience of otherness in England, which Boland experienced as a daughter of the Irish ambassador to London in her childhood in the 1950s. She learnt to modify her vowels in London, depending on the company she was in (see Boland, 1997).

Although Boland writes about homesickness, her women leave the nostalgic space and the past-oriented temporalisation. If nostalgia means to look backwards at something that has been forgotten and deserted, and an attempt to recreate a painless relationship with it, immigrant communities often practise an extreme version of this process. Using Stuart Hall's concept, Nira Yuval-Davis (1997: 46) refers to the lifestyle of many British immigrant communities as cultural fundamentalism, or freezing of cultures, which means stopping the natural fluctuation of cultural influences as the only way to survive from one's culture shock. It is interesting in terms of my analysis that Irish feminist poets use almost the same concepts about Irish nationalism that Yuval-Davis has noted in the context of Islamic immigrant communities in Britain. Why do they speak about freezing, paralysis and standstills in both locations?

Paula Meehan's 'cobwebby state, chilled vault' in *Don't Speak to Me of Martyrs* gives a similar impression of 'spookiness' as Boland's *Mise Éire*. The poem proceeds vertically: 'up there' is a fanatical male demagogue speaking about the will of the people and freedom, but the basement hides the bloodshed of the struggle, the skeletons that no one sees in daylight. 'Up there' absolute terms can be used, but when one comes down from the platform, concepts become blurred:

> Up there on the platform a man
> speaks of the people: of what
> we need, of who we really are, of how
> we must fight to liberate ourselves.
>
> (Meehan, 1990: 74.)

The platform could be seen as what is commonly known as national consciousness. A psychoanalytical interpretation of the poetics of space here would be that 'up there' is the superego, a consciousness about how things should be, whereas the lower levels of the poem appear as the unconscious. The female subject listening to the demagogue escapes to her world of daydreams and starts to swim 'down' in her memories:

> Down through the cigarette smoke
> the high windows cast
> ecstatic light to the floorboards
> stiletto pocked and butt scorched
>
> but now such golden pools of sun to bask in there.
> *I am fish,*
> *water my demesne.*
>
> (Meehan, 1990: 74)

The woman ignores the demagogue's monolithic will and identity of the people. After a nomadic daydream the woman gets back to the 'surface', to 'an ordinary room', a kind of intermediary space between the speaker's platform and the 'chilled vault'. Whereas the light of the meeting was 'ecstatic' and there were only candles burning in the church, a fluorescent light shines in the ordinary room and reveals to the woman every banal detail of her everyday existence:

> I push back to the surface, break clear,
> the light has come on, fluorescent,
> and banishes my dreaming self.
> It is after all an ordinary room.
>
> (Meehan, 1990: 75)

The blank space makes it possible to stop talking about martyrs. Inhabited by ordinary people, there is more space for historical variation than in the other places of the poem (political meeting, school, vault, the killing of martyrs in 1916, the national museum, childhood home, church):

> And we are ordinary people.
> We pull our collars up and head
> for the new moon sky of our city
> fondling each whorled bead in our macabre rosaries.
>
> Don't speak to me of Stephen the Martyr
> the host snug in his palm
> slipping through the wounded streets
> to keep his secret safe.
>
> (Meehan, 1990: 75)

If no one reminds her of martyrs, she can walk the streets of Dublin without thinking of those who were killed or wounded there. She is no more interested in the martyrs' secrets, about what 'really' happened on the streets during the Easter Rising in 1916. She wishes to live in a more anonymous city space.

Benedict Anderson's concept, 'imagined communities', is closely connected to memory and amnesia. Newborn nation states always create coherent stories of origins to hide the linguistic contingency in which the citizens live:

> Disintegration of paradise: nothing makes fatality more arbitrary. Absurdity of salvation: nothing makes another style of continuity more necessary. What then was required was a secular transformation of fatality into continuity, contingency into meaning. As we shall see, few things were (are) better suited to this end than an idea of nation. If nation states are widely conceded to be 'new' and 'historical', the nations to which they give political expression always loom out of an immemorial past, and, still more important, glide into a limitless future. It is the magic of nationalism to turn chance into destiny. (Anderson, 1991: 12)

If the birth of nation states, along with the outbreak of industrial capitalism and scientific rationalism, indicated an ideological revolution against the churches' economic, political and cultural dominance, memories reaching beyond the coming of Christianity were often an essential building block of an imagined community. What was not remembered had to be recreated – a past full of contingencies became a story of the fate of the nation.

Feminist writers often elaborate on historians' critique of the nation states by revealing the gendered sets of assumptions behind national imaginings. The mainstream literature on nationalism (see Anderson, 1991; Hobsbawn, 1994; Gellner, 1994) still maintains the male perspective, in which women are nameless icons in the photo appendix, or relegated to the footnotes as wives, mistresses and daughters of great men. If one is ignorant of its limits, one easily concludes that women hardly ever acted independently in nationalist movements anywhere in the world.

However, the point of feminist writing is not to fill in gaps but to find new forms of expression and theoretical viewpoints. Poets seem to have a more fluid space than historians, who write from an established position and choose their topics because of their academic value and relevance. If imagined communities deal with myths, legends and daydreams – phenomena that cannot be objectively proved – it seems possible to analyse them only by detaching oneself from any truth claims. This is the poet's preserve, not the historian's.

Antiseptic Space

Máighréad Medbh does not place hope in the national project taught at Irish schools. For her sick Ireland, the nation-state is an antiseptic space that 'reminds her of nothing'. There are no signs of a glorious past or a promising future – the 'tidy house' leads to total amnesia:

I am Ireland / and I'm sick
I'm sick of this tidy house where I exist/
that reminds me of nothing
not of the past/not of the future
I'm sick of depression
I'm sick of shame
I'm sick of poverty
I'm sick of politeness
I'm sick of looking over my shoulder
I'm sick of standing on the shore/
waiting for some prince to come on the tide

(Medbh, 1993: 59–60)

The last lines refer to the old *aisling* tradition, romantic poetry in which women were often sad, lonely figures waiting for men who had gone to sea. In a similar way to Eavan Boland in *Mise Éire,* Medbh rebels against the old representations of passive womanhood. The difference between the two other poems is that, in *Easter 1991*, none of the elements of the imagined community lures the female subject. Whereas Boland and Meehan portray *nation-ness* with ambivalence, Medbh is only disillusioned:

> I am Ireland/
> and I'm not waiting anymore.
> (Medbh, 1993: 60.)

After seventy-five years, the static icon is tired of waiting for the prince, or the achievement of the 'national interest'. Instead, there is an angry woman who speaks for the first time without whispering. After listing Ireland's sicknesses, she does not draw a map of a feminist, post-Catholic, or postnationalist island but leaves the rest to the reader's imagination. Ireland is travelling in an open space, and the direction is not yet predictable.

Displacement, Feminism and Open Spaces

The female subjects in the three poems are all displaced: the reader is led into a radically open *now-time* full of possibilities and uncertainty about the future. Boland's *now-time* is a place where the English language creates 'imitations of what went before', translations that tame the original. Medbh's *now-time* is raw everyday realism – poverty, drugs, domestic violence and hypocrisy. Meehan's *now-time* is lit by a fluorescent lamp, under which one cannot drift off into the world of daydreams. In a sense, all poems deal with the loss of a safe national narrative, women's symbolic divorce from simplistic analogies between the Celtic past (origins) and a future (destiny) built upon it.

The poets do not erase the richness of the Irish past but reflect on the role of history in women's lives today. It becomes clear that women have little time for a history full of 'totems', 'old dactyls' or the operations of 'medical men' if they want to change their lives. The past exists but only as 'passable imitations'. A critical approach to one's history involves modifying one's political memory, questioning the periodisations of the past, and in the case of feminist writers, examining power relations from the perspective of gender, for example by following Adrienne Rich's idea of politics of location. The expressions 'I won't go back to it' (Boland), 'I'm not waiting anymore' (Medbh), 'Don't speak to me of martyrs' (Meehan) are powerful negative outbursts. The poets do not deny the meaning of 'national' history but they perceive these events from a partial position that demands less commitment to an ideology of oneness. Every move towards an original culture is a move towards deeper amnesia. One century after Yeats' and Gonne's mystical search for roots, Ireland has been divided into two, and the struggle for the origins of culture has ended in civil war. The peace treaty in 1998 did not stop cultural fundamentalism in one night.

The feminist movement in the Republic of Ireland has not yet been an open forum for discussion about the idea of the nation. Feminist activists in the Republic consider the acute, everyday issues, such as reproduction, the feminisation of poverty, women's health and education as more central than 'patriarchal' national history. On the other hand, Northern feminists often feel excluded from the materialist discussions of their Southern sisters, because in their lives history is concretely linked to the questions of peace and security. There is still a division in the feminist space of the island between the interests of the womb and border.

The poems cited here are moving towards the unknown, perhaps to a place where poetry as storytelling could function as a bridge between the materialist demands of today (the womb) and the need to know one's past (the border) – perhaps to a space where different conceptions of the birth of the nation and Irishness as a mentality could meet together peacefully and where a strictly 'tagged' national identity will finally dissolve.

Notes

1. Paula Meehan is the author of *The Man Who Was Marked by Winter* (The Gallery Press, 1991), *Pillow Talk* (The Gallery Press, 1994) and *Mysteries of the Home* (Bloodaxe Books, 1996). I should like to thank the poet for permission to reprint excerpts from her 1990 version of 'Don't Speak to Me of Martyrs'.
2. The article is a development of my MA thesis in Political Science at the University of Jyväskylä, Finland, entitled *Finding a Voice Where They Found a Vision. Time, Place and Politics of Location in Contemporary Irish Feminist Writing* (1997).
3. Máighréad Medbh is a performance poet who has published two collections of poetry: *The Making of a Pagan* (Blackstaff Press, 1990) and *Tenant* (Salmon

Publishing, 1999). A further collection will be published by Salmon Publishing in 2001/2. I should like to thank the poet and the Feminist Collective for permission to reprint excerpts from 'Easter 1991'.

4. In the 1937 Constitution, women's place was defined as the keeper of the common good in the following words: 41.2.1 In particular, the State recognised that by her life within the home, woman gives to the State a support without which the common good cannot be achieved. 41.2.2 The State shall, therefore, endeavour to ensure that mothers shall not be obliged by economic necessity to engage in labour to the neglect of their duties in the home (*Bunreacht na hÉireann*).

PART III

VISUAL SPACES
EMBODIED PLACES

Figure 15.1 Pieter de Hooch, *A Woman with a Broom and Pail in a Courtyard*, c1658–1660, 48.2 × 42.9 cm. Courtesy of Sotheby's, London.

CHAPTER 15

THE VIRTUAL INTERSECTION: A MEDITATION ON DOMESTIC VIRTUE

Jorella Andrews

In a little-known courtyard scene by the Dutch seventeenth-century painter Pieter de Hooch (Figure 15.1) – a work that has been predominantly housed within private collections[1] – a lone woman is depicted having emerged from the relative darkness visible through the gateway behind her. She carries a broom and pail, her overskirt is hitched up, her head is down. Clearly, she intends to carry out a domestic task, yet she seems strangely poised between motion and motionlessness. As insistently present in the work as she is, is a geometrical slant of light – a 'virtual pathway' – over which she has just stepped...

Simply entitled *A Woman with a Broom and Pail in a Courtyard*, this painting dates from between 1658 and 1660 and was made while the artist, a native of Rotterdam, was resident in Delft. It is one of a series of images first produced by de Hooch during this period depicting mainly middle-class women at work within spaces designated as domestic. Interestingly, by focusing upon the domestic in this way, de Hooch was entering into a territory which, before mid-century, had remained relatively unscrutinised by the eye, and untouched by the brush, of painters. Indeed, in the early decades of the century this subject had been almost exclusively the province of draftsmen and printmakers (notably the printmaker Geertruydt Roghman (1625–c.1651–57)), with the Haarlem artists Dirck Hals and Judith Leyster probably being the first to experiment with such scenes in oils (Sutton, 1998: 68).

A Hermeneutical Context

The overt (some would say nominal) subject-matter of paintings such as the de Hooch concerns the so-called virtuous middle-class woman – or more accurately *married* woman or *housewife* (the *deughdelijke* or *weerde vrouw*). This distinctively Protestant ideal of womanhood was energetically promoted within the popular culture of the United Provinces or Dutch Republic. Informed by both Lutheran and Calvinistic doctrines of virtue, which emphasised industry and moderation, and came to regard economic success and domestic stability as evidence of virtuous living (see Fromm, 1997: 77), it found expression not only in painterly form, in popular prints and in moralising emblem books, but particularly in the voluminous literature on the subject of domestic conduct that had accumulated since the 1520s. This was consumed in great quantity by a literate public from the end of the sixteenth century onwards. Of these, one of the most widely disseminated was Jacob Cats' *Houwelyck* (*Marriage*), a manual addressed to a female readership, which reinforced patriarchal ideals concerning the roles women should play in society as their lives progressed from the state of *Maecht* (maiden) to *Weduwe* (widow), and also presented what Cats called the appropriate 'masculine counter-duties'. First published in 1625, and illustrated with emblematic engravings by Adriaen van de Venne, it was aimed predominantly at women of the regent class and the *haute bourgeoisie*. However, the production of cheaper editions ensured that it reached a much wider public; in fact, twenty-one editions of *Houwelyck* appeared during the seventeenth century, with what has been estimated as some 50,000 copies in circulation by the 1650s (Sutton, 1998: 69–70). The primary message being communicated to women in this kind of literature was that the role assigned to her sex – her civic as well as divinely pre-ordained duty – was to create and maintain order, cleanliness and harmony within the home, and to train her daughters and servants to do the same.[2]

It is as a source for reflection upon the nature of domestic virtue, and indeed, more generally upon the nature of virtue itself, that I approach the courtyard scene by de Hooch. However, the question I must first explore concerns the nature of the relationship between such *painterly* representations of domestic virtue, the literature to which they are thematically connected, and what would have been the lived experiences and attitudes of women in the Dutch Republic at this time. Repudiating the view that such images were straightforward representations of everyday life in the Dutch Republic during that period (a view popular until, and particularly in, the nineteenth century), certain contemporary commentators (most notably Eddy de Jongh), favour iconological readings of Dutch seventeenth-century painting. As such, they emphasise the symbolic connections that may reasonably be expected to have existed in the minds of painters and their audiences between the popular textual, and text affiliated visual material on domestic virtue, and their supposed high art equivalents. Consequentially, what Roland Barthes (and Svetlana Alpers after him) have called the 'reality effect' of such works – their apparent emphasis upon the figural as against the discursive, and upon what, in Philips Angel's *Lof der schilder-konst* (*In Praise of Painting*) of 1642, is called the *'waerneminghe van d'eyghen natuyrlicke dinghen'* (observation of the actual natural things) – is thought at first sight to obscure the symbolic, allegorical, and frequently moralising messages that actually constitute these paintings' raison d'être. Thus, significant use is made of popular cultural sources as aids to interpretation.

Other commentators (principally Alpers) repudiate iconology with its emphasis upon so-called 'disguised meanings', and its tendency to appropriate popular visual and textual sources as interpretative aids without adequately attending to the perceptual, material, formal and other differences distinguishing the production and reception of particular paintings, prints and texts. Instead, they take seriously, and seek to make appropriate sense of, the specific modes of picturing the world evidenced in painted works, effects achieved through the observational and imitative procedures praised in much of the admittedly scant seventeenth-century Dutch theoretical literature on painting.[3] Works like de Hooch's domestic scenes, therefore, are principally regarded as occasions for artists to explore those issues of a strictly painterly and technical nature that were reputedly paramount at the time, that is, to experiment with the construction of a *particular kind* of illusionistic space through an approach to perspective that has been defined in certain spheres as adding 'actual viewing experience to the artificial perspective system of the Italians' (Alpers, 1989: 27). Such a methodology involved, *inter alia*, particular attentiveness to the action and effects of light as it came into contact with different kinds of surface, filtered through different media, and illuminated different kinds of architectural space. (Such concerns, it is argued, were particularly provoked by the latest technological advancements in the area of optics, and the widespread interest of both painters and their audiences in the worlds being opened up by the various optical instruments and devices that were being experimented with – lenses, microscopes, telescopes and the camera obscura.[4]) When Alpers writes specifically on de Hooch, she intentionally makes paramount the architectural features of his works, and his depictions of space and light (1999: 95–98). Sutton concurs with Alpers' noniconological approach: 'de Hooch's general pattern of disregard for specific emblematic or metaphorical dimensions ought to elicit caution and skepticism' (Sutton, 1998: 75). However, as he had put it a little earlier: 'to say that [he] used symbolism only sparingly is not to suggest that his art was value-free or devoid of didactic or moral content' (Sutton, 1998: 68).

A third perspective located, we might say, somewhere between the two positions just described, would admit to the ideological nature of seventeenth-century Dutch genre paintings, while also taking seriously their *painterly* characteristics. Qua *painterly*, their psychological effects upon viewers could not simply be regarded as analogous to that of the domestic literature upon its readers, or the text-inscribed popular prints upon their consumers. As Mariët Westermann puts it, the *realist strategies* employed by artists certainly made 'depicted situations or relationships seem natural and immutable, hence true', thereby helping 'to create and maintain a largely middle-class consensus about the values that structured, or should govern life in the Dutch Republic' (1996: 99). But this did not erase a frequently intrinsic ambiguity or undecidability of *overall effect* which served to 'invite contemplation of domestic virtue' and place 'the responsibility for locating meaning … with the viewer' (Westermann, 1996: 124, 128). Having said this, however, many genre paintings of the period, including de Hooch's, seem at first sight to complement rather than problematise the views put forward in the literature. Particularly through formal devices – through the creation of a unified space achieved through a diffused and harmonising use of light and colour, and through compositions often organised around strong horizontal and vertical axes[5] – they appear visually to duplicate 'the quiet and harmonious household prescribed by Cats and others' (Westermann, 1996: 124). This seems to be particularly the case with de Hooch's interiors. Some of his courtyard scenes of women at work, with their greater informality and more active displays of industriousness, evoke a somewhat less insistent orderliness. Nonetheless, again largely through a more or less unified treatment of light and colour, they too succeed in producing an immediate sense of quiet, bourgeois contentment.

What sets *A Woman with a Broom and Pail in a Courtyard* apart from de Hooch's other courtyard scenes, is not only the comparatively emphatic formality and simplicity of its structure, but particularly the unusually dramatic interplay among architectural space, light and the female figure. It is this interplay that interests me. What are we to make not only of the sharply defined 'pathway' of light that has been included in the image – this 'virtual intersection' – but also of the depicted act of having 'stepped over' it? In what ways might these factors affect our interpretation of the picture, taken, as I have already indicated, as an occasion for reflection upon the nature of domestic virtue? I have no clear answer. What I will offer instead is a series of alternative readings based upon differently articulated explorations of the painting's compositional as well as iconographic and ideological elements. My methodology, in other words, is to juxtapose, to bring into conversation, those aspects of Dutch seventeenth-century genre painting that tend either to be segregated, and discussed only in parallel within the art-historical literature, or are treated oppositionally and placed in competition one with the other.

Domestic Virtue as Disempowerment?

Here, then, is a courtyard – a location regarded as an extension of the internal realms of the home, but nonetheless on its very edges. It is, according to one commentator, that region where the pure is particularly in danger of contamination from the impure: 'The dross of the earth comes right to the threshold of the house and must be vigorously scrubbed away' (Lokin, 1996: 114). Within the emblematic tradition such spaces were symbolic of the soul, that other inner world regarded as vulnerable to contamination but through the 'portals' of the senses (see de Jongh, 1995: 202–204). Here, too, is the woman, with light bathing her face and body, strangely poised, as I have said, between mobility and immobility. Had she perhaps hesitated for an instant and considered relinquishing her task, to follow instead the path of light which leads out through the open doorway to the sun filled landscape and distant city? Who can tell? Significantly – indeed, uniquely, where de Hooch's courtyard paintings are concerned – the woman is pictured alone and apparently unobserved. The fact of her aloneness, coupled with her stillness, make it difficult to interpret her demeanour with any degree of precision. Indeed, in the only recent commentary on this painting I have been able to discover she is described merely as being 'very conscious of her civic duty to purge the street and her courtyard of any stain' (Lokin, 1996: 114).

Certainly, one aspect of the work in particular may lead us to interpret it as a celebration of resolution and faithfulness to duty: although the woman's body is placed slightly to the left of the composition, her illuminated brow, downcast in submission and acceptance (perhaps) and leaning slightly forward, is located precisely at its centre point. We might even want to treat this point of illumination upon her face as symbolic of her virtuous state. In this case, the presence in the image of what I have called the 'virtual pathway', together with the woman's depicted act of having stepped over it, might be understood as a testimony to her determination to put duty before pleasure, industry before rest.

However, a profoundly negative reading of the picture, again based upon compositional factors, is equally justifiable. We might want to argue that by stepping over the pathway of light, the woman has literally passed over the opportunity to reject the drudgery demanded of her. That she has displayed a lack of courage in throwing off imposed limitations. By thus failing to exchange a life of duty and restriction for one of spontaneity, she has effectively reduced herself to the level of the fowl feeding to the left of the image, her functioning, like theirs, being governed solely by inbuilt instincts and nonreflective responses to external conditions. Indeed, her posture – head down and body tilted slightly forward – seems to echo that of the creatures that share her space.

Further, if we examine more closely the composition within which the woman is framed, we see that the courtyard is represented as a space from which there is, for her, no exit. Not because of any physical barrier, it is suggested, but due to conventional ones. The expanse of landscape, with the barely perceptible city in the distance, is revealed to us as rigidly contained by the small, symmetrical form created by the doorway and the side of the house. This area is further subdivided, vertically by the two tree trunks and horizontally by the canal and dark edge of field further back. This sense of confinement is intensified by the fact that, despite the picture's low horizon line, little of the sky is visible. Rather, its expansiveness is obscured by tree tops and the solid mass of the house.

So, are we then to understand this image as equating a life of domestic virtue with one of limitation, lack of courage and dehumanisation? Wayne Franits, in a recent study of Dutch genre paintings, seems in no doubt that the lifestyle prescribed for women within seventeenth-century Dutch culture was one of restriction and oppression. In justification, he refers to the way in which both religious and socio-economic developments had reduced the options available to women.

In the first place, with the religious shift that had occurred to a Calvinistic form of Protestantism, the Dutch Reformed Church had become the officially recognised state Church. Catholicism had been outlawed (although, with over one third of the population remaining Catholic, it was unofficially tolerated so long as it was practised clandestinely), and the convents and monasteries closed down.[6] Arguably, these developments were as tied to socio-political as to strictly religious concerns – that is, with the still young Republic's attempt to construct a sense of identity distinct from that of Catholic Spain, which had had dominion over the territory of the Low Countries, and from which independence had been gained through a series of revolts in the second half of the sixteenth century. (The Treaty of Münster, formalising Spain's recognition of Dutch independence had been signed only in January of 1648). For Schama, in fact, it is particularly with respect to a patriotic compulsion to clearly establish, maintain, and indeed police, the boundaries between national identities that this iconography of domestic hygiene is best understood (Schama, 1991: 378 ff.). In any case, a pressing social and theological need seems to have arisen to construct a model of ideal womanhood alternative to that of Catholicism.

Most significantly, whereas Catholicism had associated woman's highest religious calling with that of a celibate life within a cloistered order,[7] Protestantism, as we have seen, associated it with the home, and with her service of, and submission to, her husband. The Catholic model had its deficiencies, but arguably it did make available to women of a certain class a broader range of acceptable lifestyle possibilities and modes of social and intellectual interaction. Incidentally, an interesting parallel between the cloistered woman of Catholicism and the domestically cloistered one of Protestantism appears in the work of certain Protestant writers and theologians, for whom the virtuous married woman of Protestantism may properly be regarded as retaining, within the context of married life, an original state of virginity (see Sutton, 1998: 71).

The second factor that Franits identifies as contributing to the oppression of seventeenth-century Dutch women, relates to the gradual rise of capitalism which had occurred during this period and which, he writes, 'eventually transformed families from the older, feudal type of self-sufficient units of production and consumption in which husbands and wives worked jointly, to units in which production and consumption became separated, the former being identified with men and the latter with women' (Franits, 1993: 64). This shift, he argues, resulted in the disempowerment of women, who found themselves increasingly relegated to (and confined within) a private, domestic sphere, cut off from creative and productive engagement within the realm of the public and political. If it was indeed the case that the practice of the Protestant model of virtue resulted in the disempowerment of women, then this would point to a terrible disjunction between the practice of virtue on the one hand, and its etymological meanings on the other. For the Dutch word *'deughdelijk'*, like the English word 'virtue' (from the Latin, *virtus*), has etymological connections with the concepts of power, force and courage.[8]

Franits's argument concerning the oppressed condition of Dutch womanhood is founded upon his claim that during this period the realms of the private and public, the domestic and the civic, were regarded, and experienced, as sharply differentiated. According to other commentators, however, they were in fact seen as problematically interconnected. Mariët Westermann points out that contemporary writers regarded the domestic household as a microcosm of the larger polity, with the resource management (by women) of the former, having implications for the resource management of the latter (1996: 118). Could it have been largely due to this recognition of interconnectedness that so much emphasis was placed upon ensuring, through ideological and educational means, that women remained faithful to their duties of harmonising and stabilising the home environment?

According to Simon Schama, the male population was likely to have been in possession of an uncomfortable, indeed paranoid, awareness of the power that the culture had, no doubt inadvertently, invested in the hands of women (and ultimately women of low social standing). He cites, in partial justification, a riddle that was doing the rounds of the Amsterdam taverns in the 1640s:

> *Question*: How is it that the Devil rules Holland?
> *Answer*: Why, because Amsterdam rules Holland; Burgomaster (Andries) Bicker rules Amsterdam; Mevrouw Bicker rules the Burgomaster; Mevrouw is ruled by her maid, and the Devil, you can be sure, rules the maid.
> (Schama, 1980: 5)

Space, Illumination and Virtue

If, on the one hand, the courtyard is represented as a place of containment, on the other hand, it is also represented as an expansive space, without clear limits, and containing numerous internal entrances and exits. In visual terms it is the most open structure in the painting. It is impossible to judge how far it extends, indeed the imagination has a propensity to wander beyond its limits, making it a realm of unknowability – and also of possibility. It is also a place open to illumination. Indeed, here spaciousness and illumination are tied together. The 'virtual pathway' is, after all, the compositional device *par excellence* where the construction of a forcible illusion of space is concerned. Further, the house (located deeper within internal space) is not as impenetrable, bounded or closed as it might at first appear. Windows set high in the bright wall to the left and in the section of dark wall facing us, both reflect light and allow it to enter within. The light itself, of course, is of an order and reality alternative to, and greater than, the man-made. Within the context of an awareness of such factors, the woman's intention to fulfil a pre-determined task, while also aware (physically and perceptually) of the invitation of sunlight and open doorway to do otherwise, might imply at the very least not only her recognition that other possible behaviours run alongside her own, but also a deeper recognition that to have ceased working and to have gone outside, for instance, would not have been to exchange mindless duty for freedom, but, as is the case in every situation, one set of limitations and possibilities for another.

Perhaps, then, at issue in producing an interpretation of this painting is our understanding of the nature of the woman's awareness both of the expansiveness of the space in which she is located, and of the illuminatory capacities of the light that enters it. But certain aspects of this painting suggest that this is something of which only the painter is cognisant. For arguably, in this work, the capacity to see is located less in the woman than symbolically, through the artist's depiction of the curved, eye-like container which rests on its side on the bench to the right and slightly behind her. This container, open to the light and reflecting it, particularly on its interior surfaces, seems to be receptive in a way the woman is not. The woman, head lowered and eyes in shadow, seems blind by comparison.[9]

Now, at least two conflicting interpretative possibilities present themselves, this time concerning the relationship between virtue and visual perception. The first implies a negative view and is provoked visually, within the painting, by the woman's strange stillness. For might she not be understood as having been halted not, admittedly, by something seen, but by something (once) heard? Has she not something of the posture of someone listening intently, not, perhaps, to an audible stimulus, but to sounds or words reverberating within her memory? Taking now a theological perspective, associations with the Calvinistic pre-eminence of the ear over the eye are inevitable. 'In Calvin,' writes Michalski, 'the ear seems to acquire an almost divine connotation, the eye only a human and earthly one, both on the level of philosophical deliberations and ordinary mental associations. In fact for Calvin the ear stands for the soul, the eye for the senses' (1993: 55). Might one interpretation of this image be as a Protestant rendering of the Annunciation?

It is significant, however, that within other Dutch seventeenth-century cultural contexts, and specifically within the intellectual and scientific climate of the day, the virtues of visual perception were much celebrated, with the complexities of the visual world functioning as a source for fascinated debate among painters and their public. This was a period which saw the beginnings of empirical science as we understand it today, and fundamental to this mode of research was the belief that visual perception, as opposed to acts of supposedly pure intellection, were the primary means of accessing knowledge about the basic nature of reality. According to Vasco Ronchi, this position was particularly informed by a change in mindset in the area of optics, such that the use of optical technology, of lenses, was now taken seriously as a means of pursuing this quest. Having previously been regarded generally by scientists and philosophers as devices that deceive by distorting reality, they were now being used to open up the previously unknown and unexplored, but apparently infinitely expansive, regions of the very small and the very distant (Ronchi, 1970: 95–97). (The dramatic and destabilising effects of these researches, particularly in the area of astronomy, are well known.)[10] Perception itself was seen as receptive in nature. As Kepler had written in 1604 regarding what he saw to be the mechanics of vision (and leaving questions concerning its psychology to others), 'vision is brought about by a picture [*pictura*] of the thing being formed on the concave surface of the retina.'[11]

According to this emphasis upon the importance of visual perception, to refuse to see was to refuse to be receptive to knowledge or truth concerning the nature of self and world. This brings me to my final point. If we read the patch of light within the painting as a virtual pathway inwards (an entering, a movement within and towards, rather than an exit), requiring an attitude of openness or responsiveness, then the woman's act of stepping over it might be understood as a sign that she is unreceptive to revelation, to the possibility of an alteration in mindset regarding the nature of her locatedness within the world, and thus to change. This might in turn have implications with respect to the meaning of the painting. More to the point, the aspects of the work which I have made the focus of my discussion – the 'virtual intersection', the 'stepping over' – may be seen to articulate certain tensions and contradictions inherent to contemporary perceptions of female virtue, and more generally to Calvinistic conceptions of virtue.

The fact that the woman is shown apparently caught between motion and motionless, might be reworded to say that she is caught at a point of tension between activity and receptivity. The psychoanalyst Erich Fromm, writing on the Calvinistic association of virtue with unceasing human effort and industry, points out that this seems at first to be a contradiction, bearing in mind that the central tenet of this doctrine is that of predestination. But he goes on to infer that such industriousness had an important psychological function since it served as a mechanism enabling individuals to 'overcome [the] feeling(s) of doubt and powerlessness' that were inevitable within that particular belief system, given that it was, above all, prognostic in nature. 'The irrationality of such compulsive effort', he writes, 'is that *the activity is not meant to create a desired end but serves to indicate whether or not something* [i.e. salvation] *will occur* which has been determined beforehand, independent of one's own activity or control' [Original Emphasis] (Fromm, 1997: 78).

The activity at issue in this painting is that of sweeping – a task that hardly seems necessary, judging by the pristine condition of the courtyard. Sweeping was an activity given specific symbolic meanings in a number of religious texts, both Protestant and Catholic, from the seventeenth century, and earlier. Frequently, the broom was associated with spiritual and moral purity and according to one writer (Oomius), 'discipline in the home, that is, spiritual and moral assiduousness, is the broom that cleans it, preparing it to receive God's presence' (Franits, 1993: 98–100).[12] But here, the emphasis, once again, is upon human effort. In a contemporary Jesuit emblem, by contrast, it is the Christ Child who 'sweeps a heart clean of all iniquity'. Here, presumably, the human task – the virtue required – is that of allowing this procedure to occur. But if we take Fromm's analysis to be convincing, this particular kind of receptiveness, this kind of openness to possibility and change, may have been difficult to cultivate within the Calvinistic system of the time.

Notes

1. The painting was, however, on loan to the Scottish National Gallery of Art in Edinburgh for a period of some years.
2. Aristotle's writings were significant for humanist and Protestant theories concerning marriage, and he was 'among the first ancient philosophers to expound this theory of the dichotomous nature of the sexes; he postulated that men, with their robust character, were best suited to work outdoors, while women, because of their natural timidity and weakness, were best suited to work in the home' (Franits, 1993: 68–69).
3. See edited volumes by Freedberg and de Vreis, 1991 and Franits, 1997 for accounts of relevant art-historical debates from the seventeenth-century onwards.
4. For accounts of seventeenth-century optics see Ronchi, 1970 and Lindberg, 1976.
5. See Wheelock (1977: 279–280) on the differences between de Hooch's and Vermeer's treatments of composition, and on the relationship in their paintings among space, the environment and the human figure.
6. For instance, the former nunnery, the St. Agatha Convent in Delft, was offered as accommodation by the Delft regents to William, Count of Nassau and Prince of Orange (leader of the rebellion), the latter having made Delft his residence, and base of operations in 1572.
7. Erasmus and other theologians and humanists endeavoured to overturn established Catholic doctrines that exalted celibacy by championing matrimony as an honourable state for humankind, ordained by God. See Franits, 1993: 66 and Sutton, 1998: 68.
8. Here, it is also worth noting that if the home was regarded as *the* space of female labour, it was not exclusively so. The working space of many

Dutch painters of the period, for instance, male as well as female, was located within the home, rather than at court or in a separate studio (Alpers, 1997: 65).

9. For an alternative reading of this kind of pictorial scenario see Crary, 1996: 25–66 ('The Camera Obscura and Its Subject').
10. In his lecture 'Of Other Spaces' of 1967, for instance, Michel Foucault wrote that 'the real scandal of Galileo's work lay not so much in his discovery, or rediscovery, that the earth revolved around the sun, but in his constitution of an infinite, and infinitely open space' (Foucault, 1986: 23).
11. Cited by Alpers, 1989: 34. The text in question is Kepler's *Ad Vitellionem Paralipomena.*
12. For a detailed iconographic study of this topic see de Jongh, 1995: 194–214.

CHAPTER 16

'ANXIOUS PERFORMANCES': AESTHETICISM, THE ART GALLERY AND THE AMBULATORY GEOGRAPHIES OF LATE NINETEENTH-CENTURY LONDON

Andrew P. Stephenson

What performance where will... compel a radical rethinking of the psychological presuppositions of gender identity and sexuality? What performance where will compel a reconsideration of the place and the stability of the masculine and the feminine? And what kind of gender performance will enact and reveal the performativity of gender itself in a way that destabilizes the naturalized categories of identity and desire.

Judith Butler, *Gender Trouble*

Within dominant accounts of the formation of modern sexual identities in late nineteenth-century London, the role of the art gallery in providing a sympathetic venue for the liberating visibility that Aestheticism offered to young women and to lesbians and gay men has remained largely unexplored. Given the imaginative centrality within Aestheticism of flamboyant sartorial styles and extravagant performativity; given its privileging of 'feminine' fashionable display and the pleasures of conspicuous consumption and given its sanctioning of 'feminised' homoeroticism and overt theatricality for men and women, perhaps surprisingly, the social and sexual dynamics of the art gallery have remained hidden and underexposed.[1]

Using recent theories of performativity as outlined by Judith Butler and Peggy Phelan as well as drawing on studies of late Victorian sexual desire by Eve Kosofsky Sedgwick and Richard Dellamora, I shall argue that the Aesthetic art gallery (or art exhibitions that showed work by leading members of English Aestheticism in carefully installed and design coordinated aesthetic environments) constituted a crucial discursive space within which the fluidity of modern sexual identities were compellingly dramatised (see Spencer, 1972). As art critics and writers aligned the aesthetic experience with imagined empathetic unions across artworks and between viewers, and as they validated particular types of public masquerade and exhibitionism as signs of an aesthete sensibility, the art gallery registered as a fashionable space in which to encounter alternative interpretive communities.

Interpreting the art gallery experience as a liberating and empowering form of ritual developing at a historical moment when modern notions of sexuality were in the process of being defined, artists, art writers and spectators came to acknowledge the formative role that pleasurable identifications and sexual desire played in constituting identity and its social repertoires. Within public performances, subtleties of bodily deportment, gesture, eye contact and dress were carefully perused as part of a daring and self-fabricated act that outwardly signified inner aesthetic sentiments carrying resonances of secret and repressed sexual desires. Given the status of the gallery space as a location for exhibiting modern social and sexual manners, it is apparent that gender became increasingly approached not as a fixed binary of biological or anatomical oppositions, but in more fluid terms and open to dimensions of theatricality: what Judith Butler has termed gender as 'a corporeal style, an "act", as it were, which [was] both intentional and performative, where "performative" suggests a dramatic and contingent construction of meaning' (Butler, 1990: 139).

Taking the art gallery as a revealing symbolic site, I shall propose that in Aestheticism's radical rethinking of gender norms as historically shifting and culturally contingent, it marked out a significant disruption of earlier Victorian disciplinary and proprietorial regimes. In its challenging of the 'natural' and the 'conventional', Aestheticism's sexual politics (in a distinctively modern way) also choreographed revised homo-heterosexual categories and re-textualised male and female bodies, gay and straight, in terms that had previously been considered perverse within the public imaginary. Significantly, it was at this moment that the 'dangerous sexualities' of the 'New Woman', the lesbian and the homosexual dandy were constructed in the literature of Western modernity as emblematic; as resonant and revealing figures that questioned traditional social roles from positions on the margins of urban life (Felski, 1995: 14 and Adams, 1995: 2–3).

Alongside these repositionings, as earlier notions of distinctive gendered spheres centred on oppositions between masculine/public/urban and feminine/private/suburban were shown to be less entrenched, Aestheticism initiated new metropolitan social circuits for women and gay men to be seen in. The ambulatory spaces of the West End of London, forbidden and dangerous territories for single women earlier in the nineteenth century and precarious locations for lesbian women and homosexual men at any time, became part of modern social and sexual geographies in which contemporary forms of consumerism and fashionability were apparent. The art gallery, alongside the department store, the theatre, the private library, the concert and lecture halls, public parks and certain Anglo-Catholic churches, was incorporated within these urban itineraries of visual pleasure, leisure, spectacle and self-display (Walker in Orr, 1995: 70–85).

Like the department store, the aestheticised interior of the art gallery with its integrated installation design and colour coordination, as well as its adoption of new technology and commercial devices, eagerly anticipated what kinds of meanings and allusions negotiated between and across viewing subjects might be generated; what type of viewing practices and modes of engagement between display and spectator would be permissible and what forms of interpersonal communication, visual and verbal, cross sex and same sex, would be appropriate and decorous.[2] Considering the sophisticated knowledge of complex social protocols that this demanded, the popular press, not surprisingly, offered prior guidance and exemplary role models in revealing narratives aimed primarily at younger, often suburban, readerships.

On 29 May 1878, the London weekly *The World: A Journal for Men and Women* published such a short story for its expanding female readership with a middle class young woman as its central protagonist.[3] It provided an insight into the modern English women's unrestrained attitude towards urban spaces by highlighting her confident metropolitan mobility. Entitled 'Pamela in Piccadilly', it was a narrative based on the visit of a suburban woman (probably in her twenties) to London to go shopping and to call on family and friends. A tale of what today we might call conspicuous and pleasurable consumerism, it involved her travelling unchaperoned by train and overnight accommodation (probably staying at a hotel such as the Midland Grand Hotel or Langham's which had separate facilities for women). Pamela lunched at an ABC tearoom and dined in the early evening at Verrey's, Grant's or Simpson's. In gaps between appointments and to recover after the exhaustion of shopping in department stores on Oxford and Regent streets (notably John Lewis which opened in 1864; Liberty's in 1875 and no doubt eagerly awaiting D.H. Evans which would open in 1879), she made use of the facilities such as the Berner's Club or de Vere Hall rooms which were resting places for single women with female superintendents. Calling in at bookshops and collecting her orders from one of the private lending libraries, Pamela may have purchased and flicked through a few of the contemporary magazines which outlined the expanding entertainment opportunities and educational facilities for women in London, noting down the current offerings of a few art exhibitions and galleries.

What is revealing is that the circuits of urban tourism which Pamela followed were represented by the *World* as neither unusual nor especially remarkable for 1878. Instead, 'Pamela in Piccadilly' repeats a familiar, somewhat clichéd, set of modern trajectories for young women in and across London. What the narrative does underline, however, is a more flexible attitude towards urban culture and modernity, stressing the assured mobility, social freedom and shifting status of the single woman in the English metropolis (even if, as many feminist writers have correctly acknowledged, such an experience was not without its physical and sexual dangers). Pamela as a savvy participator in the metropolitan spectacle provides another frame of reference in the representation of English 'modernity'.

Moreover, as Lynne Walker has shown (1995: 74–6), it is clear that Pamela was not an isolated case. By the late 1870s, in sharp contrast to even ten years earlier, it was not uncommon for middle-class women, in large numbers and using public transport, to traverse the West End of London going in to what were once restricted access areas of the city. Visible as workers, students, shoppers and tourists, women also frequented museums, art galleries, concert and lecture halls, alongside hotels, tea rooms, restaurants, department stores and libraries. Whilst not symbolically central nor the main occupiers of London's male-dominated thoroughfares, women were an increasing and conspicuous presence on the capital's social scene and had adopted effective social strategies for avoiding male effrontery.

Significantly, Pamela's knowledge of the complex social geographies and sexual codes of the metropolis does not register as first-hand. Rather her familiarity, as the article makes explicit, is from the burgeoning popular and illustrated press (readily accessible in the suburbs and the provinces through the extensive and speedy distribution networks). Even if the *World* overstated the issue by asserting that: 'provincial life has ceased to exist...now all the young women are educated up to metropolitan standards... Every one [of them] is more or less a traveller... Her knowledge comes from the press and from photographs', there was some accuracy in the argument that mass circulation literature and popular journalism, aided by a growth in illustrative reproduction and photographic technologies, had enhanced women's access to the subtleties of metropolitan spatial and sexual semiotics. Mediated through the dynamic spaces of advertising, fashion and consumerism, London's sights/sites fascinated, not least, because of the exposure to contemporary forms of social spectacle and sexual identity which it provided.

With this claim in mind, it becomes evident that the authors of such topical travelogues, like many of the writers of the behind the scene exposés about artists lives and the love rivalries over female models, were primarily professional middle-class men such as 'Rita' whose popular serials 'Told in the Studios' and 'Brothers of the Brush' were published in the 1890s (see *Strand Magazine*, 2, July – December 1891: 352). Although there were a growing number of women writers, these male journalists re-cycled what had previously been the social identity of the *man about town* with its 'masculine' mode of address and confident urban mnemonics, to a growing provincial and often female readership. More likely than not, the writer of 'Pamela in Piccadilly', like the editors of these illustrated weeklies, was alert to the interest in modern social and sexual manners and was wise to the sales potential (and earnings) that such vivid cross gender impersonation could secure.

To explore this further, let us follow our heroine into an environment where, according to the *World*, 'the modern Pamelas are to be seen in considerable force': the art exhibition.

The narrative of 'Pamela in Piccadilly' continues: meeting her father at the Royal Academy, the young woman is 'vexed' by what she sees displayed there and refuses to remain in 'the dreary annual exhibition'. Confidently voicing her disdain out loud, Pamela declares that 'English art is so little progressive and so content to remain in the weary old groove'. Incidentally, this is an opinion which showed that Pamela was a regular subscriber to the magazine since she repeated almost verbatim the damning review of the Royal Academy show contained in the *World* some three weeks earlier as being of 'indifferent quality; indeed a poorer collection of pictures has scarcely been seen in the galleries of Burlington House' (see *The World. A Journal for Men and Women*, 8 May 1878: 9).

Dragging her father out of the Academy, 'we're off' she shouts 'in search of imagination and poetic culture'. Following an itinerary which Pamela's father believes 'she can only have learned about in magazines', they rush up New Bond Street and go into the grand entrance of the Grosvenor Gallery (Figure 16.1). Only recently opened to media acclaim in the previous year (May 1877), the gallery's second May exhibition was on display (see Newall, 1995; and Casteras and Denney (eds), 1996).

Upon entering the gallery interior (Figure 16.2), Pamela and father take stock of the paintings. The father is convinced, incorrectly, that he is in 'a loan collection of early [Florentine] masters' since the works close to him show images of 'pallid and angular maidens' reminiscent of the Renaissance era. After being informed that this is not the case, the old man becomes confused and anxious. Pamela, with catalogue in hand intervenes: 'My daughter set me right by reading from the catalogue the very modern names of Burne-Jones, Watts, Morris and Whistler. I took a chair and sat down to study Burne-Jones's wonderful productions'. This being the May 1878 Grosvenor Gallery exhibition, these were probably *Laus Veneris* (1873–78) and *Le Chant d'Amour* (1868–77) amongst others, as they had attracted extensive press attention (see Casteras in Casteras and Denney (eds), 1996: 81–6).

Hearing his daughter's arguments being confirmed by 'wild utterances' from other gallery-goers, the father finally declares: 'I heard for the first time of the "inner dualities", "sweet sensuousness of expression", "gracious tonality" and "passionate splendour!"' This contemporary parable concludes with the father not only becoming enlightened about the work and aesthetic theories of Burne-Jones and other modern English artists, but with the realisation that his daughter is, along with many other young women in the Grosvenor Gallery, a member of this new breed of 'modern Pamelas of the aesthetic type'.

Figure 16.1 Intended Facade of the Grosvenor Gallery, New Bond Street, *The Builder*, 5 May 1877, p.453 (LD.60). By Permission of the British Library.

Figure 16.2 The Grosvenor Gallery of Fine Art, New Bond Street, interior view, *The Illustrated London News*, 5 May 1877, p.420 (LD.47). By Permission of the British Library.

It is evident that, throughout the story, there are a range of anxieties and potential threats being articulated, some explicitly whilst others are veiled, in relation to the new femininity symbolised by Pamela. These point up the instability of gender identities which this new art and its aesthetic sanctions. One aspect relates to the altering attitude of women towards art galleries and exhibition venues as public spaces for fashioning and displaying modern social and sexual identities. Art galleries like the Grosvenor Gallery (from 1877), the New Gallery (from 1888) and the Grafton Galleries (from 1893) appealed in part because of their proximity to London's shopping districts and to its leisure and educational facilities. Through their support for women artists (notably the Grosvenor, which showed work by Marie Spartali and Evelyn Pickering in 1877) they no doubt attracted some of the expanding number of women artists (over one thousand women identified themselves as professional artists in the census of 1871 (see Marsh and Nunn, 1998: 12)). They had also successfully inserted themselves into the city circuits and calendar of the fashionable woman about town.

The growing number of female consumers interested in art increased the profits that might be made from the one shilling entry charge to exhibitions. In response, galleries provided facilities specifically to attract women. As the popular magazine the *Queen* noted in an article dated 18 May 1878 on 'Refreshments for Ladies in the Grosvenor Gallery', 'the existence of the refreshment room during the past year has been highly useful to many thousand visitors, especially to those ladies who [are] far distant from their homes'. From 1880 its facilities were expanded further with the Grosvenor Gallery opening a ladies drawing room and by 1885 it had a 'new and commodious ladies reading room' and a library (Gillett, 1996: 56).

Moreover, exhibition venues replicated the layout and interior decor of domestic spaces, transforming their commercial showrooms into more intimate interiors that mirrored the taste of the private patron (incorporating silk damask wall-coverings, antique furniture, Liberty draperies and oriental rugs). Acknowledging that such 'private' installations demonstrated discernment and offered informality, this refurbishment especially benefited the appreciation of the small-scale easel painting which was presented as a valuable decorative addition to the private home.[4] As Henry James wrote in a review of the Grosvenor Gallery published in the *Galaxy* in August 1877, the overall effect was to distance the dealer's room from associations of commerce and trade by evoking the exclusive atmosphere of a private collection. As James noted, 'In so far as these beautiful rooms in Bond Street are a commercial speculation, this side of their character has been gilded over and dissimulated in the most graceful manner' (Sweeney (ed.), 1989: 139). Likewise, earlier in 1875 the London art dealers Agnews' new premises had abolished formal counters and instituted an intimate drawing room ambience with elegant interior design and settees believing that this relaxed environment encouraged a tasteful and aesthetic mode of viewing and art appreciation.

Increasingly, art galleries and dealers engaged positively with the lessons of consumerism, showing a familiarity with new styles of presentation and marketing pioneered elsewhere in the commercial sphere. Capitalising on the appreciation of smaller groups of works by the same artist or by groupings which placed related artists together (as the Grosvenor Gallery did in the West Gallery in 1877 by showing Burne-Jones together with his followers, John Melhuish Strudwick, John Roddam Spencer Stanhope and Walter Crane) such innovative presentation formats were intended to move away from the conventions of mid-Victorian models of viewing which (as at the Royal Academy) packed in artworks thereby encouraging quantitative over qualitative interactions, and an overall rather than particular syntax of display.[5]

Alert to updated consumerist trends, artists, independent art groups and art dealers recognised that gallery design using carefully harmonised colour installation and modern natural lighting facilities (aided by gas-lighting and electricity – at the Grosvenor Gallery from 1882–83) could be employed to good effect to launch, in the manner of a trademark, an easily recognisable in-house style and brand name: Aesthetic modernism. A greater stress upon coordinated frames and colour installation harmonies (following a trend set by Impressionist artists and imported in Whistler's use of a total colour coordinated environment at the Flemish Gallery in 1874 and at the 'Yellow and White' exhibition at the Fine Art Society in 1883 – see Bendix, 1995: 205ff); the use of tinted or individually decorated frames and mounts cultivated an aesthetic awareness of the importance of all aspects of the environment to the artistic effect: a lesson informed by Aesthete 'art furnishings' articles in the expanding number of home decoration journals and 'how to' manuals which saw it as a virtue of sophisticated cosmopolitanism.

Finally, there is an awareness of the new forms of artistic biography circulating within the popular press, and later in New Journalism, supported by the *Künstlerroman* (artist-novel), celebrity interviews and the biographies of the widows of artists (see Tickner, 1994: 46–7, 70–1). These were supported by art catalogues and by the growth of the monograph, artists' biographies and lifestyle literature which encouraged belief in a recognisable signature style and an approach based on a cult of international celebrity. Popularised accounts of Aesthetic theory also acted to disseminate the democratic and liberating potentials that the Aesthetic environment and artwork, and the proximity to like-minded aesthetes, offered.

With these ideas in mind, I want to move away from Pamela as an exemplar of the problematics of women's 'modernity' within visual culture, already admirably mapped out by many feminist scholars (see Tickner, 1994; Cherry, 1993; Nunn, 1987 and Pollock, 1988). Instead, I want to turn to the way in which Pamela's father represents these spaces in order to examine the threat to patriarchal authority which his daughter's recently found aestheticism entailed. Continuing with 'Pamela in Piccadilly', after Pamela's brief lecture on Aestheticism and English art, the father's attention turns to the Grosvenor Gallery's audience 'whose dress and comportment he finds perplexing'. In exasperation, he questions Pamela about how he should interpret these odd men and women; how he might assess their social rank and position in the light of their modern appearances, odd conduct and eccentric physiognomy. He asks her, somewhat furtively, 'What mysterious creatures are these that linger over [such] strange conceptions [of]...dreadful crude yellows with frightful dabs and sage greens?' And addressing the reader directly, the old man then declares that he is 'haunted even now by these sad, silent, sexless things that do duty for men and women, so long and lean and all so supremely weary and haggard'.

What is being presented in this scenario is not only the conflict between older and modern conceptions of dress and public decorum, but the disjunction between traditional manly/womanly proprietorial regimes and more modern approaches to sexual identity and physiognomy. For the father, subscribing to mid-Victorian conceptions that saw physical appearance, racial characteristics, bodily deportment and dress management as outward signs of an 'inner' moral integrity, the audience at the Grosvenor was 'undecipherable'. One corollary of this was a fear that modern 'masculinity' (like modern 'femininity') might not be the result of some immutable sexual core and inherited race identity, but a mode of performance that was dependent upon the conditions and dynamics of intersubjective interpretation for its conviction. In other words, that English masculinity depended upon being seen and recognised as convincing in the eyes of others and against their sexual norms (see Stephenson, 2000).

Presumably it was this radical – performative – notion of the inscription of sexual difference and the liberating potential it offered for fashioning updated, fluid gender roles which appealed to Pamela and underpinned her 'enthusiasm' for modern art. And it was this difference in the ethical and moral assumptions about art and sexuality that underpinned the old man's 'confusion'. For Pamela's father, as unschooled in 'decoding' modern social manners, fashion styling and sexual roles as he was in the ability to appreciate English Aestheticism's artistic vocabulary and its associated art theory, the audience at the Grosvenor Gallery were ambiguous: 'sad, silent...long, lean...supremely weary and haggard'. Rather than *being* men and women (in the active bodily and biological mid-Victorian system of signification that he understood) they appeared 'perverse', 'unhealthy' and 'sexless'; androgynous anatomies without clear manly definition, and women lacking any semblance of conventional womanliness. All hollow cheeked and attenuated bodies; as he phrased it, 'that do duty for men and women'.

The father's fears were confirmed when he then turned to the evidence of Burne-Jones's *Le Chant d'Amour* and *Laus Veneris*. As many conservative critics had pointed out, Burne-Jones's figures showed explicit signs of 'softness', sensualism and androgyny; representations that confused the conventional boundaries between masculine-feminine definition. The women appeared languid and motionless; the men lacking in energy and will: effeminised and emasculated. In its July issue, the *Magazine of Art*'s critic repeated this evaluation denouncing the male figure in *Le Chant d'Amour* as 'unmasculine': 'its strenuous paganism emasculated by false modern emotionalism' (*Magazine of Art*, 1, July 1878: 81).

For the old man, who saw the moral and ethical responsibility of the artist being symbolised in a skilful naturalistic transcription of appearance and physique, and who insisted upon painting's referentiality to the outside world (as he had seen in the works displayed at the Royal Academy) Burne-Jones's images were 'de-realised' and 'melancholic'. Moreover (and the man may have had the makings of the connoisseur in him) their self-conscious artificiality was confirmed by the fact that they looked like, but were not, 'real' Renaissance masterpieces. As 'sham' reworkings, the paintings deferred the present into the petrified past of Tannhauser and Arthurian legend disrupting earlier artistic languages and disciplinary regimes to refashion 'unnatural' sexualities that re-textualised both knights' and damsels' bodies in ways that seemed morbid and perverse. For the father, it was all too much.

By contrast, for Pamela, who asserted the conviction that modern art was autonomous and its terms of reference linked to aesthetic values and beauty, Burne-Jones's works subscribed to a thoroughly self-conscious and sensual 'modernity' (and in this sense, it was Henry James who put his finger on it in his review published in the *Nation* in 1878 when he referred to them in a distinctly modern usage as 'conceptions, representations' (Sweeney, 1989; 164). Moreover, English Aestheticism marked out an updated and modernising approach to the past, one that paralleled the way young women were now a conspicuous and active part of city life. They were more in evidence in art gallery and exhibition spaces than ever before and eager consumers of fashion, trends in home decoration and the illustrated press.

By asking Pamela to clarify what she saw in the work of Burne-Jones and put into language her sense of English Aestheticism's effects, the father desires to 'see' through the eyes of another and according to the 'feminised' frame of reference of a Paterian and Swinburnian sexual-aesthetic ideal of culture (Dellamora, 1990:112–4). Whilst what he hears in response are the popularised catch phrases of 'inner dualities', 'sweet sensuousness of expression' and 'passionate splendour', it is a form of enlightenment and social discourse to which the younger suburban readers of the *World* might well have aspired.

As the ambulatory dynamics of public space and social manners were shown to be more flexible, so galleries and exhibition venues in the West End of London became conspicuous sites of and for modern forms of consumerism, fashionability and display. Such realignments, as I have argued, not only generated modernising subjectivities for women (and men), but choreographed revised masculine–feminine and homosexual–heterosexual definitions. Whilst 'Pamela in Piccadilly' opens up opportunities for the examination of gender identities and the representation of sexual politics in the late 1870s, we also need to be alert to the possibility that yet again (as the *World* and its male editors and its journalists, and as the art gallery dealers and entrepreneurs surely knew) such a metaphoric appropriation of 'woman' and the frameworks of the 'feminine' might be another means of reproducing and reinstating the dominant discourse of the 'masculine' at a moment of crisis.

By the 1870–80s, although the art exhibition could be a dynamic performative space invoking a liberating modern aesthetic and transformed modes of pleasurable and eroticised spectatorship, it was one that had become aligned with practices that were becoming predominantly the preserve of white, middle-class professional men: male artists, male designers, male couturiers and male journalists who wrote on and lectured about aesthetic matters in art, fashion, interior design and good taste for women. In 'remasculinising' these areas under more rigid regimes of 'professionalisation', these men actively and self-interestedly appropriated the 'feminine' within an all-encompassing aesthetic taste consonant with their beliefs (see Callan in J. Attfield and P. Kirkham (eds), 1989: 151–64). At the same time, by not approaching modernity from the acknowledged position of patriarchal authority (as exemplified by Pamela's father) they assumed the insightful ventriloquism of the 'feminised' man.

Significantly, it is at precisely this historical juncture, and against the expanding mobility and increased visibility of women's dynamic social experience of the metropolis that, as Christine Buci-Glucksmann has argued, 'the feminine' (identified with the figures of the prostitute, the 'New Woman', the lesbian and the effeminised dandy) is allocated a significance by men within symbolic representations of urbanity as 'an allegory of the modern' and as 'the inevitable sign of a new historic regime of seeing and "not-seeing"; of representable and unrepresentable' (Buci-Glucksmann, 1987: 221, 220–9).

Finally, I want to briefly examine the experience of one male aesthete in these metropolitan circuits and to underscore how the art gallery proffered a public platform for spectacular performance. On 31 April 1877, the twenty-three year old Oscar Wilde travelled up from Oxford to attend the private showing of the Grosvenor Gallery prior to its first Summer exhibition. He was also present at the grand formal opening the next day (see Ellmann, 1988: 75-8). Undoubtedly, Wilde would have been aware that a sizeable section of fashionable and aristocratic London society would be present and that the opening would generate a considerable amount of press attention as well as lengthy art reviews. The impressive architecture and rich interior decoration of Grosvenor Gallery provided Wilde with an ideal arena for self-advertisement.

To attract attention to his careful dress management and to make his London debut particularly noteworthy, Wilde had his tailor make a fetching two-tone coat in bronze/red cloth, the back of which was shaped like a cello. Wilde's artful choreography and sartorial manipulation acknowledged the crucial role that clothes, alongside body language, deportment and gesture played in articulating a conspicuous and creative presence. At the same time, such self-conscious artistry made explicit the contrived nature not only of Wilde's act, but of exhibitionism and narcissism as an integral, if often overlooked, feature of masculine identity. What Wilde's enactment exposed was that modern masculinity was a form of play acting – a masquerade – within which the male body as a site of artificial grooming and cosmetic manipulation remained central, but 'unseen'. As a negotiated performance dependent upon the eyes and judgement of other men and women, such flamboyant display evidently ran the risk of being seen as an overidentification with the artificial, the decadent and the 'feminine'. Location and audience, as Wilde surely knew, were crucial for maximum effect.

In the Grosvenor Gallery's meticulously orchestrated and sumptuously decorated interior spaces and in front of canvasses by leading members of English Aestheticism, Wilde's performance would not just draw attention to himself (and generate copy and media celebrity), it would also register, to some at least – 'the modern Pamela's of the aesthetic type' and their like-minded male friends, if not their fathers – as an alignment in which exhibitionist personal style and aesthetic theatre infringed not only the divisions between art and life, but contested conventional boundaries between masculinity/femininity and between homosexuality/heterosexuality in a distinctively modern way. Moreover, Wilde's performativity, like Aestheticism's art theories, engendered new ways of thinking about social and sexual identities; both proffered alternative models which modern metropolitan experience and its emerging opportunities for participation urgently demanded.

To conclude, what my reading of the cultural choreography of late nineteenth-century Aestheticism and the Grosvenor Gallery underscores, is that changes in art consumption practices with updated modes of installation and display, altering modes of representation of the art world and its expanding female art audiences, the enhanced visibility of marginalised groups in the popular press, and new, sexualised approaches to art and aesthetics were all part of broader social and sexual trends. Not immune to these wider shifts, the art gallery constituted one of these modern ambulatory spaces. Aestheticism's liberating aesthetics and the attraction of the art gallery as a site of modern social and sexual mores were influential both in getting young women out of suburban hearth and home and up to town and in encouraging alternative forms of transgressive sexuality to be conspicuous in fashionable London venues.

A central paradox, however, was that the success or failure of any performance, like the impact of English Aestheticism's cultural politics, was ultimately measured for its achievement in the eyes of others. Nevertheless, tracing the performative dynamics of the art gallery, and mapping its place in metropolitan ambulatory circuits, discloses more than might at first be apparent about the cultural politics and sexual geographies of late nineteenth-century London. From the mid-1880s, as public surveillance of urban spaces intensified, so the 'New Woman', the lesbian and the homosexual man (alongside the prostitute) attracted increased legal attention. By the time the Grosvenor Gallery closed in 1890 medico-legal pathologies of deviancy and decadence were already being put into place and these distinctive metropolitan sexual circuits were posed as a powerful threat to the dominant moral, social and sexual codes of late Victorian Britain. As an increasingly antifeminist, homophobic and racist atmosphere became prevalent within contemporary English culture, 'what performance where' became a strategic ploy in the public demonstrations and political campaigns of the suffragette movement and 'what kind of gender performance where' became crucial as a strategy of survival for lesbians and gay men in the increasingly sexually repressive and dangerous ambulatory geographies of the British capital.

Notes

1. These studies include Showalter, 1991; Ledger and McCracken (eds), 1995 and Adams, 1995.
2. For studies of the London department store as a space of cultural consumption, see Nava in Nava and O'Shea (eds), 1996: 38–76.
3. 'Pamela in Picadilly', *The World. A Journal for Men and Women*, 29 May 1878, 9. All subsequent references to this story are from this source.
4. These arguments about installation are indebted to Martha Ward's study of French art exhibitions during this period. See Ward, 1991: 599–622.
5. For evolution of the art gallery interior, see Dulwich Picture Gallery, 1992.

CHAPTER 17

You want to see? Well, take a look at this! Ethical Vision, Disembodiment and Light in Marcel Duchamp's *Etant Donnés*

Chris Horrocks

> Hence it comes about that the gaze is the instrument through which light is embodied and through which... I am *photographed.*
>
> Lacan, *The Four Fundamental Concepts of Psychoanalysis*

Etant Donnés: 1e La Chute d'Eau, 2e Le Gaz d'Éclairage (*Given: 1st. The Waterfall, 2nd. The Illuminating Gas*) was Marcel Duchamp's final work of art. Begun in 1946, completed in 1966, and installed in the Philadelphia Museum after his death, the work was a clandestine project. Its exposure initiated a reappraisal of Duchamp's significance within histories of modernism, and instituted re-interpretations of his biography and oeuvre.

The purpose of this essay is to assess the synthesis of psychoanalytic and existentialist interpretations of *Given*. They remain valuable tools for examining the projective and identificatory processes involved when trying to understand the relation between the art object/image, the subject and the gaze. However, my contention is that these readings pay insuf-

Figure 17.1 Marcel Duchamp (1887–1968) *Etant Donnés: 1e La Chute d'Eau 2 e Le Gaz d'Éclairage*, 1946–66.
Mixed media assemblage, height 238.75 cm width 175 cm.
Courtesy of Philadelphia Museum of Art: Gift of the Cassandra Foundation, Photocredit: Graydon Wood, 1996.

ficient attention to the significance of the linkage between the formal aspects of this installation and the specific visual engagement of the viewer. By problematising psychoanalysis my purpose is neither to reject its contribution nor reduce the work to an empiricist, antitheoretical, object oriented stance. Instead, I wish to show how the articulation of a specific artwork's perception, its description and its interpretation might be analysed from a perspective that tends to be present but marginalised in psychoanalysis. This perspective is phenomenological, and emphasises the constitutive role of perception while diminishing the prevailing tendency in readings of *Given* to link vision with desire, language and the unconscious. I will argue that these analyses do not interrogate the function of visuality in relation to the specific constituents of the work such as lighting and form, in their imbrication with vision as a situated and embodied activity of the viewer.

However, my critique attempts to avoid the phenomenological reductionism that 'embodiment' often signals when reifying the presence of the body. Instead, I suggest that a close phenomenological reading permits a description that recasts the body in a complex relationship where, in the case of *Given*, the body is disembodied, or taken beyond itself. Embodiment has a disembodied dimension, and the phenomenological content of Lacan's psychoanalytic model reveals this.

Interpretations of *Given* often identify key themes that indicate an association between the visual qualities of this work and the viewer's constitutive and reactive role in relation to them. In critical responses to this artwork, these themes are generally presented as problems of interpretation rather than perception. The work is read as being resistant to meaning (it will not divulge its secret), open to different, equally persuasive readings, or illustrative of one overarching theory, generally psychoanalytic or existential in character. Texts on *Given* often identify a contradiction in which the assemblage is either perceived as a referentially overloaded and confusing aggregation of visual codes, syntactical systems and symbolic orders or as a dense visual perturbation through ambient or perceptual inconsistencies.

However, these readings also indicate another aspect of the relation between perception and meaning, and vision and knowledge. This is *Given*'s status as a site of mediation between the eye and symbolic articulation, where themes of ambiguity, ambivalence and slippage define the assemblage as refusing the domination of the viewer's eye. These themes can be registered in a phenomenological dimension, where ambient and formal aspects of the work are 'bound up' with the embodied eye of the viewer, in order to critique explanations that privilege the function of unconscious desire and voyeuristic guilt.

However, while casting light on the phenomenological context of psychoanalytic readings I should emphasise that these hermetic or evasive qualities do not emerge as a consequence simply of a slippage between vision, object and language in semiological, psychoanalytic or phenomenological domains. Rather, they are historically and intentionally installed by Duchamp, and are inherent to the work. Additionally, the psychoanalytic interpretation of the assemblage as an enigma or secret is invited by *Given*'s morphology and the mode of its perception, because it must be viewed through two eyeholes in a barn door. The work is organised in terms of currencies of forbidden, the tabooed and the voyeuristic. A constellation of refusals, prohibitions, impasses and bars on meaning and knowledge (carnal or conceptual) brings *Given* into alignment with specific modes of exegesis. These either attempt to account for the work using psychoanalytic theory, or intersect with it by employing literary or art-critical forms that provide 'open', poetic responses.

I now turn to the theorised role of the gaze in order to discuss the problematic relation of dominant psychoanalytic and existential approaches to the work. These, I argue, attempt to constrain the work to an ethics of the gaze, and therefore delimit and devalue the phenomenological currency of *Given*.

Texts by Krauss, Jones and Silverman, which draw on Lacanian and Sartrean theory, variously present the work as a 'partial demonstration' of the exteriority of the gaze beyond the sovereignty of the subject. Here, the look of the viewer becomes lured by a scene that exposes the conflictive identity of this subject, whose imaginary identification denies the otherness through which the symbolic order is organised. The subject is forced to see its reliance on the other which it normally rejects as the radically other in order to maintain its illusory wholeness, and defy its lack.

Silverman, for example, claims that *Given* deconstructs the normative model of identification and disavowal that assimilates what is desirable about the other to the self, and exteriorises what is despised in the self as the other. Instead, the assemblage reveals the otherness of the desired self and the familiarity of the despised other, permitting the viewer to 'grasp the objectivity of the *moi*, and to recognise him or herself precisely within those others to whom he or she would otherwise respond with revulsion and avoidance' (Silverman, 1996: 170).

These Lacanian versions are significant because they expose the relation between *le regard* of the viewer and his or her place in the gaze of the others (Lacan says there are many gazes behind a work of art), where the subject's look is trapped in the signifying scene. However, I suggest that the Lacanian and Sartrean approaches of such writers reduce *Given* to a normative and proscriptive mechanism that conflates epistemological and ethical categories (knowledge and moral conduct) without enquiring how this process is constituted.

For example, Krauss claims that viewer's voyeurism is itself put 'on stage', in mirror relation to the female's genitals behind the door. Thus the subject is split in an identificatory moment, seeing himself in what he lacks, and turned into an object in the gaze of the other, in the 'shame' of being observed observing: 'To be discovered at the key hole is, thus, to be discovered as a body[...] As for himself, this thickened, carnal object produces as the content of his consciousness, the carnation of shame' (Krauss, 1993: 112). At first sight this reading appears to illuminate embodiment's role in the construction of the subject in relation to the Other. However, I suggest that it only presents *Given* as a one-dimensional illustration of an equally limited reading of the body, which only exists here insofar as consciousness is aware of it as shameful in the eyes of the other. Krauss's reductivism does not confront the generative embodiment that the 'voyeur's' eyes constitute. In other words, I contend that in this case the act of perception cannot be reduced to a consciousness of shame, which finds its expression in the body (Krauss's 'thickening'). The act is also one in which the eye is 'led out' of itself, becoming disembodied by dint of its interaction with the scene. Paradoxically, this perceptual disembodiment draws the viewer's attention to the embodied dimension of looking, as I shall describe below.

For Silverman, the production of the eye identifies the signifiers that mark the presence of the gaze in the 'screen' of the work. This is a process through which subjects register their misrecognition and acknowledge the instability of their constitution in the field of the other. Such is the case for the subject who takes his reflection for his self and his image, or assumes his presence to himself in language as an 'I' (1996: 170).

She states: 'It can only work ceaselessly [to] undo the projections through which it rids itself of lack, and the incorporations through which it arrogates to itself what does not belong to it.' Her project is to reinstall an ethical relation to the other, in a 'battle against ourselves' (1996: 173). Jones aligns this recognition with a gendered encounter between subject and object, which renders borderlines of sexual identity unstable and seductive, according to linguistic constructions of gender (Jones, 1994).

Such readings, however, are characteristic of the politico-ethical turn in Lacanianism since the 1970s. For example, Silverman discusses the ethics of the 'productive' look, which 'becomes operative not at the moment when unconscious desires and phobias assume possession of our look, but in a subsequent moment, when we take stock of what we have just "seen", and attempt – with an inevitably limited self-knowledge – to look again, differently' (1996: 173). Duchamp's *Given* is seen to rehearse this form of ethical recognition in an aesthetic domain. She suggests that 'visual texts can give us the task of effecting' this negotiation at an unconscious level. However, I suggest that the conception of *Given* as a visual training session for a self-reflexive recognition of our illusory relation to the other (invariably overdetermined by gender) annexes art to a pedagogy for the eye and unconscious. This view is difficult to sustain if one asks how it is that we can recognise that the (linguistically constructed) unconscious can be made available for such training, or altered through such education.

Thus, a contradiction exists in these accounts of *Given*. These writers emphasise vision, the gaze and specularity yet relegate the visual study of the work itself. This analysis would reveal how the constitutive and embodied vision of the viewer cannot be removed from the work's morphological, ambient and spatial construction. While emphasising misrecognition and the 'productive look', the readings are so intent on providing the normative and theoretically systematic model of self, eye, gaze and other that the work of both *Given* (i.e. the 'gaze' of Duchamp) and the activity (rather than 'task') of the viewer are taken for granted. This is not merely an ascetic refusal of the pleasures of the eye, or an aversion to the 'objectness' of the work, although these charges could be laid at the door of these versions of *Given*. Instead, it is a consequence of inattention to the work's relationship with language or, more precisely, the relation between what is seen and the complex process through which it becomes linguistically categorised.

In other words, while these theories rehearse sensitivity to the 'other' of *Given* they actually act upon it coercively. Instead of approaching such art objects as precisely staged, situated and specific modalities that are produced in a complex dynamic between the acts of perception, description, and interpretation, they choose to legislate for the work as effortlessly as possible (no 'task' here!) within the discourse of a disinterested recognition of an ethics of the unconscious. Silverman's reference to images as 'visual texts' is perhaps indicative of the desire to relate the object to its linguistic structure without considering what is excluded in terms of the perceptual specificities of the image for the constituting vision of the viewer as desiring subject-in-front-of-art.

However, my critique does not entirely reject the Lacanian method, but seeks to reorient it towards its phenomenological content and acknowledge not just the value of Lacanianism (in its less ethical inscriptions) but also the historical context. This is because Duchamp knew Lacan, who conversed on anamorphosis (using Hans Holbein's *Ambassadors* of 1533) and the rational, geometrical grid of the chess board. Indeed, this chess grid is installed beneath *Given*. Lacanian readings are therefore intrinsic to the construction of the work. Moreover, Lacan owned Courbet's *The Origin of the World* (1866), which was a visual source for *Given*. In a tantalising passage in Lacan's *Four Fundamental Concepts of Psychoanalysis* he also discusses the role of art criticism in understanding the images. He says, 'yet someone who is close to me, and whose views count for a great deal with me, told me that he was very troubled when I embarked on something very like art criticism' (Lacan, 1998: 109). While he was not explicitly referring to Duchamp at the time of that 1964 seminar, it relates to Duchamp's view, expressed to Arturo Schwarz in 1966, that 'The content or the value of a painting cannot be evaluated in words... You cannot interpret one form of expression with another form of expression. To say the least, you will distort completely the original message, whatever you say about it' (Schwarz, 1969: 562). This is not to claim that the work is hermetically removed from language but to insist that the link between object and language, perception and meaning is more complex than reducing visual distortion to an abstracted ethics of looking.

Turning from the theory of the work to its description, I want to examine how, in Lacan's phenomenological setting, *Given* operates. In *Given*, the lighting is liminal and contradictory. In Duchamp's words, it maintains the phenomenon of 'ultra-rapid exposure' or 'extra-rapid exposition' (a snapshot of an instant within a continuum of events) by which he defined some of his art. Octavio Paz says:

> the gas lamp burning in the sunlight; its weak, flickering flame makes us doubt the reality of what we see. The lamp produces the darkness that Duchamp demanded for the ultra-rapid exposure; it is the reflective element that makes the work enig-

> matic. The enigma lets us glimpse the other side of the presence, the single and double image: the void, death, the destruction of appearance, and simultaneously, momentary plenitude, vivacity in repose. The zero is full; plenitude opens up, it is empty. (1990: 177–8)

Paz claims that the viewer perceives the light of *Given* as darkness. The assemblage therefore constitutes a problem that is as much one of visual perception and visual effects as unconscious desire. Indeed, it invites us to consider not only the crucial embodied activity of the subject's eye, but how the eye and the intentionality of the viewer become hooked into or taken up by the work rather than govern it. The effects that Paz describes are the 'lures' by which the viewer becomes enmeshed in the work.

Lacan discussed these effects in relation to Merleau-Ponty's phenemonology. However, Lacan uses Merleau-Ponty's discussion of lighting not in order to illuminate the relation between light, eye and body but merely to provide him with a metaphor for the position of the subject within the gaze.

For example, Lacan suggests that perceptual effects correspond to the crucial function of what he terms the 'screen', which is defined as the locus of mediation between the gaze (i.e. the world that looks at me), and the desiring subject's grasp of reality and position in it (1998:107–8). Lacan links light to desire by describing an example of a lighting effect that dominates us and directs our gaze, such as a beam of light so pronounced (like a milky cone) as to conceal what it illuminates. The insertion of a small screen makes the light retreat and the objects within the cone of light emerge. However, while the screen blocks the light, it is invisible because the ambient light masks it. In other words, the subject is always placed in relation to a reality that appears marginally by dint of a screen that remains unseen. The screen is, in essence, the mediation between the light of the gaze of the other (including in this case Duchamp and the gazes under which he labours), and the 'picture' of reality that the screen designates for the subject. It should be understood that this picture is not a literal one, but is descriptive of the positioning of the viewer within a spectacle.

In short, Lacan reverses the 'geometral relation' in which the subject is the sovereign and source of the look, and for whom the world is situated in advance at a distance. Instead, he emphasises how 'that which is light looks at me', grasps the subject and puts him or her in relation to a domain of vision.

Lacan states that this process of capturing the subject can always be observed in a painting, 'which is not the case in perception' (1998: 108). This is because a painting already exists in relation both to the gaze of the artist, who has composed this image as a fascinating game, and the 'gazes behind'. Again, these gazes are the desires of others towards whom the artist orients his or her mediation. The viewer, in front of the picture, is elided as the subject in relation to this screening of desire. In fact, the viewer feels 'rather out of place in the picture' (96). The subject's relation to things through vision, and ordered in the figures of representation, ensures that 'something slips, passes, is transmitted, from stage to stage, and is always to some degree eluded in it – that is what we call the gaze' (1998: 73).

Whereas Lacan states that the gaze is constructed as 'the thrust of our experience, namely, the lack that constitutes castration anxiety' (73), Duchamp provides a perceptual and embodied staging of the elusiveness of the gaze, which is not reducible to lack at the level of unconscious desire or anxiety. The lack here is not prior to vision, and it is not merely implicated with it; it is mobilised by the enmeshing of the embodied eye with the world through the judicious techniques that Duchamp has employed in the 'screening' of *Given*. The eye in the assemblage is conceived not in subordinate relation to the gaze, but as an organ in the perceiving body that is bound up with the work (which is not to dispute the role of the gaze, desire or lack in the constitution of that organ). The question, therefore, is not the relation of the eye to desire, but of the eye's encounter and negotiation with the work.

I therefore suggest that the theorisation of the gaze in the texts discussed at the top of this essay delimit the function of lighting or the 'point of light' that Lacan presents. These readings assume that light, from the world or the subject, is a specific, located and directed quantity, like a ray which hits the viewer or is directed from his or her eyes as a beam. This conception has as its corollary the assumption that the light is directed or controllable. In fact, Lacan's reading is more diffuse than the 'hard' light of such interpretations. In terms of the function of the screen, mask or opacity, Lacan states that 'what is presented to me as space of light, that which is gaze is always a play of light and opacity ... the point of gaze always participates in the ambiguity of the jewel' (1998: 96).

However, Lacan can also be accused of reducing light and vision to a rather schematic role in his discourse. For example, in order to dramatise the prior function of desire and the gaze, and to demote vision to a secondary role, his critique of Merleau-Ponty tends to overemphasise the latter's concern with the constitutive presence of the subject and the primacy of the eye. Lacan diminishes the role of the 'enmeshing' of the embodied subject with the world. Referring to Diderot (86), Lacan makes a distinction between the look and the gaze: vision is not simply visual, because the blind can 'see' using sticks or hands. While for Lacan this opens up the possibility of the gaze as being extrinsic to the organ of the eye, and a function of desire rather than sight, Merleau-Ponty sees the distinction as relegating visual perception to an inferior status. Lacan's geometrical bias towards perceptual vision, which sees it as subordinated to the process of establishing relationships by use of a straight line between points, expunge light of its indispensably deceptive qualities of refraction, colour and reflection. Merleau-Ponty therefore reinstates vision as a perception in which touch and vision are co-extensive. This is not to suggest that Merleau-Ponty is reducing perception to a factual account of consciousness where colour or lighting are distinguishable from the object of perception; they remain bound up with the entirety of perception, including touch, sound and smell. These textures of light, Cathryn Vasseleu states, following Merleau-Ponty, 'cannot be explained by a range of empirical variables, such as the way a thing appears in the light, the kind of light, its position in relation to other things. A belief in the prior identifiability of all these relations in perceptions is maintained by ignoring that their identification as different components of perceptional relations can occur only after the fact of perception' (Vasseleu, 1998:44).

As Lacan's use of Merleau-Ponty's beam of light demonstrated, lighting, for example, demonstrates the 'connectedness' in experience of a thing's properties. Light can be background or ambient but also an object of perception (as in a beam), having a colour or atmosphere. However, it cannot be extracted from the intentionality that is experienced by the subject as being co-existent with the phenomenon. Thus, Merleau-Ponty stresses the fact that light for the seer is not looked upon but inhabited. He states that 'Light's transcendence is not delegated to a reading mind which deciphers the impacts of the light-thing upon the brain and which could do this quite as well if it had never lived in a body' (Merleau-Ponty, 1964: 178). The eye is not an instrument but an organ. Importantly, Vasseleu stresses:

> the eye which sees things through the coincidence of light is replaced by the knowing-body as condition of lighting. Lighting is the lining of what it is that we see, the assumed intermediary directing or supporting our gaze. *We* do not see. We perceive in conformity with a carnal light that already knows and sees, because it is not detachable from the things we see. Lighting supports our gaze as a background of sensibility. (1998: 46)

At this point we can approach Duchamp's work not only as an exercise of the articulation of the gaze with unconscious desire, but of embodied perception bound up with its object, which pays particular attention to the role of light and other qualities that are coextensive in the work. However, this requires consideration of *Given*'s phenomenological dimension in relation to its textual description, in order to indicate how light is turned from texture to text.

These texts describe and attempt to account for perceptual confusion in front of *Given*. For example, Octavio Paz said, 'All is real and verges on banality; all is unreal and verges – on what?' (1990: 96).

Molly Nesbit draws our attention to the fact that our attention is not drawn to what should be most obvious:

> There is not enough here to sustain the common graphic interest, if one cares to really look, but in large part it's because the rest of the scene bursts. Something else besides shame leads the eye back by the nose… Erotic matter colors the air we breath through the peephole, it is everywhere everywhere everywhere [sic], in the darkness, in the velvet, not locked in the tiresome theoretical stranglehold eyes have been made to have with, for example, cunts. The physical separates from the literal. Don't ask, accept. Given: eyes must wander. (1993: 159)

Jean-François Lyotard's intention is to characterise the work as ambiguous and ambivalent:

> You put your eyes in the holes in the Spanish gate, you see a vulva all lit up by a 150-watt spotlight, hairless, and you think you see whatever you want to see. So what did you want to see through the holes in the door? That's just it, after seeing this female hole, you don't know anymore. That and not that. You thought you had wanted to see that, but you notice that you no longer want to think so. Holes onto a hole. What's there to see about a hole? (1990: 2)

These descriptions tend to present the subject as perplexed by the emptiness of the artifice presented to them: there is nothing much to see and the viewer is therefore 'led on', in an active visual exploration that seeks to fill in the scene. The outcome of this observation is the self-reflexive response to the retinal properties of the work, which stand in contrast to the conceptual foundations of Duchamp's oeuvre up to that point. These descriptions are related back to the self-awareness of the body ('breathing' in the scene) linked with the act of seeing that is particular to *Given*. However, the relation of the viewer to the visual properties of the work is not phrased in terms of the eye's control over the event, but as the compulsion of the eye to be mobilised by the scene ('eyes must wander'). The visual indeterminacy of the diorama, its objects and its scotopic or dim light may be associated with Merleau-Ponty's description of the corporeal eye in its unintentional moments of flux, abandon or disempowerment. In the *Phenomenology of Perception* he describes passive, ungazing vision which is dazzled by light with the loss of an identifiable orientation of the seer in relation to it. Here, light becomes an invasive foreign body from which the eyes recoil in pain, 'blinking and watering senselessly on alien contact ... an unintentional dissolution of or tear in the field of vision' (Vasseleu, 1998: 50).

Vasseleu compares this evacuation to Bataille's pineal eye, in its 'excessive illuminations of an improper body which, far from adhering to any intentional formation, are so grotesquely ambiguous in their shameless proliferation of coherences that they make reason shit and vomit' (1998: 49). This reading of the eye's expenditure, as a kind of energy discharge (Bataille, 1991: 77) is, however, burdened by Bataille's primatial vision of humanity, and his symbolic association of the eye with the sun.

Comparing Bataille with Merleau-Ponty, Vasseleu contends that the latter does not extend this reading to associating, for example, the blink in bright light with an abandonment of vision or 'a shedding of everything, including a being unable to recollect itself in a fluidity without scope' (49).

However, I suggest that in the original passage Merleau-Ponty is at least highlighting the function of 'passive vision' (1962: 315), and indicating that there are other modes of vision that operate in tandem with qualities or textures of light in the work of art. These particularly apply to a three-dimensional, electrically lit scene such as *Given*, which can be precisely organised in order to exist on a liminal or threshold position between such registers. This modality permits (or induces) the viewer's constituting vision to fluctuate between these fields, in what Duchamp had dismissed in his earlier, conceptual phase as a 'retinal shudder'. Bataille's vision of the pineal eye is too extreme to accommodate these more subtle modalities of light.

Lacan, however, provides an intermediate example that relates to perceptual properties of *Given*'s light. His contention that vision, in relation to space, does not subscribe to the order of the visual (which can be established geometrically without the inclusion of optics), follows from his reference to Merleau-Ponty on the function of light. Lacan states that 'It is not in the straight line, but in the point of light – the point of irradiation, the play of light, fire, the source from which reflections pour forth. Light may travel in a straight line, but it is refracted, diffused, it floods, it fills – the eye is a sort of bowl – it flows over too, it necessitates, around the ocular bowl, a whole series of organs, mechanisms, defences' (1998: 94). As Lacan says, the organ of the eye is always presented with a multiplicity of functions, including detecting a faint star 'only if you fix your eye to one side' (1998: 102). *Given*'s light shares this 'ocular liminality'.

In 1967, Fried's critique of theatricality in art included the example of the consciousness of distance between a person and a minimalist art object within a darkened room (1995:128). This gave rise to a disquieting and embodied estrangement that was bound up with the object. Descriptions of *Given* are phrased in terms of this presentation to experience. Its trickery, mimicry and trompe l'oeil effects draw on the viewer's body and the light levels also catch his or her breath. However, because this involves a 'laying down' of the gaze, the embodied eye retains in its activity a removal from the control of the subject. The viewer leaves the body, escapes its voyeuristic mode, and moves over the scene ('clairvoyantly', according to Paz), and the gaze is allowed to rest while 'eyes wander'. For Lacan, the artist gives the viewer the option, phrased thus: '*You want to see? Well, take a look at this!*'

Indeed, the gaze of the viewer is lost to the orchestration of the scene, and the eye is disembodied precisely because it is caught in a lure of the diorama, and removed from the desire of the viewer. This produces the misregistration between eye and gaze: on the one hand, 'you never look at me from the place from which I see you'; conversely, 'what I look at is never what I wish to see' (Lacan, 1998: 103). The shuttling between embodied and disembodied vision, and between the centre and the edge of the visual field, is a feature that is particular to this work. The principle of an embodied but textured light, which lures the eye rather than directs it or overwhelms it, extends to the morphology of the scene, where perception is ambivalent.

Turning to art-criticism of *Given*, it is important to note that the work is constructed along similar lines of indeterminacy, and that even seemingly neutral description is trapped in the division of *Given* according to the normative act of naming its elements. As Amelia Jones states, the work disruptively projects a fantasy of erotic seduction onto the notion of structure or linguistic dualism (1994). Indeed, Nesbit describes the sexual organs as 'dry, stretched almost beyond recognition, and bloodless (why do some at this point speak of violence?)' (1993: 159). Lyotard claims that the right breast and shoulder are male in structure, and that the genital area has a swelling which suggests a scrotum (1990: 9). Schwarz suggests that the absence of pubic hair indicates that 'the Bride is very young [and] her debauched posture gives the viewer the impression that the Bride has just reached an orgasm' (Schwarz,1969: 561).

These ascriptions, and seemingly unproblematic conversions of the materiality of *Given* into names, demonstrates both the perceptual slippage Duchamp has instigated and the unawareness of the import of attributing descriptive terms to the visual event. At this point, issues of projection, identification or difference (the stuff of psychoanalysis) can be introduced in order to explain why Copley describes the twigs under the figure as faggots (1969: 36), why Schwarz claims the posture is profligate, and why Van Schepen states that the legs of the 'nude' are 'splayed directly in front of the spectator/participant in a brutally confrontational manner' (1992: 69).

Thus, having acknowledged the relative value of psychoanalysis, we should be aware of its discursively coercive function in some instances. It is at this point that we enter the field of discourses of vision which, for example, Michel Foucault claimed was absent in Merleau-Ponty's account (Jay, 1986). For example, Schepen interprets the work as an act of perversion, in which the world is made an undistinguished mass of self and other to erect a fantasy of omnipotence as a regression in the face of castration anxiety, not to mention an incest taboo (1992: 53–75). For Schepen, Duchamp's description of the twigs on which the figure lies as 'boughs frosted in nickel and platinum' is indicative of a repressed wish to regress to an anal, pre-genital stage. These 'descriptions' then permit the 'decoding' of the work and the artist according to the regulative, normative regime of the discourse of pathographical Freudian psychoanalysis.

In conclusion, although the task of ethical Lacanianism is to reveal the relation between image, vision and unconscious, it reduces the work to an illustration of the psychoanalytic topology without attending to the means through which *Given* embodies such processes, or presents them to experience. It leaps precipitately from the work to language without considering the given-ness of the work to the eye of the constituting viewer. This viewer is enmeshed in a particular act that cannot be entirely reduced to a prior and innate activity of the ethical gaze, desire or look in the domain of representation.

Psychoanalytic or existential theories of the gaze and desire provide necessary tools to prevent art criticism from assuming that, no matter how sensitive or descriptively 'neutral' to the work it appears, it cannot repress the function of difference, projection and identification on which such readings are founded. However, such methodologies should themselves be held as potentially reductionist. Even though attempts have been made to provide an embodied, carnal reading of the task of vision in relation to *Given*, these are too rapidly consigned to illustrations of theory, or to an ethics of the gaze. Merleau-Ponty acknowledged the viability of this intellectual and 'sensible quality' which accompanies perception as a peculiar product of an attitude of curiosity and observation. This product appears when 'instead of yielding up the whole of my gaze to the world, I turn towards this gaze itself, and when I ask myself *what precisely it is that I see*' (1962: 226). Yet, he knew that its employment 'does away with the spectacle properly speaking.' The latter, specific, situated but interpretable encounter between the constituting, embodied yet disembodied gaze of the viewer in unity with the formal and ambient specificities of *Given* therefore merits more consideration than its interpreters have given hitherto.

CHAPTER 18

Lost in Space between East and West: Roots behind the Iron Curtain

Marja Keränen

What Border? What Identity?

Nation state borders are said to be weakening with the processes of globalisation, such as European integration, the 1989 collapse of socialist systems, and the bipolar world order of the Cold War.

The border discussed here is the Finnish–Russian border before and after the collapse of the Iron Curtain. One of the changes brought about by the opening of the border was that the Karelian population of Finland, who left their home sites during the Second World War, could now visit these places. The space that had existed only in the idealised memories of former Karelians for forty-five years now became a part of observable 'reality'.

This essay is about a trip 'back to one's roots' in Karelia, and how memory and identity is transmitted in diaspora from one generation to another. Through this, I was led to ask whether my trip was actually about travelling in space or in time? And, furthermore, what alternatives were on offer for Karelian identities now that the Paradise imagined in memory is lost? This essay is, therefore, also about the meanings given to space and the regulation of these meanings by the defining of national territories and the borders of nation states. Do identities really need to be territorially regulated and spatially rooted? Do we actually need to regain the lost land?

Where Precisely is this Border?

For nearly 50 years, from the Second World War until the Change and the collapse of the Soviet system, the border between Finland and the Soviet Union was strictly controlled. Finns could visit the Soviet Union, but mostly in groups and in regulated areas and programmes well planned in advance. Russians would come to Finland in Ikarus buses, looking distinctly identifiable dressed in a different colour range, and moving around in groups. Spotting Russians by a whole semiotic system of cultural differences was simple.

For some time the most effective way to insult a Finn was to assume that we had been part of the Soviet Bloc. Some of the time other people's assumptions about Finland's geopolitical position may have been amusing; at other times they were not. As the misunderstanding conflated Finns with socialism, poverty, and a satellite status as part of the Soviet Union, the proximity of the border had decidedly led to a fear of contamination. In effect, the mainstream Finnish world-view has us facing the West, with our collective back towards the East.

This geographical and geopolitical location has offered a version of Finland's place in the world, which has necessitated accentuating, and underlining, the difference and separateness of Finland from the Soviet Union/Russia. The most hidden – and the most obvious – secret in Finland is that we are indeed close to the East, close to Russia. While contexts change, foreign policy still remains conditioned by this proximity, recently demonstrated in our eagerness to join the European Union and the European Monetary Union in order to demonstrate that we belong to the West.

Some versions of this geopolitical position would represent Finland as a bridge-builder between the East and the West, with special ability to transmit and translate between different cultures. This public relations version, circulated mainly for commercial purposes, is largely unfounded or at least contradictory amongst the wider population. Few Finns, for example, have been willing to learn Russian.

The Finnish–Russian border is now the European Union border at which the gap in living standards on each side is the biggest in Europe. In the context of European transformations of integration and disintegration, Europe's border with the East has been displaced and renegotiated in recent times.

Where is the Border between East and West?

Since it is no longer clearly divided by the Iron Curtain, the question arises as to where Europe ends and, by the same token, to decide who belongs to the community and who is '*extracommunitari* and, effectively extraterrestrial' (Morley & Robins, 1993: 3–6; also Turunen, 1998). Karelia, the area on the Finnish–Russian border, is one location where the problem of marking the boundary between East and West is acutely present, and where each and every act of significance is predetermined by the East–West coordinates. (Figure 18.1)

National and ethnic identities are products of a piecemeal invention of homogeneity. Since it is so often said that Finnish identity is a homogenous one, the conception prevails that multiethnicity and multiculturalism happens somewhere else far distant. Regional identities within the state borders are assumed to be insignificant, amusing and picturesque details devoid of political significance.

In a canonical literary work in Finland, Väinö Linna's *The Unknown Soldier*, the faiths of a company of soldiers gathered

Figure 18.1 *Coat of Arms of the Province of Karelia*, c.1562. A symbolic representation of the confrontation between East and West, (Rancken & Pirinen, 1949: 61).

from all parts of the country, speaking the various dialects and characterising the 'typical characters' of this or that region, are homogenized into a common version, orchestrated to speak with a common (although univocally male) voice of the nation. If national identity is a result of the piecemeal production of homogeneity, what preceded it? We must consider what the various ethnicities integrated into Finnishness were and the history of Karelian identity as one of these ethnicities. More precisely, what are and what were the multiple Karelian histories? Whether there ever was an ethnic Finland pertains to the more general question of when differences become ethnicised. A Balkanisation of identities, while not even remotely likely in Finland, would not be a happy prospect.

Remembering the Lost Land

One result of the Second World War was that Finland lost parts of its territory to the Soviet Union, and the population of these areas (more than 400,000 people, or about 10 per cent of the Finnish population) was deported to other parts of Finland (Forsberg, 1995: 202–223). One of these was the Karelian Isthmus, where my mother came from. She came to central Finland, where she met and married my father. Before this, my father had spent five years of his life at the Eastern front. When he returned in 1945, he was twenty-three years old, she was twenty.

The Karelian population was evacuated, and settled all over Southern Finland. At the outset, the Karelian exiles met with hostility in many places. They were called Russians (*ryssä*), which, in a country that had just lost the war to Russia, was stigmatising. As their loss of homeland was also considered a national tragedy, the Karelians were assimilated into mainstream Finnish culture without overwhelming difficulties. I, for example, a second-generation half-Karelian daughter, did not particularly think of myself as Karelian (see also Sallinen-Gimpl 1989 and 1993 on Karelian identities).

The image of lost Karelia was mediated to me by 'things' and 'talk' such as picture books my parents got as wedding presents or family albums with pictures of relatives posing for the camera on sunny beaches and standing by their bikes in flowery dresses. Stories were told about relatives and former neighbours. There were weddings and funerals with many fiercely talkative and joyful people switching to the Karelian dialect as soon as they met each other, and switching back to 'normal' Finnish again when the party started to fade from their memory. Among Karelians, an altogether more talkative and merry bunch than the rest of the Finns, even funerals would eventually turn into laughter and joy at meeting each other again.

After the war, the image of the lost Karelia was represented as idealised, a green and rich land where birds sang and it was always summer. It was the lost home that my aunt would dream about for the rest of her life.

I still have an illustrated map of Finland from my second grade in school, collected bit by bit as part of an effort to teach us the importance of saving our pocket money. Much later it occurred to me that the map of Finland I learned and internalised was different from the one that my mother had learned in school. The borders of the country had seemed natural and eternal and it never occurred to me that they could have altered in one generation.

Yet I knew that something existed across the border. There was a fairly popular literary genre dealing with Finnish war activities on the Eastern border during the Second World War. (Some of the war fought against the Soviet Union was defensive, some was not.) This genre of war literature was popular with the war veterans, amongst others. Some of it was documentary, fighting the same battles fought during the war again, and displaying maps of the movements of Finnish troops in the battles of Summa or Ihantala. I knew that the places existed across the border, but I could not really imagine where they were located. They existed in my imagination, mediated by books, maps, or films, but not really anchored in any specific location.

After the war, many kinds of publications reconstructed images of the lost land of Karelia. Local histories were written. Photographs were collected and published as books. Autobiographies were gathered from the former inhabitants by each and every community association. A popular type of publication among the diaspora Karelians was a catalogue, hundreds of pages long, listing in detail all the farmhouses and families that used to live in a particular area, this or that municipality 'over there', as it had been organised before the war (Kiuru, 1981; Henttonen, 1984; Anttonen, 1988; Vanhanen, 1993; Anttila, 1994; Vanhanen, 1996).

The encyclopaedic activity of listing in detail every location, every occupancy of land, may have been helpful for the first generation of exiles in order to maintain an inner map of what was there; to document and perhaps correct a false memory; to catalogue every individual so that no one would be forgotten. From the point of view of a second-generation Karelian who had never seen the place, the activity of identifying places and people 'as they were then' seemed obsessive. Reconstructing the lost land in detail seemed like a post-diaspora fabrication.

In spite of all this activity of reconstruction of bygone places, the first Finnish visitors to Karelia after the border opened did not know what to expect. What would they see? How would they orient themselves in this territory, now a wilderness from their point of view?

Maps of the lost Karelia had become almost like Samizdat literature, secretly distributed from hand to hand. Pre-war maps of the ceded areas of Karelia had been handed over to the Soviet Union as part of the peace agreement and the first official maps were reproductions of these. Producing maps for the use of 'Heimat' or homeland enthusiasts proved to be a problematic venture. In a few years, however, up to date maps were published in cooperation with the Russian side (Haltia, 1998a; Kemppinen, 1992; Jaatinen, 1997).

The first maps that circulated among the visitors were wrinkled photocopies of maps on which all the place names were in Russian. Where there used to be a specific 'place', perhaps a village, there might not be one. Instead, new 'places', maybe a *Kolhoz,* would have appeared in new 'spaces'. (Russification of names in the Karelian Isthmus had been implemented by an administrative decision in 1948 – Haltia, 1998a: 12). After the Finnish population had been deported, new people from other parts of the Soviet Union had moved in. Old Finnish names were not translated into Russian, new names were invented.

Not only were places renamed or turned into non-places. The history of the Karelian Isthmus had been rewritten from a Russian point of view. The new population had no knowledge of a previous Finnish occupation of their region. The City of Vyborg had been called 'an old Russian town' in history books and city memorabilia (Haltia, 1998a; Haltia, 1998 b).

A Journey to Paradise Lost?

After the relaxation of border control in 1989, freedom of movement was extended on both sides. The Karelians, who had emigrated almost fifty years before, could now visit their home regions.

In May 1997 my mother and I made a journey back to Karelia. Starting very early in the morning from the region of Häme in central Finland, our bus reached our 'home region' of Vuoksenranta about midday, having passed through the Russian border control fairly early in the morning. When the bus finally reached the home village of our family, the older passengers started identifying places: 'This is where the family of so-and-so lived. From here you could go to the farm of such-and-such.' There was almost a competition for who could remember most and correctly identify the places, roads and houses of the former village. There was also disagreement and negotiation on this or that location and who had lived there. A disagreement on the exact location of a bridge actually continued afterwards, in telephone calls between participants and in later accounts of the trip for family members who had stayed at home.

How can a place be identified if it has changed completely? The roads were probably in the same places as before, but in bad condition. There were still fields, although not cultivated, and forests, although not looking quite the same. Some traces in the landscape still bore the scars of the war that had ended fifty years ago. Next to the eagerly expected flowers blooming and trees bursting into leaf you would find trenches in the forest. A bunker and a defensive line made of stones marked some redundant historical borderline.

Only some of the travellers on the bus could have had memories of the old spatial organization of the village. Remembering the significance of places was, of course, possible only for the generation that had lived in Karelia in their youth. This first generation had a splendid ability to map the terrain and orient themselves in a space that did not seem to contain anything, as if guided by a virtual map almost totally disconnected from the requirement to represent any kind of reality, with no reference point to a space or a territory.

This nothingness, this emptiness of space also allowed the Finns to orient themselves in the Karelian forests without quite seeing and realising that this now was somebody else's place. The virtual map of past memories allowed them not to see the Russian people that now inhabited the area or that this was a Russian village now.

Although most of the buildings had been destroyed, the village church was still there, badly ruined. The Finnish Heimat travellers, devastated by its bad condition, had started to clean up the church, putting iron fences across the door so that not everybody could enter, building a pulpit and new wooden pews, and bringing in birch branches to decorate it. In their small ways they had started to reoccupy the church, a symbolic place of their own.

Not much was left of my mother's childhood home. Remains of the stone foundation of the house, a depression in the terrain where the shed used to be, a well, and the upright of a swing. On the Karelian question, the question of returning the Karelian Isthmus to Finland, my mother would say, 'No, there's nothing left there' (Figure 18.2).

Figure 18.2 *The Site of My Mother's Home in Karelia,* May 1997.

Versions of Karelian Identity – Spatial or Virtual?

My highly personal and emotional experience of the journey back to Karelia with my mother has been shared by thousands of others. During the past ten years of the open border, such trips have become very popular, and thousands of diasporic Karelians have visited their former homes in the Karelian Isthmus. In the course of these trips, the first generation has passed on some of their memories and experiences to the second and even third generation. The Heimat travellers are increasingly people without their 'own' memories or lived experience of the place/space. Their experience of Karelia has been formed at second hand.

The stories told about the trips, although very personal, are mostly told in very similar ways, following the same course of narration (Kotitie, 1995; Heikkinen, 1998: 4; Sihvo & Sallinen, 1990). However, it is not obvious what the final significance of this experience might be, or how to put it in context. How does the sense of paradise lost change when you actually see what is left? One obvious consequence is demystification.

The lost land of childhood memory is precisely that, memory. Another consequence may be the urge to have Karelia back, to regain control of the territory.

The issue of reclaiming the Karelian Isthmus is an evergreen topic in post-war Finnish foreign policy. For quite some time talking about Karelia was politically unwise. Now talk is possible without the speaker seeming to be a revanchist lunatic; opinions simply differ.

Karelia has been a part of the national narrative through the years, a cornerstone and boundary marker of Finnish nationalism. It has been a deepfreeze for long-gone nationalist sentiments. 'Karelia' is also a brand of lager. The label on the bottle displays the same heraldic image of two opposed arms, the symbol of the meeting of East and West that dates back to at least 1562. The iconography of heroic masculinity is still available to the advertiser and can be put to use as a celebration of nationalist sentiments (Figure 18.3).

During the early years of Finnish nation-building in the late nineteenth century, Karelia signified the place of the origin of Finnishness, the Finno-Ugrian peoples' route to the territory now called Finland. It was the site of 'original' culture undisturbed by modernity, a site where ethno-logists would have a field day.

Having been an explicitly nostalgic place of remembrance and yearning, the land of song and poetry, Karelia remained exotic during the post-war years of closed borders. The rare visitor was authorised by their experience to document and convey the wondrous visit to others who could not cross the border. Even when the aim was to depict the realities of the Soviet Karelia of the time, Karelia would be turned into myth, or later, kitsch (Ripatti, 1985; Nieminen, 1988; Lindstöm, 1979; Haataja & Lintunen, 1990). Beyond the border, Finns could find the exotic ethnic Other, their own unconscious, an endlessly rich well of semiotic meanings.

However, Karelia exists not only as a boundary marker of Finnishness. There is another Karelia behind the border, The Republic of Karelia, a peripheral region of Russia in which some of the population speaks Finnish or Karelian and have

Figure 18.3 *Win a trip to Switzerland*, an advert for Karelia lager shortly after Finland won a medal in the ice hockey world championships in 1998.

their own cultural institutions. The Karelian population living in the Karelian Republic is fighting for its existence, language and cultural institutions. Some strongly urge the codification of the Karelian language in its own right – as if thereby starting the process of nation-building all over again, just as other nations have done, starting to strengthen their identity precisely when the population base is diminishing and fairly scattered.

This Karelia has remained invisible to Finns, but the reverse is also true. Russian discussion about returning Karelia to Finland is largely stalled. Since the Russian version of history has been rewritten and does not acknowledge Karelia as in any sense Finnish, there is no agenda for that debate. The Iron Curtain has prevented both sides of the border from seeing through to the other side.

Not only is there an incongruity between the two versions of Karelia, one Finnish, the other Russian, divided by the border. 'The problem of many Karelias' (Heikkinen, 1996: 16) is evident in ways of naming the place and in versions of its history from times much earlier than this century. Karelia stands for a diffuse geographical area composing the Karelian Isthmus, Ladoga Karelia, Border Karelia and Petsamo, often called Karelia with no precise geographical reference. Neither was there ever a clear identity among the Karelians. In the border area between Finland and Russia, Karelia became characterised as part of one or the other, dependent on point of view (Heikkinen, 1989). Various political projects on both sides attempted to Russify or Finnify the place at various times (Haltia, 1998a). As a contested territory over time, the boundaries of Karelia were always in flux. Even what was meant by 'boundary' did not remain the same (Hämynen, 1994: 17–27).

Thus, there is a considerable instability in naming Karelia and difficulty in deciding which version one is talking about. Heikkinen (1996: 34) claims that this change represents a shift in the whole field of the many Karelias, not merely the deinstitutionalisation of two Karelias on opposite sides of the border. It is less and less possible to look for unified versions of Karelian identities. The relaxation of the border and the disappearance of the Iron Curtain have allowed us to see versions of Karelia both beyond the border and in history. Karelia has always been a contested territory, where borderlines shift and cultural influences mingle.

Neither is there anything special about Karelians as a population divided in two by a nation state border. As Heikkinen points out, quite the contrary, it is difficult to find a border that would not cross the homelands of some other ethnic group or population (1989: 367). Although the experience of exile and changing borders is unique to each people, the feelings generated are universal.

However, new versions of Karelia have started to emerge. New kinds of cross-border traffic, developmental aid, economic cooperation and business interests arise from concepts of regional Karelias on both sides of the divide (Tykkyläinen, 1995; Saarelainen, 1994; Kortelainen, 1997). New European Union funded research projects have been founded for the promotion of border research and cooperation. Recent guide books for tourists show things from the point of view of the other beyond the border, preparing the traveller for what will be encountered and how it should be interpreted, retranslating the names of places Russified in the 1940s (Sellainen on Viipuri, 1993; Kemppinen, 1992).

After ten years of an open border, seeing Karelia has turned from an emotionally charged mythical experience into something more of a tourist trip. The visitors have become interested in areas other than just their original home. Karelia attracts people for other reasons. Rebranding Karelia, however, may not have been easy. When asked about what 'sights' or tourist attractions 'my' home village could offer, the village association could point out the former locations of a few archaeological sites, the site of a stone age village and a place where the remains of a 9000-year-old fishing net were found. However, just like the 'sights' of later years, they were simply not there (Jaatinen, 1997: V–VIII, 50–51).

In a realist foreign policy discourse, talk of Karelia was determined to be talk of a piece of space, the territory that was ceded in the Second World War (and not, incidentally, about redrawing the boundary where it was drawn in, say, the peace agreements of 1323, 1595 or 1811 (Kirkinen, 1976). In this discourse, talk about Karelia was bound to be about the occupation of space and would, by the same token, constitute a speech act comparable to stepping on the land mines at the border. Talk about territory becomes talk of retrenchment. It activates the impulse to control a territory instead of seeing other possibilities.

My second-generation diasporic Karelian identity does not need a territorial anchor. It is not dependent on territory or control of space. Karelia is constructed in mental space, in the practices that transmit Karelian identity from one generation to another, the family albums, the diverse literary genres, the stories told, the weddings and funerals where family and kin are not only continuously kept up but also constantly transformed. Identification by village may still remain even in exile. Whenever I say that my mother is Karelian, people will ask, 'Which village?' But I know that village exists only in a virtual reality.

If Karelian identities, then, are virtual rather than spatial, there are good grounds for constructing new and more inventive Karelian identities. I would suggest the following: a Cosmopolitan Karelianism as represented, for example, by *Värttinä* – a group performing music which is now called 'world music', rooted but also cosmopolitan; a Carnival Karelianism, as represented by Leningrad Cowboys, a travesty of locatedness between East and West, and Karelia as multicultural urbanism, rewriting versions of history that describe Karelia (especially the city of Vyborg) as multicultural before the Iron Curtain. It is a description of Karelia as a melting pot, like Finland, a gathering of many kinds of people, rather than a purified space or an ethnically cleansed territory.

Lost in Space? Lost in Time?

My newly purchased map of Karelia, bought at the marketplace in Vyborg in the Karelian Isthmus, lists places in both Russian and Finnish. The map has been drawn for the audience of Finnish returnees, to meet their expectations of what is significant. It has been produced by Russians, realising the existence of this specific market niche and a real demand for maps (discussion with Martti Haltia, 22 July 1999). As the former official Soviet version constructed Karelia's history as clearly and indisputably Russian, this can only be interpreted as the Russians adapting to the perspectives of Finns.

Not only are place-names given in both Finnish and Russian. A dual temporality is written on the map that shows where Finnish places used to be, but have been destroyed, or where they used to be and still partly are. I am less sure of whether it actually shows where Russian places now are, where people live, and what counts as significant on their maps.

A temporal reading of the map might explain this amazing ability of Heimat travellers to cross the border as if to a mythical alien territory, trying in small ways to regain control and symbolically reoccupy it. Walk in the forests and in the landscape of one's memories as if there was no present time, only a stage of forests and fields that recall the old place, beyond the normal coordinates of time. Memory guides both what you see and what you do not see.

The map also draws multiple lines for the border between Finland and Russia, one for a peace agreement of 1323, another one for 1595, and a third for 1811. The name 'Iron Curtain' does not sound entirely accurate for a border that was redrawn and relocated on numerous occasions.

Karelia, space is a floating signifier, and many times are simultaneously present. The ambivalence and difficulty of deciding what to make of the Karelian territory activates a time warp for interpreting the 'nothingness' of visible reality. 'There is nothing there.' While this time warp allows the first generation to return to and remember their childhood, the trips in themselves increasingly bring new and varied conceptions of the territory, making it possible to reconcile the pictures in the family album with the wasteland actually seen.

The journey brought me to see myself as ethnic. Having come to realise my ethnic identity, it seems to me that Finnishness – previously represented as a monolithic identity – is composed of all kinds of ethnic identities, each of 'us' being half of this, a quarter of that, and a few percent of every thing. This does not constitute a basis for territorial purism.

Reactivation of ethnicity throughout Eastern Europe can be seen as both reactionary and liberating. Being lost in time, we want to stabilise the nation-space. As the European Community expands to the East, to Central and Eastern Europe, 'we' are not the only ones to ask these questions. Looking at the space/time conjunction at the boundary between East and West, I will have to remember that although my diasporic Karelianism is virtual, the small vegetable patches that keep the Karelian villagers alive are very real.

CHAPTER 19

MAKING SPACES VISIBLE: ALISON WILDING'S EARLY SCULPTURE

Fran Lloyd

> *'...whilst firmly placed in our world the sculpture should take us out of it, offering a glimpse of an alternative order...this happens by making and doing processes...'*
>
> Alison Wilding, *Entre el objecto y la imagen (Between Object and Image)*

Alison Wilding came to public attention in the early 1980s as part of what has come to be called New British Sculpture, which included among its practitioners Tony Cragg, Richard Deacon, Bill Woodrow and Anish Kapoor. As frequently happens, New British Sculpture was defined in opposition to its immediate predecessors. The sculpture of the 1970s could be broadly characterised as, on one side, that of an older generation concerned with formal issues, and on the other, of a younger generation who sought to extend the definitions of sculpture to include the processes and actions of the body as in the walks of Richard Long. Negotiating both of these positionings and earlier sculptural traditions, New British Sculpture was associated with sculpture firmly placed on the ground (rather than the pedestal), signalling sculpture's move, from the 1960s, into the physical world as part of a located cultural space (see Newman, 1982).

What is most marked in the early critical reception of these sculptors' work is that, while Cragg and Woodrow, for example, could be discussed in terms of a situated social sphere (post-industrial Britain and urban experience), or Anish Kapoor and Shirazeh Houshiary in terms of cultural identity, Alison Wilding's early work (of which relatively little was written by comparison) was consistently described in terms of the private and the secret – the 'other' (see McEwan, 1983).

The catalogue to the exhibition, *The Sculpture Show* (at the Hayward Gallery on the South Bank and at the Serpentine), which helped to consolidate this grouping in Britain, is typical: 'her sculpture makes us aware that it is the product of an intense and slow communion within the privacy of the studio and as a result perhaps decrees that the nature of our personal response is best left private also' (Crichton, 1983a: 57). The accompanying guide for visitors is equally evasive: 'While Wilding clearly refers to the appearance of the natural world through her intense communion with her materials ... her work remains essentially private in nature and impossible to characterise' (Crichton, 1983b: 4).

The language links Wilding's work with the private, the natural and the secretive, and suggests a forbidden or secretive quality which cannot be articulated or named. Although her work differs from that of the other New British sculptors in certain crucial ways, the terms of description do appear to be a reinstatement and reiteration of the 'separate spheres of gender' which has long associated the male with public spaces and the female with the private. In this context, I want to question this reading of Wilding as *inarticulable*, impossible other, existing outside of language (a language of exclusion often used in relation to women artists) and reposition her work within the social and public sphere by investigating the specific conditions of its production in Britain in the late 1970s and the early 1980s.

Sculpture has been a relatively untheorised area within the discipline of art history, particularly in Britain, and, until relatively recently, little attention has been paid to the issues of positioning through gender, race, class or sexuality in relationship to the production and reception of sculpture, and its histories. Drawing upon recent approaches to visual culture as performative, negotiated and situated, I want to focus on Wilding's work as a visible site/sight in which, and upon which, multiple cultural and gendered positionings were (and are) visibly enacted, and to highlight a series of relationships which have been suppressed or forgotten in the received histories of British sculpture. Accepting that there is no neutral, free zone of the studio, immune to the effects of the outside world, I want to start from the premise that Wilding, as a sculptor and a woman, is already positioned within the social as a gendered subject, and that her work is, in part, a conscious and continuous renegotiation of this positioning as an embodied subject.

Firstly, it is necessary to briefly consider the state of sculpture in the early 1970s when Alison Wilding, like several of the sculptors mentioned, trained in London. These years were marked by fierce debates about the nature of sculpture (see Harrison and Cooke in Neff, 1987) On one side, an older generation, led by Anthony Caro, produced large-scale, abstracted metal sculpture premised on formal concerns while, on the other side, a younger generation, such as Richard Long and Gilbert & George, sought to redefine sculpture as a critical activity that extended beyond the aesthetics and geographies of the studio, and included the performativity of the artist's body/bodies. What was at stake was sculpture as a form of self-referential modernism, or sculpture as part of an 'expanded field' of life, perceived as part of a radical avant-garde, which questioned traditional categories and naturalised languages (see Seymour 1972, and Krauss, 1979).

Alison Wilding, who attended the Royal College of Art in London from 1970–73, was well aware of these debates and firmly positioned herself in the 'expanded field' rather than the 'macho' metal camp, as she called it (Wilding interview, 1998). In fact, both groupings were male dominated, as Wilding knew well, but one offered a more questioning approach to making and meaning. In order to begin to situate Wilding, I want to initially focus on an early work, *Without Casting Light on the Subject* of 1975 (Figure 19.1), produced within two years of leaving college. Originally shown with the accompanying text at a public opening in her studio, the work is now known only through the photograph. Like much of the more conceptually inclined expanded sculpture of this time, Wilding uses simple, everyday material: the material of language in the text, the colloquial saying in the title, and the recognisable household/studio objects, such as the table and the desk lamps. The text foregrounds a series of actions and processes as seemingly logical steps in an experiment which is explained in precise detail. However, as the text is read, it becomes clear that it does not 'explain' the work; reason does not cast light on the subject. Equally, the disconnected lights, even if they were connected, could not reveal the surface of the objects, either from above or from below: no light can be cast on the objects.

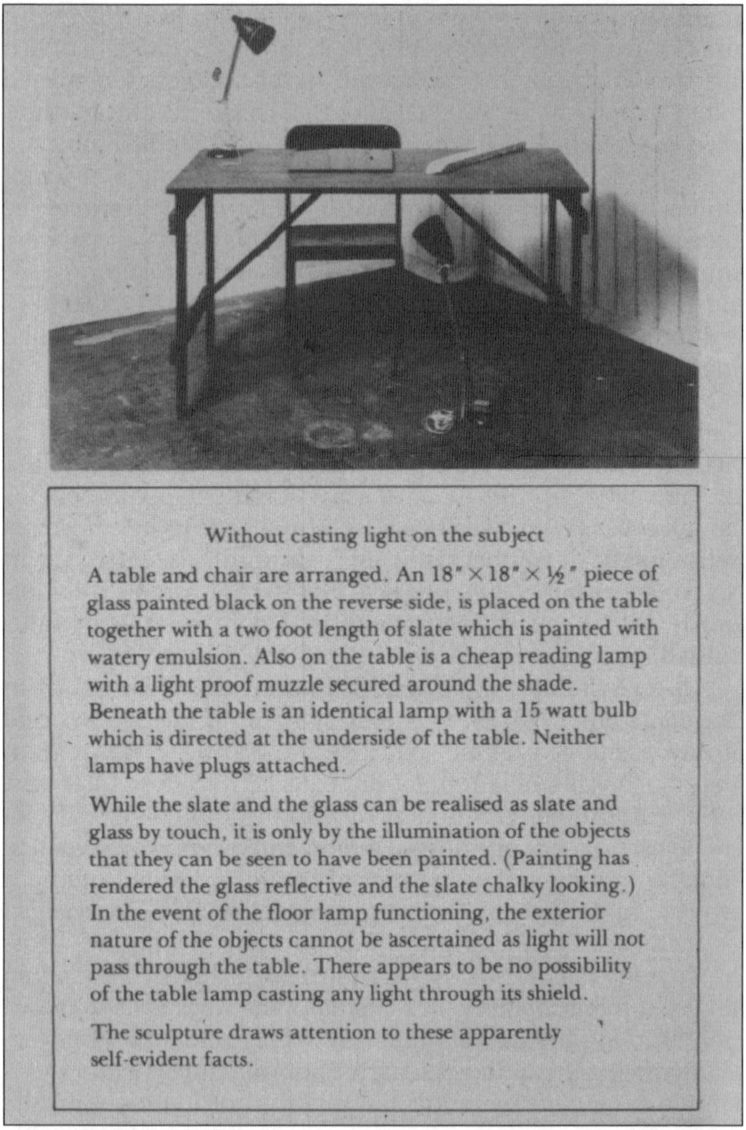
Without casting light on the subject
A table and chair are arranged. An 18" × 18" × ½" piece of glass painted black on the reverse side, is placed on the table together with a two foot length of slate which is painted with watery emulsion. Also on the table is a cheap reading lamp with a light proof muzzle secured around the shade. Beneath the table is an identical lamp with a 15 watt bulb which is directed at the underside of the table. Neither lamps have plugs attached.
While the slate and the glass can be realised as slate and glass by touch, it is only by the illumination of the objects that they can be seen to have been painted. (Painting has rendered the glass reflective and the slate chalky looking.) In the event of the floor lamp functioning, the exterior nature of the objects cannot be ascertained as light will not pass through the table. There appears to be no possibility of the table lamp casting any light through its shield.
The sculpture draws attention to these apparently self-evident facts.

Figure 19.1 Alison Wilding, *Without Casting Light on the Subject,* 1975 (destroyed), Mixed media with text. Courtesy of Alison Wilding.

If light and reason are unable to function in this work, the senses prove to be equally as unhelpful. Sight is unable to distinguish between the two materials on the table (the glass and the slate which have been painted to create an illusion of something else) while touch produces a different kind of partial knowledge. Thus, in effect, the spectator is presented with a series of propositions, or alternative systems, which make us question how we know or experience the world and, furthermore, as Lynne Cooke notes, point to 'the fallibility of the senses and the limits of knowledge' (1985: 6).

A further level of oppositional play is enacted in the title, which casts doubt on the subject as distinct from the object. In traditional art history, 'subject' refers to the content of the work (the subject matter) but here it also suggests the artist as subject vis-à-vis the work as object. The separation between subject and object, which has been central to Western thought, comes under pressure. In this sense, *Without Casting Light* is deliberately confounding and, in common with much work of this time, it undermines what Lyotard would later call the 'grand narratives' of the Enlightenment. However, as I will argue, the work can be further situated by an exploration of the specific conditions confronting Wilding as a gendered subject and artist.

Within Western art, women have long been the object of the male gaze and rarely the active subject, as John Berger showed in his ground breaking work of 1972, *Ways of Seeing*. By 1975, the year of Wilding's work, issues of visuality and visibility were high on the agenda for a number of interrelated reasons. The early 1970s saw the beginning of various feminist art interventions in Britain which centred initially on questions of women's visibility and representation both within the history of art, and 'woman' as sign in contemporary visual culture. In 1971, the American writer Linda Nochlin posed her famous question 'Why Have There Been No Great Women Artists?', while in 1975, Laura Mulvey published her classic essay on the male gaze in *Screen*. Given, as I have argued, that Wilding was aware at this time of the problems of working with objects as a female subject and of the gendered identifications with the materials and languages of sculpture, these crucial issues about site and sight, and how women artists could intervene in what had been shown to be a patriarchal system of representation, raises the question of what it meant to produce sculpture as a female in Britain in 1975.

If one takes Hilary Robinson's argument that to be a woman artist is automatically to transgress codes in Western society, then to be a woman sculptor, where sculpture is predominately a male practice, is doubly transgressive (1987: 139). For various historical reasons, as Fiona Carson notes, there have been fewer female sculptors than painters, and fewer still had been 'rediscovered' by the mid 1980s, let alone the 1970s (2000). For example, although Barbara Hepworth was described on her death in 1975 by *The Guardian* as 'probably the most significant woman artist in the history of art to this day' (Florence, 1996: 34), it was difficult to see her in this light as she was either ignored by feminist historians as part of a masculinist modernist tradition, or seen within normative art history as a poor relation to Moore. Meanwhile, Germaine Greer's widely publicised book of a few years later, *The Obstacle Race* (1979), was on 'the Fortunes of Women Painters and their Work'. In fact, it is only since 1989 that the gender of Meret Oppenheim, long famous for her fur-lined cup and saucer, or the work of Louise Bourgeois have been given critical attention, and only since 1996, for instance, that the work of Barbara Hepworth has been reconsidered in terms of gendered positioning (Curtis, 1996).

Furthermore, in the 1970s, sculptural practice in Britain was one of the most gendered spheres. Like painting, it was associated with a male-dominated tradition, a private as opposed to collective activity, and with a modernist emphasis on medium and 'pure' expression. It was seen as helping to maintain the very categories and hierarchies of art history – the artist (universally male), genius and individual expression – that feminist writers were beginning to show had excluded women (see Nochlin, 1971). This was visible in the major Hayward Gallery exhibition of 1975, *The Condition of Sculpture,* where only four out of forty artists chosen to represent the current state of sculpture were women (see Parker and Pollock, 1987: 22 for details of the resulting petition).

Thus it is not surprising that, of the many women artists associated with feminism in the 1970s, trained within an art school system that had adopted modernist values, several rejected painting and sculpture in favour of photography, performance or conceptual art, which were widely associated with an adversarial avant-garde practice and less burdened with history. Undermining the dominant forms of modernist abstraction which inscribed art as 'purely an optical experience' (gender free and universal), feminist art practice in Britain became dominated, as Amelia Jones has shown, by a particular form of poststructuralist signification where the traditional categories of painting and sculpture became increasingly positioned against the supposedly more radical 'document' work (Jones, 1996: 34 and 155–6) and women artists were urged to 'resist visual pleasure' which was associated with the male gaze (see Parker and Pollock, 1987: 29 and

232–248). Thus for a period during the 1970s 'this produced a "negative aesthetics" among certain feminists, a radical distanciation from any aspect of the spectacle and visual pleasure, a distrust of the visual image, of the iconicity especially of women' (Pollock, 1998: 79).

Of the women sculptors working at this time, one of the most notable and influenticial was Eva Hesse, whose work was known in Britain through the international art magazines such as *Art in America*, exhibitions, and particularly the writings of Lucy Lippard (1976 and 1979). However, her tragic life of being born a Jew in Germany, enduring the traumas of the war and illness until her early death, combined with the publication of her diaries, led to an almost exclusively autobiographical reading of her work, ignoring her negotiation of a grand male tradition and its materials.

Thus, to be a woman sculptor who wished to make objects was a particularly difficult position in the 1970s in Britain. Precedents would be linked with male counterparts in the way Hepworth was to Henry Moore, or risk the marginalisation of Hesse to nature and biography. In the context of recent feminist interventions, there was much work that deconstructed the dominant images of women or explored taboo areas, but there was little work or writing that could offer some model for a consideration of gender issues in the making of sculpture, which was regarded as a rearguard, as opposed to resistant avant-garde, activity. Equally, it was only in 1978, following several petitions, that five women were invited to select the 1978 *Hayward Annual* (organised in direct protest to an Allen Jones' exhibition of fetishist sculpture), and that *Studio International* devoted an issue to women's art.

In this context, *Without Casting Light* can be seen as a powerful representation of the site of the gendered artist's studio – the place of making objects – where Wilding provides both a critique of the 'normalised' (masculinist) values of the 'mastery' of sight, associated with power over the object, and points to the ambivalent and difficult positioning of the female subject who, absent from critical history, cannot see a way of making. Foregrounding sight and site, the major determining factors of visibility in the art world, Wilding points to the absent presence of the woman sculptor as active subject and introduces issues of relationality and the relativity of experience which undermines objectivity (see Jacobus et al. for a discussion of the interconnections between the practices of science as objectivity, distancing and the construction of masculinity). In effect, through the disjuncture between the subject and object, the work disrupts this privileging of one over another and raises the question of who is the subject.

In 1978 Wilding moved to a new studio (after a period of not producing work) and it is the works made in this new space, shown in public spaces in 1979 and 1980, that I want to focus on. Firstly, I want to briefly discuss *Untitled (with bag)* of 1979, a complex work which no longer exists except through photographs taken in Wilding's new studio space. Significantly, the work consists of four distinct forms which use all the different boundaries or edges of the studio: 'a silk bridge' of aluminium rod sewn into silk, fixed into the wall at one end and suspended from the ceiling; a 'strip of white rubber suspended' in the corner from ceiling to floor; a long aluminium rod, encased in a tube of 'French knitting', which curved out from the wall to the floor, and a black small bag attached to the wall.

Compared to *Without Casting Light*, it is evident that Wilding has moved into making the total space of the studio the site for her work. Using this already given space, she maps it out by articulating its boundaries and she changes it. In a recent interview with the author, Wilding interestingly recalls that 'the corner was emphasised and altered by having the strip of white rubber suspended from it ... it was "de-cornered" in a way. I felt that I was using and describing and outlining every single part of the space of my studio' (Wilding interview, 2 March 2000; all subsequent quotes are from this source).

In addition to making the space visible, it is striking that all of the elements used here are transformed by oppositional means – whether the aluminium rods sewn into the silk or concealed by the French knitting, the 'de-cornered' corner, or the 'white plastic bag that was painted black'. Thus the space of the studio becomes the site for questioning the gendered materials and forms traditionally associated with the 'separate spheres of culture', and Wilding both subverts and negotiates these through the performative and embodied acts of making. Clearly aware of the recent work of Eva Hesse and Carl Andre's floor pieces, Wilding can be seen to be making a space for herself by negotiating the materials and processes associated with both radical 'masculine' and 'feminine' art practices at this time.

Furthermore, in the context of the previously noted feminist development of 'negative aesthetics', without directly imaging the female body, the work carries the marks of making while, at the same time, allowing visual pleasure to become part of the work which Wilding refers to as follows: 'I always thought that making that silk bridge thing and getting it to make the right sort of curve... I understood something about what was beautiful... I'd wanted to excise any ideas of beauty as an aesthetic from the work. But I allowed it to come in and it was OK.' On the oppositional use of materials, she goes on to say that 'I think the change can be physically or visually enjoyed'. Thus, from a space of uncertainty and inactivity, Wilding had moved into a space of discovery and it was this work, shown at the end of 1979 in *New Sculpture* at the Ikon Gallery in Birmingham, that Wilding later ascribed the number one to when she began to keep an inventory of her work.

In November 1980 Wilding exhibited in *Eight Artists: Women: 1980* at the Acme Gallery, London,[1] which was part of an unprecedented year of public visibility of women's visual culture in Britain. The ICA, under the exhibition directorship of Sandy Nairne, presented three major feminist exhibitions from November to December: *Women's Images of Men, About Time* and *Issue*, an international selection of women's art by the American feminist Lucy Lippard; *Women's Own* (a women's film season); and a weekend conference entitled *Questions on Women's Art* (see Parker and Pollock, 1987). All of these events were, in part, differing responses to the previously mentioned *Hayward Annual* of 1978. *Eight Artists,* which Wilding participated in, included painting and sculpture, was organised to coincide with the second ICA exhibition, *About Time,* which focused on film, video and photography (see Parker and Pollock, 1987: 235). This juxtaposition of what was considered the more radical feminist artistic practices in *About Time,* against the more traditional forms of painting and sculpture, was an intentional strategy. They were all advertised together and presented to compliment each other.

That the presentation of *Eight Artists* was part of a strategic feminist/women's cultural intervention is further emphasised in the catalogue. The introductory statement by Claire Smith, the organiser and one of the participating artists, makes it clear that the exhibition is about women who still choose to paint or sculpt and how they position themselves against and through the existing poles of male practice and dominant feminist practice. As she states: 'women artists who are reluctant to make work with an overt political content or application, even though they may identify and sympthasise with feminism, have been left with the alternative of adhering to the traditional hierarchical procedures, and instead of having greater freedom, this has led many women to feel more oppressed about the scope of their creative inclinations' (*Eight Artists*, 1980: unpaginated). Smith then continues by distancing the exhibition from the 'hairy cubist' style (presumably as a reference to dominant modernist male practice of the time) with its dogmatic adherence to maintaining old hierarchies and safeguarding their territory.

Curiously, *Eight Artists*, although presented and reviewed as part of the above mentioned 'women series', has been forgotten by feminist and nonfeminist writers alike. In part, eclipsed by the popular success of *Women's Images of Men*, other reasons for this forgetting lie in the specific debates which were dominant at the time, and which have subsequently shaped its history. As previously mentioned, the dominant feminist debates in the late 1970s centred on the gaze, the imaging of women and the associated strategy of 'negative aesthetics', exemplified by Mary Kelly's *Post Partum Document* of 1976. This tended to polarise debates between painting and imaging, and consequently sculpture was, to a large extent, ignored. *Eight Artists*, however, did not just present painting and sculpture – it was presenting nonfigurative or 'abstract' works. Without getting caught up in the debate about these various terms, the key point is that abstraction was, and still is, a difficult area for women artists. Given the perceived links of abstraction and modernist (male) practice in the 1970s, it was difficult to see how such work could be shown to engage with gender issues, and it is only recently that feminist writers and artists have begun to question this forbidden territory where, as Betterton states (in reference to painting), 'the idea of the body of the artist, female embodiment and female subjectivity' are central to this exploration (1996: 94).

By showing her work in *Eight Artists*, Wilding is clearly working within and negotitiating current debates about different forms of art practice: which are the most avant-garde and which are most suitable or effective for women artists? As Cooke notes, her inclusion in this exhibition 'forced Wilding to consider the problem of making sculpture for contexts other than her studio and for situations that contained very diverse kinds of work' (1985: 7). Thus, contrary to the previously noted received view of Wilding's work as personal and private, in positioning her work with regard to both an emerging body of dominant feminist work in Britain (which favoured a deconstructive approach) and the pervasive, and more importantly, institutionalised forms of modernist male practice (whether those of the formalist kind or those associated with the avant-garde practices of conceptual art), I want to show how she negotiates the issues of gender through her work at a particularly pivotal public moment in contemporary British art.

Of the five works that Alison Wilding exhibited at *Eight Women*, I want to discuss two. The first is *Untitled (with bags)*, 1980, (Figure 19.2) which Fenella Crichton succinctly describes in the introductory catalogue essay as: 'Two serrated paper bags have been reconstructed in brass sheet and placed inside a meandering zinc stockade. They still carry with them memories of their original use but now they have been made to stand upright, comical and yet triumphant, within their own protective space' (*Eight Artists*, 1980: unpaginated). As with the previous works, the sculpture works on several interconnected levels. On the level of materials, she once again uses metal associated with the previously discussed 'macho' tradition of welding. However, Wilding's process is not an industrial or welded one; they are hand cut and shaped so they carry the traces of the artist's body. In this case, the material is undisguised and, within the category of alloy, the zinc can contrast with another, the brass. Propped against the other, the two bags are also linked at the top by the often overlooked element of tissue paper which heightens this subversion of materials.

Figure 19.2 Alison Wilding, *Untitled, (with bags)*, 1980. Zinc, brass foil and paper, 24 × 131 × 160.5 cm. Arts Council Collection, Hayward Gallery, London. Courtesy of Alison Wilding.

Untitled also subverts normalised perceptions of sculpture and its relationship to space. Usually, the sculptural object is placed or imposed on to space where it occupies a space or territory as a solid, and consequently hides the space it occupies. By placing the object or materials *across* space in this floor based work, Wilding makes visible the space that is usually hidden by sculpture. The bags, or containers, inhabit the centre and are protected, surrounded or restrained by another boundary, the small wall of zinc. This draws attention to the space between the objects, which is made visible (rather than hidden), and the relationship of one material to another, one surface to another, and the complex interconnections of light and shadow. In effect, it establishes relationships both between the different forms of solid (the bags and the outer edge), and between the interior and exterior spaces.

Not only is the relationship between the centre of the piece and the boundary or margin made explicit, but the question of which is inside or outside becomes problematised. As Wilding notes 'I think a bag is a beautiful way to describe a volume – something that holds nothing or something... it can do both things'. Similarly, the outside of the bags, for example, are inside the outer wall, and the outer wall acts as a skin which is both simultaneously an inside, in relation to the bags, and an outside in relationship to the spectator. Importantly, the unhierarchical placement of the forms does not privilege one form above another and I would suggest that the spectator, looking down upon the work, is presented with questions about relationships *between* things, within and across the categories of metals, space and solid, which include that of the spectator's body.

Without imposing a linear reading on Wilding's work, she can be seen to return to some of the questions posed in the earlier works about subject/object, about gendered positionings in order to reconfigure them. If *Without Casting a Shadow* prompts the spectator to consider two oppositional positionings which finally refuse an either/or resolution, *Untitled (with bags)* can be seen to refer to relational and multiple interconnections, and changing points of vision which cross space and destabilise a unitary positioning. In her discussion of Wilding's later works, Hilary Gresty refers to a 'complex and oscillating visuality' (1993: 15) which I would argue, from a phenomenological point of view, is also an important part of the effect of this earlier work. Without using the literal body, the work evokes the body through its deployment of space and boundaries, not as a fixed, given object, but as a negotiation between and through other objects in the world. From the point of view of the artist (given the then current feminist debates about the female body as object), the fetished female body is absent, although the traces of its active presence are in the work, and it is the body of the spectator which has to negotiate and interact with the first of Wilding's floor based, bipartite objects in real space, deciding whether to step over the outer wall or respect its space and so forth.

Other commentators on this work have described it as 'separate and self-contained' where the relationships within the work 'are largely internally circumscribed. Thus they do not depend on the participation of the viewer in either a physical or an emotional sense' (Cooke, 1985: 8). In contradistinction, I am arguing that this interaction is a crucial part of the work in the way that it alludes metaphorically to the body, surface and boundaries. The *object and its spaces* both interact with the space around it and evoke the body as a site/sight of temporary embodiment in space; of tissues, skins and surfaces. This is particularly evident in the photograph taken of it in the artist's studio in 1980, where the scarred floor, within and outside of the object, together with the twist of tissue paper provides a 'ridiculous' support. I would therefore suggest that, as Cooke notes, this work shifts the 'attention from the individual components to the relationships that bind them' (1985: 12) but that these relationships extend into the spectator's space. Thus Wilding destabilises the unitary subject of the viewing spectator and highlights a process of changing relationships, and the interactions between and within the object/subject.

The last Wilding work I want to focus on is *Untitled* of 1980, (Figure 19.3) which is literally an example that has crossed from the threshold of the visible to the invisible and back again. Recently, when discussing the making of *Untitled (with bags)* and commenting on the usually hidden, interior space of sculpture which this sculpture makes visible, Wilding referred to its 'companion' piece which was also shown in *Eight Artists*, as one of the other two untitled works. Impossible to know from the title and not previously reproduced, the no longer existent work is now visible through its photograph. Slightly smaller than *Untitled (with bags)*, *Untitled* is in effect the interior space of this work made visible in the almost minimal skin of the dark rubber sheet. Placed in the centre are two strips of zinc, 'wrapped around something' to form cylinders that were 'continuous ... one was open and one was closed with a piece

Figure 19.3 Alison Wilding, *Untitled,* 1980. Rubber, zinc, glass and paper, 17.5 × 135 cm. Courtesy of Alison Wilding.

of glass painted black. And then between them ... they were supporting a piece of black paper'.

No longer needing a surrounding separate boundary, the rubber defines the space of the work, its edge and its skin, and the hidden space of sculpture (revealed by the previous work) now becomes the object/subject of visibility. And the negotiation of space, and the process of mapping it, is made highly visible. As Wilding notes: 'I don't remember when I did this talking about negative space but that is what it was, it was another way of seeing this [*Untitled (with bags)*]. Sort of turning it inside out, but the language is different now to talk about it.'[2]

Several writers have discussed Wilding's later works, which utilise a play of object/space, light/shadow, subject/object, in terms of '*L'écriture féminine*' which emerged within French feminism as an attempt to reconsider Lacan's psychoanalytic theories of the female as absent 'other' or the passive recipient of the male gaze (see, for example, Althorpe Guyton, 1988). However, within the framing of this essay, I do not want to pursue Wilding's work in terms of Julia Kristeva's 'dark chora' or the different approaches of Luce Irigaray and Hélène Cixous to 'the feminine' in culture, although their theories of embodiment, which do not privilege the mind/body duality or sight (the mastery of the gaze) may be appropriate. Reminded of Lisa Tickner's important article on feminist body art of the

1970s, in which she states that 'Living in a female body is different from looking at it, as a man', I want to return to the question of the early reception of Wilding's work (1978).

Looking back to the mid 1970s from the position of the present, I have argued that Wilding's work was problematic because it transgressed certain dominant norms of male sculpture, but was equally not containable in the dominant modes of feminist art or indeed 'feminine art'. Seen, therefore, as a secret space, it was relegated to the much rehearsed gendered sphere of the private, the inexplicable and, in effect, to the normative spaces ascribed to the female subject within a largely patriarchal art world of the late 1970s. However, far from being 'essentially private' and outside of culture, it is clear that Alison Wilding's work embodies quite specific cultural meanings.

Focusing on issues of gender and making, I have argued that her work is situated, that it negotiates and seeks to disrupt dominant discourses which, by their nature, attempt to impose fixity. Equally, through her use of materials, processes and forms, I suggest that her work is performative in the sense of actively negotiating meaning in the making of the work, and that through these actions Wilding destabilises the binaries of male/female sculptural practice, of active subject/passive object, inside/outside, solid/space, public/private, and disrupts the either/or in favour of the relative and the relational, firmly situated in space. Finally, in discussing the making of visible spaces, it becomes apparent that other spaces are revealed – the forgotten spaces of specific histories, their interelationships with other histories, and their continuing effects on the present.

Notes

1. *Eight Artists: Women: 1980* at the Acme Gallery, London. Part 1, 3–25 October 1980 included Shelagh Cluett, Emma Park, Jozefa Rogocki, Claire Smith. Part 2, 31 October–22 November 1980 included the painters Mikey Cuddihy and Sarah Greengrass, the sculptor, Margaret Organ and Alison Wilding, who showed five works.
2. The connections with Rachel Whiteread's work, which is discussed in the next essay, is quite striking. Wilding taught Whiteread at Brighton and at The Slade School of Art, and she worked for a while as Wilding's assistant. For further discussion of floor based works and sight/site see Fer, 1997, and Malvern, chapter 20 in this volume. I would like to thank Sue Malvern for bringing Briony Fer's article to my attention.

Chapter 20

Hidden Spaces and Public Places: Women, Memory and Contemporary Monuments – Jenny Holzer and Rachel Whiteread

Sue Malvern

This essay discusses the hidden spaces of memory in public monuments. In particular, it examines two projects from the end of the twentieth century. The first is Jenny Holzer's *Lustmord,* a work originally commissioned in 1993 as a set of artist's pages for the magazine of *Süddeutsche Zeitung,* Munich and subsequently remade in various versions including its projection onto a war memorial. The second is Rachel Whiteread's proposal for a Holocaust memorial for the Judenplatz, Vienna – a project which won a limited entry competition in 1996 and is finally completed. One of the issues that intrigues me is the role now played by women in this particularly androcentric form of public art. Given the current preoccupations and anxieties about monument-making, why have women – traditionally neither the subjects commemorated nor the makers of monuments – begun to be invited as the preferred artists for commemorative projects to impossible subjects such as the Holocaust?

Maya Lin, the maker of the *Vietnam Veterans War Memorial* in Washington, is a kind of progenitor or precursor for the emergence of women as ideal monument-makers for a genre which finds itself in crisis about both the forms and the meaning of commemoration. However, there is a difference here because Lin won an open-entry competition for the monument and her entry was selected without her name or her gender being revealed. Rather, her status as a woman artist has tended to legitimise retrospectively the forms of her memorial proposal as somehow ideal, indeed essential, for representing the trauma of a lost war and the wounds it had inflicted on American national self-identity.

I want to start off the issues raised here somewhat obliquely, however, with a discussion of Carl Andre's floor pieces such as *Equivalent I – VIII*, 1966, or *144 Magnesium Square*, 1969. These very flat minimalist floor sculptures have been read in a number of ways. Firstly, they have been seen as works which flatten out any notion of interiority or interior psychic space, as a refusal of the notion that works of art somehow express the inner emotional life of the artist. As Rosalind Krauss put it: 'The ambition of minimalism was, then, to relocate the origins of sculpture's meaning to the outside, no longer modeling its structure on the privacy of psychological space but on the public, conventional nature of what might be called cultural space' (1977: 270).

Secondly, these works have been characterised as a new kind of object which has something both painterly and sculptural about it but which is 'neither painting nor sculpture' (see Judd, 1975: 181). This was sometimes associated with a tendency for sculpture to get closer and closer to the ground by erasing or absorbing the pedestal, where the pedestal was understood as something that set sculpture apart, in favour of sculpture as simply an object in the world. What then made it readable as art was its context or site-specificity, for example its being shown in an art gallery.

Thirdly, such floor based sculpture has recently been rethought as figuring invisibility or blindness as a condition or corollary of visibility or vision. Briony Fer states that such floor-based sculpture 'steals from the field of vision that mass or height that had conventionally characterized sculpture' (1997: 276–77). The interest of this reading of floor-bound sculpture, if we return briefly to Holzer and Whiteread, is that there is indeed something blind about the blocks or bunkers represented in both these works, while both forms insist that the object's blindness is not concealing some sort of secret space or hidden interior. This is signified by the inversion of Whiteread's casts of book shelves and the door. The inside is on the outside. In Holzer's virtual village for the web-site version of *Lustmord*, the doors open onto negative interiors (see Ruf, 1996: 101–02).

Fourthly, Andre's floor pieces have also been described as 'razed sites', by David Bourdon in 1966 (the reference is found in Fer's article), again suggesting crushing, demolishing or levelling something down. He was referring to Andre's *Lever* which the artist himself deliberately referenced to Brancusi's *Endless Column*, itself a First World War Memorial erected in Romania. Andre intended *Lever* to deflate the phallic logic of the *Endless Column* but he had also started to describe his work as a 'cut in space'(Bourdon in Battcock, 1968: 103–4).

The strangest and most difficult response of all to Andre's floor sculptures, however, appeared in a statement by Eva Hesse, a few months before her untimely death at the age of thirty-four, made towards the end of an interview with Cindy Nemser. Nemser asks: 'What do Carl Andre's floors represent to you?' Hesse replies: 'It was the concentration camp. It was those showers where they put on the gas' (Nemser, 1975: 195).[1] Because the interview begins with Hesse's own account of her rather traumatic biography – her pre-war flight from Germany as a Jewish refugee, the suicide of her mother, her own illness with a brain tumour – it has often conditioned the reception of her art so that it is read as the expression of her life, as if her work were the voice of the hysteric (Chave, 1992: 112–3). It has also been used, and perhaps misused, to implicate Andre's work in a rhetoric of power and oppression (Chave, 1992: 107; see Chave, 1990). But what I want to extract from this statement is Hesse's attribution of imagery to the 'razed sites' of Andre's floor pieces. In particular, she invokes two distinct spatial metaphors: one, the camp as extension or field and, secondly, the shower block as obstacle or bunker. But at the same time as figurative references are invoked they also suggest the impossibility of visualising these. Both these forms, extension or field and obstacle or bunker, appear in Holzer's and Whiteread's projects (at one stage Whiteread's monument was going to be sited on a glass platform).

All this might serve as a preface for considering a crisis in monument-making and it would suggest reading such a crisis as one of the conditions of modernism or modernist art. Space became the dominant trope for thinking about architecture in the late nineteenth century but in modernist thinking the spaces of modernity were particularly associated with transparency and mobility. Space, light and transparency stood for rationality and the abolition of dark superstition. Space and light also represented cleanliness, hygiene and the elimination of dirt. In the post-war housing tower block every resident would have his or her quota of sunlight and the dark and unhealthy slum would be abolished. Transparency and space would also open everything to scrutiny, abolishing the distinction between inside and outside, public and private (see Vidler, 1995). Such an understanding of modern space was antithetical to the traditional monument and the association of architecture with public authority. Modernist ideas about space were also set in opposition to the pseudo- and historicist monumentalism of fascist states in the 1930s. Linked to the experience of the Second World War and the Holocaust as incommensurable and unrepresentable, the compulsion nonetheless to mark the occurrence of traumatic events produced a new form for the contemporary monument as a self-effacing object or an antimonument, termed in German the 'Gegen-Denkmal', the countermonument or the monument against itself (see Young, 1993: Chapter I).

An early prototype for this kind of antiphallic or self-effacing monument again appears to be Maya Lin's *Vietnam Veterans War Memorial* 1980–82, designed as two horizontal walls inserted into the ground and meeting to form a V-shape. It is read as a scar or a wound, sometimes as a vagina (Mitchell, 1994: 381). The controversy it generated, and also its popularity, are attributed to its antiheroic form. It is read metaphorically as representing the trauma of the American defeat in Vietnam. And because it seems to embrace its visitors and to embody an invitation to touch, it appears to be opposed to the implacable authority of traditional monuments set on pedestals. Lin's monument is therefore read as a critique both of the Vietnam War and of traditional monumental form. But the monument, by commemorating the 58,000 American dead, commits a massive act of amnesia when set against the estimated three million Vietnamese dead.

Moreover, in an interview given in 1985, Lin said of her monument: 'I wanted to work with the land and not dominate it. I had an impulse to cut open the earth ... an initial violence that in time would heal' (quoted in Abramson 1996: 704). In effect this statement, that the monument first accomplishes an act of violence that is healed in time, reiterates the most basic function of war memorials. All memorials, but particularly war memorials, whatever their form, first embody, literally give body, to the wound sustained by the symbolic order in the act of war precisely in order to make visible that which needs to be healed, if the symbolic order is not itself to be ruptured or torn apart by the violence it has sustained. In other words, war memorials stand for the symbolic death that follows literal death as necessary for the completion of acts of mourning, rather like the funeral lays the body to rest by guaranteeing that the dead live on in the minds of the living (see Žižek, 1991: 23).

If this is the case, then I am suggesting that it is very problematical indeed to produce a monument or a memorial that functions as a critique of the monument. The contemporary preoccupation or obsession with commissioning memorials, particularly Holocaust memorials, at the same time as there is a massive anxiety about how these monuments ought to look, is an enormously paradoxical activity, compelled to attempt to produce a definitive answer to something that is bound never to attain closure. And this is one of the factors involved in the choice of women artists, such as Whiteread and Holzer, to represent a community innocent of complicity in the failed forms of past monuments and therefore capable, it seems, of somehow being able to speak authentically.

The most dramatic version of the monument which simultaneously attempts to critique the monument is the inverted Holocaust memorials or antimonuments produced recently, particularly in Germany. Jochen and Esther Shalev-Gerz's *Monument against Fascism*, 1986–1993, is one example of these. It was covered in soft lead and the public were invited to inscribe their names, defacing its pristine state, as the monument was lowered into the ground over a number of years. It has now disappeared. Monuments like this intend to give form to the idea that the Holocaust is ineffable, incommensurable and impossible to represent. The imagined antithesis that guarantees the antimonument's effects is assumed to be the visibility of conventional memorials which represent a timeless permanence by commemorating the past as a lesson to be transmitted to the future. Such monuments must have an imposing presence and authority, often by reference to classical forms. They are set up in publicly significant spaces, and, by their siting and the use of a pedestal, are set outside the flux of the moment and outside time.

A number of critiques have emerged against the disappearing monument. Rebecca Comay argues that there is 'a certain grandiosity' in these 'self-effacing performances' which tends not only to reinstate 'the prestige and aura of the vanished original' but also suggest a longing for purity, what she calls 'the secret promise of the *tabula rasa*'(1997: 71). Žižek argues that a contemporary Holocaust fixation is a form of the return of the living dead because we have been unable to integrate the trauma of their deaths into our historical memory, to give them a place in the text of tradition, in effect to give them a decent burial (1991: 23). In *Mourning becomes the Law*, Gillian Rose calls this 'Holocaust piety', one which by naming the Holocaust unrepresentable, mystifies it and which conflates 'the search for a decent response to those brutally destroyed' with 'the quite different response needed in the face of the 'inhuman capacity' for such violence. In not being able to complete the project of mourning, the contemporary 'post-modern' age ends up being fixed in melancholia and deprives itself of the capacity for political action (1996: 43 and 36–38).

I want to add my disquiet about these disappearing objects by suggesting two other antitheses or counter examples to these antimonuments rather than the integrated conventional public monument which I am arguing is a fiction. The first of these might be the dismantling of monuments from the Soviet regime, often required as spontaneous acts of iconoclasm in popular uprisings or sometimes construed as vandalism by a Western Press that ignores the complex politics involved in such effacements. But iconoclasm is actually a constant problem for all public monuments. Social upheavals frequently involve the dramatic removal of public monuments which are often subject to injuries and violation as if they are the actual bodies of a people's oppressors and as though they need to be literally killed (see Gamboni, 1997).

In one sense, impermanence, and its corollary, violation or effacement, is the very condition of the public monument. For example, the Cavell monument in St Martin's Place, London, was unveiled in 1920. Buried within it is a hidden cache, a box containing a coin of King George, a drawing of Queen Mary, the story of Cavell's martyrdom and a scroll with the names of all the members of the public who subscribed to the monument. The implication is that the people who put the monument up do not expect it to survive for eternity, because the secret is the treasure hidden on the assumption that it will one day come to light. I would hypothesise that many public monuments contain such secret hordes. In a recent interview about her Judenplatz proposal, Whiteread was asked about the traces of the destroyed synagogue where her memorial was to be sited, and she stated: 'I said I thought they should be carefully excavated ... then we should put straw, sand and soil on top. When my piece was eventually destroyed, whenever that would be, the archaeological remains would still be there' (1997: 30).

The second contrary argument I want to put is that the paradox of monumental form is that its very condition is precisely to be invisible. The poet Robert Musil said: 'There is nothing in this world as invisible as a monument. They are no doubt erected to be seen – indeed to attract attention. But at the same time they are impregnated with something that repels attention' (quoted in Young, 1993: 13). When Whiteread was asked if she would have liked her temporary project, *House* (1993–94), in London's East End, to have remained, she stated: 'I would have liked it to have been there long enough for it to have become invisible. It fought very hard for its dignity, every moment it was there, and it would have been nice if people had just forgotten about it' (1997: 32).

The invisibility of monuments makes clear that they are founded as much on acts of amnesia as on remembrance. What monuments embody is the impossibility of ever making the past present to the present. This absence is the condition of all art-making. One of Jenny Holzer's *Truisms* declares: 'The desire to reproduce is a death wish'. What is never completely invisible in monuments, the thing that conditions the necessity for visible monuments to disappear from consciousness, is the dark secret hidden within, which is the violence on which it is based – such as the violent events it commemorates as well as the violence of the Law or the State – and the violation or the cut into public space it makes.

In part, this is my attempt to make sense of what Eva Hesse might have meant when she said Carl Andre's floor pieces reminded her of the concentration camp. It seems that part of this work's indiscretion is to make visible the violence of which everyone is aware but which had better be kept secret. Moreover, it is clear that public monuments are by and large invisible because they have to be willed back into visibility, for example in the annual rituals of remembrance which take place in Britain at war memorials. Moreover, in shrine making and remembrance, it is women who are often prominent as the figures of mourning. Tearing down monuments in the course of social upheaval, something which seems superficially an absurd activity and hardly a priority in the urgency of the moment, is another example of the necessity to bring back to visibility what the monument obscures, in this case the secret operations of power and the State, precisely in order to abolish it.

I have already remarked on the traditional absence of women as monument makers and the subjects of commemoration, although women are called to be present as appropriately feminine grieving figures. It might seem that the choice of women artists for contemporary commissions is to reinstate the use of weeping women as official mourners in antiquity. In this way we can delegate our most intimate emotions for someone else to perform on our behalf, without sacrificing the sincerity of our feeling (Žižek, 1989: 34–35). But if women's war experiences are to be memorialised or added to an existing taxonomy of war memorials, then what is shocking about Holzer's *Lustmord* project (Figures 20.1 and 20.2) is that it makes public that which is unspeakable – the rape of women in war. Originally commissioned by the *Süddeutsche Zeitung*, Munich, for its Sunday magazine in 1993, the work is about the rape of 30 to 50,000 Muslim, Croatian and Bosnian women by Serbian soldiers in Bosnia-Herzegovina. A version of the project was arranged as a laser projection of the texts onto the Völkerschlachtdenkmal, Leipzig as a temporary installation in 1996. It overwrites the war memorial, which was built in 1913 on the centenary of the Battle of Nations and is peopled with gigantic statues of men in armour (see Bonnet, Grudin and Werner, 1996).

In war, rape by conquering armies is an act that humiliates defeated male populations by demonstrating male impotence to defend the home. In the Bosnian war, rape was part of a strategy of ethnic cleansing, both driving people from their homes out of fear, and also impregnating Muslim women with Serbian children, an act of miscegenation. Physically and psychologically, rape takes place within the body and unlike the wound on the body, persists only as a trace or stain in the memory of an experience, an unspeakable event. Representations of rape nearly always render the victim mute. The aim of rape is 'to shatter the fantasy structure of the individual', or how she organises her identity, and for Muslim women, in particular young Muslim women, rape is a form of symbolic death, one which takes place in advance of the death of the material body (Salecl, 1994:16–17).

Lustmord relates to a genealogy of depictions of rape, but renegotiates that tradition to open up the possibility of testimony. It also extends a sense of solidarity across national boundaries and, at the same time, it does not propose to represent Bosnian women simply as victims. Because not only does Holzer mention the unmentionable, she also gives voices to rape victims, the perpetrators and an observer.

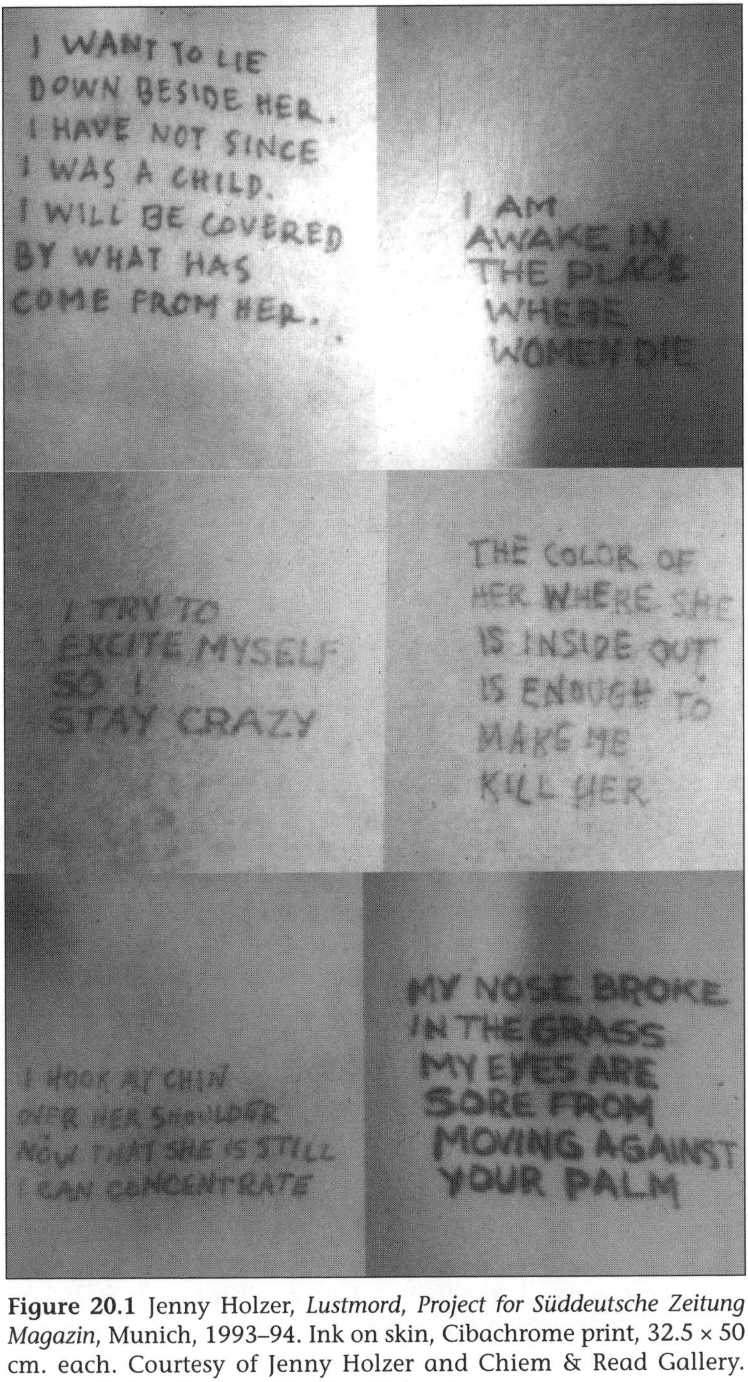

Figure 20.1 Jenny Holzer, *Lustmord, Project for Süddeutsche Zeitung Magazin*, Munich, 1993–94. Ink on skin, Cibachrome print, 32.5 × 50 cm. each. Courtesy of Jenny Holzer and Chiem & Read Gallery. ©Jenny Holzer. Photocredit: Alan Richardson.

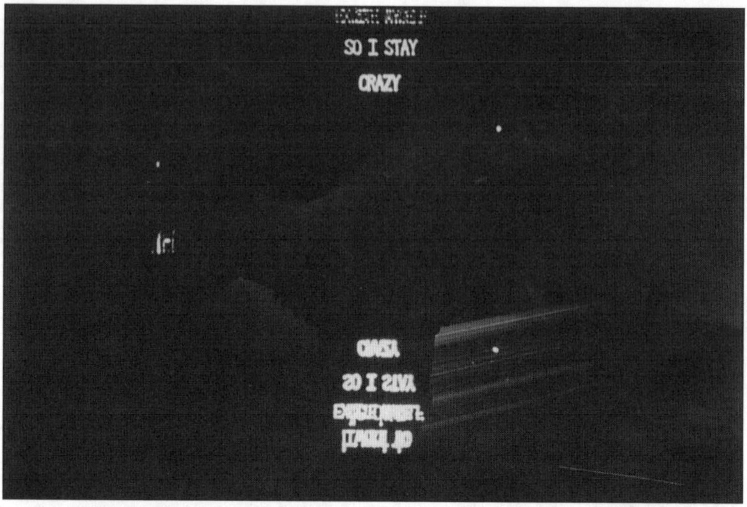

Figure 20.2 Jenny Holzer, *Lustmord, KriegsZustand, Leipzig Monument Project*, 1996, Laser projection. Courtesy of Jenny Holzer and Chiem & Read Gallery. ©Jenny Holzer. Photocredit: Helga Schulze.

For *Süddeutsche Zeitung* in 1993, a card – 'I am awake in the place where women die'– was fixed to the magazine cover. This was printed in ink mixed with the blood of eight German and Yugoslav women volunteers, which had been carefully screened before being used. It caused moral outrage and panic about fears of contamination and pollution, connected with women's bleeding and uncleanliness, and a haemophobia related to AIDS, blood tests, rituals and taboos. One person commented that the protest was greater than the outcry over the rape of Bosnian women (Smolik, 1997: 82). The other texts were written on skin photographed in close-up. These looked as though they were tattooed or like butcher's marks or the concentration camp branding.

In the version installed in the Barbara Gladstone Gallery, New York, in 1994, the words were embossed on leather in an analogy with skin and used to line a wooden framework like a chapel or sanctuary, which was very dimly lit. The installation paralleled the idea of museum display but also the notion of a tabernacle and the interior spaces of women's homes and bodies, so that to enter it is to reinvoke the idea of violation. Some of the texts have also been inscribed on silver bracelets circling human bones, which the viewer has to pick up and touch in order to read them. Holzer says they recall 'reliquaries', 'mass death' and 'women's secrets' (Waldeman, 1996: 25).

The power of *Lustmord* is that it tackles the notion of giving testimony in a way which does not privilege the perspective of any one party to the event, nor does it propose that women's suffering in Bosnia is more authentic or greater than all suffering in war. Dori Laub, writing about Holocaust survivors, refers to the inclination to silence which speakers about trauma prefer

> so as to protect themselves from the fear of being listened to – and of listening to themselves. That while silence is defeat, it serves them both as a sanctuary and as a place of bondage. Silence is for them a fated exile, yet also a home, a destination, and a binding oath. To *not* return from the silence is rule rather than exception.

The act of giving testimony and bearing witness to it, she says, thus 'includes its hearer, who is, so to speak, the blank screen on which the event comes to be inscribed for the first time. By extension, the listener to trauma comes to be a participant and a co-owner of the traumatic event: through his very listening, he comes to partially experience trauma in himself' (Felman and Laub, 1991: 57–8).

It is the witness or observer of the traumatic fact of rape in Bosnia, which I want particularly to discuss. This witness, I argue, also includes the artist and ourselves as the viewers of the *Lustmord* project, a function in which we become conscious of our shifting positions from victim to rapist to observer. Holzer has said that she began the project in order to explain the act to herself and then to other people (Joselit, Simon and Salecl, 1998: 29). Žižek has written about the fundamental fantasy of modern technological warfare, such as the Gulf War, where the reality of blood and death is blocked or suspended, reducing the observer to a pure impassive gaze witnessing a phantasmic scene. But an impassive gaze is not just one of power, the one who organises and dominates the field of vision, but also one of impotence in the position of an immobilised witness who can only look. Infected with guilt at some unspeakable horror, though it is not the gazer's fault, the impotent gaze is also a guilty gaze which in turn fuels a fascination with the victim and fantasy scenarios of rescue. These are then blocked by a split in desire between enjoyment and revulsion. The impotent gaze is powerless to act with respect to the victims of violence it observes (1994: 73–75).

Renata Salecl, who has written extensively about the break-up of Yugoslavia and the Bosnian war, discusses how a successful political discourse is one where we recognise ourselves as the addressee. It does this not by offering us images with which to identify, but by portraying us in the way we would like to appear to ourselves. More subtly, such discourses construct a symbolic space or a point of view from which we would appear likeable to ourselves, seeing ourselves as we imagine we are seen by others (1994: 33). What would it mean if *Lustmord* was a form of political discourse which deliberately set out to construct a symbolic space in which we did not appear likeable to ourselves? Would the implications of this project be that it re-enacts the shattering of the individual fantasy structures by which we make sense of the world and give it and ourselves consistency, something we imagine is experienced by those subjected to war?

But I want to go beyond Laub's invocation of the vicarious experiences of the witness to the testimony of trauma, to suggest that Holzer has refused us the promise of purification through the pleasures of catharsis and is not offering to act as our delegate mourning for the victim. In a work which never pictures the act of rape, the women, the enemy or the observer, it fails to construct a discourse in which we might appear likeable to ourselves. We cannot surrender ourselves to the secret pleasures of the impotent guilty gaze with its fantasies of rescue because the work does not speak the unspeakable with the pseudo-neutrality of an anonymous narrator standing in for us all. Instead the texts of violence are excessive, pornographic, overexposed and written directly onto the body. The shock is that the statement 'I am awake in the place where women die', printed in ink mixed with blood in the magazine, is the voice of the victim, because we ourselves 'are not all awake' to what takes place (Volkart 1997: 116).

Jenny Holzer has been termed an artist who sculpts words, but her words are sometimes so traumatic as to be unreadable. A narrative is promised which never quite coheres into an orderly progression – you are not able to achieve the right sort of distance in a refuge from the violence to which you are exposed.

Rachel Whiteread's proposal for the Judenplatz takes the form of a cast of the interior of a library so that the books appear on the outside (Figure 20.3). But a double inversion takes place, because, instead of the cast of the book-bindings, and a play of embossed and inscribed titles, Whiteread has turned the books and exposed the unopened page edges. The supporting shelf becomes an abyss. There is no promise of the pleasures of reading nor the satisfaction of the right answer to be found in its interior. The inside is all on the outside.

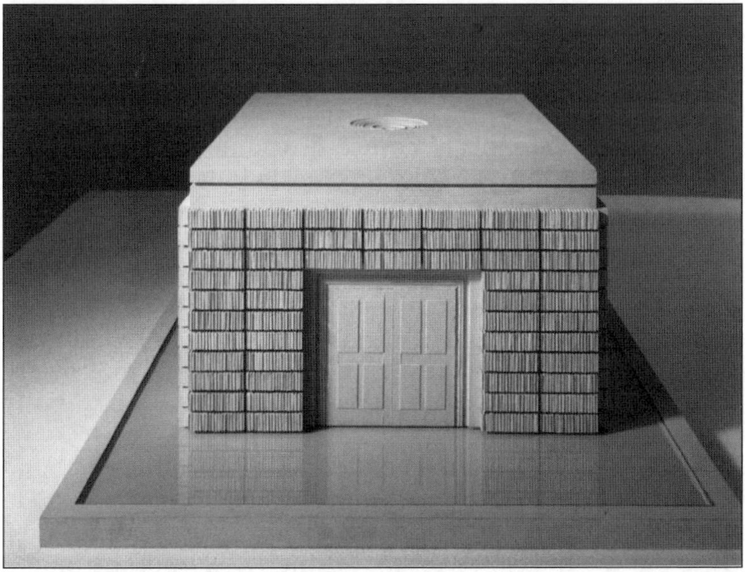

Figure 20.3 Rachel Whiteread, Maquette for *Holocaust Memorial* for the Judenplatz, Vienna, 1995. Mixed media. Courtesy Anthony d'Offay Gallery, London. Photocredit: Mike Bruce.

The inverted cast of the ceiling rose on the Judenplatz monument has been liked to the shower-head of the fake shower blocks that were the death chambers. One of the paradoxes of Whiteread's monument is that this will be invisible to the visitor walking round the memorial but it will have a witness in the site's co-monument, the statue to Gothold Lessing, erected in 1934, melted down by the National Socialists in 1939, reinstalled and eventually moved to the Judenplatz in 1982 (Comay, 1997: 65). Lessing, of course, was the author of *Laocöon* (1766) and a source for Clement Greenberg's 'Towards a Newer Laocöon', published in 1940. One text stands at the threshold of enlightenment, the other at a moment in its breakdown. Both writers attempted to police the boundaries between the verbal and the visual, and insist that visual art surrender to the limitations of its medium.

Whiteread's proposal resembles a bunker and recalls Eva Hesse's imagery of the concentration camp in relationship to Andre's floors. Whiteread's bunker is an inverted and impenetrable house of books which contains no secret interior, merely a void, like the minimalist object which steals something from vision or which refuses access to the secret inner life of the artist because there is nothing there to express. Whiteread's block will be placed on a white concrete plinth with an inlaid stainless steel inscription listing the names of the concentration camps and the simple fact of the more than 65,000 Austrian Jews, killed by the Nazis between 1939 and 1945, who can never be definitively named or counted. The memorial will relate to the traces of a synagogue in Judenplatz destroyed during the pogrom of 1420–21, when the Jews who were still free in the city locked themselves in and committed suicide, while the rabbi set the synagogue on fire. Recent excavations have brought the ashes of the *bimah*, or preacher's pedestal – a place of the word for the people of the book – to light (see Gehrmann and Greber, 1996: 104). After years of controversy and protracted delay, Whiteread's memorial was finally unveiled in October 2000.

Indiscreetly blurring the boundaries between the word and the image, both Holzer and Whiteread nonetheless respond to modernism's call for transparency and space because they have put the hidden secret that is the violence of the monument right on the outside, where everyone can see it.

Notes

1. In another published version of this interview from 1970, Hesse said, 'His metal plates were the concentration camp for me' (Nemser, 1990:196).

Conclusion: Rethinking Culture

Fran Lloyd and Catherine O'Brien

In an age of increasing mobility, whether through travel, migration, voluntary or involuntary exile or the developments of new global communication technologies, it is no longer possible (if ever it was) to conceive of culture as monolithic, as predominately associated with a singular area of activity, a homogeneous grouping of people, a fixed site of a nation or a particular geography. Culture is part of complex active and interactive relationships which are continually negotiated within and across differing spaces, places and sites/sights in a number of different ways. A heightened awareness of the multiplicity of culture, and the multiplicity of cultural identities, has had a profound effect on how we view ourselves and others.

In spite of all that has been written recently about the fragmented and contingent nature of postmodern subjectivity and identity, we locate ourselves and are located, however temporarily, through our particular histories, our cultural identities, and our embodied and often contradictory experiences in the world.

In the wake of the momentous political upheavals of the post Cold War years, this collection of essays opens up connections across centuries and cultures, through to the twenty-first century memorial to the Holocaust in Vienna. This exploration of the secret and the forbidden has shown recurrent themes in hierarchies of control, censorship, sexual power relations, the body politic, exile and death; and intersections – foreseen by the authors or discovered independently by the reader – are revealed in responses that originate in Japan, France, Ireland, England, Holland, Switzerland, Germany, Hungary, Poland, Austria, Bosnia, and on the Finnish/Russian border.

Secret spaces and forbidden places emerge in unexpected fashions and the mapping of these opens up new perspectives on the past and the present. While pointing to the multiple, continuous and discontinuous points of identification and disidentification which are engendered and embodied across the various sites and spaces of culture, they also reveal a central paradox. Visible by the demarcation of boundaries and zones of exclusion and inclusion, the secret and the forbidden continuously cross such boundaries, and are not the special preserve of either side that lays claims to them.

Operating at times as forms of protection or of preservation, they can be both disempowering and empowering, and the site of oppression and liberation. However, asymmetries of positioning exist and the secret and the forbidden are intimately bound up with questions of how we view ourselves and others as embodied subjects, both consciously and unconsciously, our desires and fears and, by extension, the spaces and places we occupy in time and space.

Notes on Contributors

Jorella Andrews is a lecturer in Art History at Goldsmith's College, University of London. She writes on issues of seventeenth-century and contemporary philosophy and visual culture, and is on the editorial board of the journal *Third Text*.

Noëlle Brick is a Principal Lecturer in French at Kingston University. Her research focuses on French sociolinguistics and her published work (with Clarissa Wilks) includes 'Et Dieu nomma la femme' in the *Journal of French Language Studies* and 'Langue non-sexiste et politique éditoriale' in *Modern and Contemporary France*.

Agnès Cardinal is a lecturer in Comparative Literary Studies at the University of Kent at Canterbury. She has written on Robert Walser, Christa Wolf, Irmtraud Morgner, Berta Lask and on women's war literature. She is coeditor of the Oxford anthology: *Women's Writing on the First World War*.

Tivadar Gorilovics is Professor of French Literature at Lajos-Kossuth University, Debrecen. Recent publications include *Recherches sur les origines et les sources de la pensée de Roger Martin du Gard*, and *La Légende de Victor Hugo de Paul Laforgue*. He is currently working on an annotated edition of the unpublished correspondence of Jean-Richard Bloch, *Lettres du régiment (1902–1903)*.

Jean-Jacques Hamm FRSC is Professor at Queen's University, Canada, and Head of Department of French Studies. His main interest is Stendhal, on whom he has published several books and numerous articles.

Valerie Henitiuk is currently a Ph.D. student in Comparative Literature at the University of Alberta, Canada, where she is researching cross-cultural spatial metaphor in women's writing. She holds two MA degrees, one in French Literary Translation and another in Classical Japanese Literature. She is also a certified translator.

Anu Hirsiaho has an MA in Political Science from the University of Jyväskylä and is currently a Ph.D. student in the Minna Canth Academy Project at the University of Tampere, Finland. She has published articles on Irish feminist writing.

Chris Horrocks is a lecturer in Art History at Kingston University and has published extensively on contemporary visual culture, including *Introducing Foucault; Postmodern Encounters, Marshall McLuhan and Virtuality,* and a forthcoming essay on science and cultural relativism in *Between Language and Culture: Crossing the Boundaries.* He is currently researching *Warhol and Performativity.*

Marja Keränen is a reader in political science at the University of Jyväskylä, Finland. She has recently edited *Grammar of the Nation-State* and works in the areas of rhetoric of inquiry, methodological issues, comparative cultural studies, and feminist political research.

Victoria B. Korzeniowska is a French lecturer at the University of Surrey. Her main research interests focus on the works of Jean Giraudoux and women's history in France, particularly the interwar years. Recent publications include 'Le Féminisme de Jean Giraudoux' in *Europe,* and she is the author of *Giraudoux: La Guerre de Troie n'aura pas lieu.*

Suzanne Langlois is an historian and lecturer in Modern European History at McGill University, Montréal, Canada and Université du Québec à Montréal. Recent articles include 'Images that Matter. The French Resistance in Film, 1944–1946' in *French History.*

Fran Lloyd is Head of the School of Art and Design History at Kingston University and has published widely on contemporary visual culture. She is the editor of *Deconstructing Madonna*, *Contemporary Arab Women's Art* and *Displacement and Difference*, and her articles include a forthcoming chapter in F.Carson and C.Pajaczkowska (eds), *Feminist Visual Culture*.

Sue Malvern is lecturer in the History of Art at the University of Reading. She has published extensively on art and war, museums, and feminism, including 'The Muses and the Museum: Maud Sulter's Retelling of the Canon' in Biddiss and Wyke (eds), *The Uses and Abuses of Antiquity*, and 'War, Memory and Museums' in *History Workshop Journal*. She is also a contributor to the *War Zones* exhibition catalogue, Vancouver, 1999–2000.

Xavier Martin is an historian of law and Professor at the Faculty of Law, Economics and Social Sciences at Angers University, France. He has published extensively on the ideology of the French Revolution and on the Code Civil of 1804.

Catherine O'Brien is a lecturer in the School of Languages at Kingston University. Author of *Women's Fictional Responses to the First World War*, her research interests are in the area of comparative literature and gender studies. She is currently completing a book on Marian imagery in French literature and film.

Gordon Phillips is a lecturer in French in the School of Languages at Kingston University. His research interests are in the area of contemporary French politics, society, and masculinities.

Andrea Rinke is a lecturer in German at Kingston University and has published widely on cinema in the former GDR. Recent publications include 'Models or Misfits? The Role of Screen Heroines in GDR Cinema' in M.O'Sickey and I. von Zadow (eds), *Triangulated Visions: Women in Recent German Cinema*, and 'Sex and Subversion in GDR Cinema' in D.Holmes and A. Smith (eds), *100 Years of European Cinema*.

Franciska Skutta lectures on linguistics and narratology in the French Department of Lajos-Kossuth University, Debrecen. Besides her thesis on Marguerite Duras' novels, she has published narratological analyses of novels by Balzac, Sand, Martin du Gard, J.-R. Bloch. Recently she has examined problems of textual coherence/coreference and thematic progression.

Andrew Stephenson teaches in the Art, Design and Film History department at the University of East London. He has published widely on British art of the late nineteenth and twentieth centuries and is co-editor with Amelia Jones of *Performing the Body/Performing the Text*. He is currently working on a study of British Modernism, 1920–40.

Magda Stroińska is an Associate Professor of German and Linguistics at McMaster University in Hamilton, Ontario. She has published on cognitive linguistics, sociolinguistics, stereotypes and the question of language and ideology.

Clarissa Wilks is a Principal Lecturer in French and Applied English Language and Linguistics at Kingston University. Her research interests are in sociolinguistics and in second language vocabulary networks. Publications (with Noëlle Brick) include 'Langue non-sexiste et politique éditoriale' in *Modern and Contemporary France*.

Tony Williams is Professor of French at the University of Hull. He is the author of numerous books and articles on Flaubert and recently edited (with Mary Orr) *New Approaches in Flaubert Studies*. He is at present preparing a survey, *Love and Marriage in Nineteenth-Century France*.

Bibliography

Abramson, D. 1996. 'Maya Lin and the 1960s: Monuments, Time Lines and Minimalism', *Critical Inquiry*, 22, 679–709.

Adams, J.E. 1995. *Dandies and Desert Saints: Styles of Victorian Masculinity*, Ithaca and London: Cornell University Press.

Ades, D. et al. 1995. *Art and Power; Europe under the dictators 1930–45*, London: Hayward Gallery Catalogue.

Alpers, S. 1989. *The Art of Describing: Dutch Art in the Seventeenth Century*, London and New York: Penguin Books.

———. 1997. 'Picturing Dutch Culture', in *Looking at Seventeenth-Century Dutch Art: Realism Reconsidered*, ed. W. Franits, Cambridge, New York, Melbourne: Cambridge University Press, 57–67.

———. 1999. 'De Hooch: A View with a Room', *Art in America*, June, 93–99.

Althorpe Guyton, M. 1988. 'Still Waters', in *Alison Wilding Sculptures 1987/88*, catalogue, London: Karsten Schubert Ltd.

Anderson, B. 1991. *Imagined Communities. Reflections on the Origin and Spread of Nationalism. Revised Edition*, London and New York: Verso.

Anttila, R. 1994. *Laatokan Karjala, Kadotettua kauneutta*, Humppila: KR-kirjat.

Anttonen, P. 1988. *Kilppeenjoki* (Kilppeenjoen entisten asukkaiden kokoamasta aineistosta toimittanut PA), Pieksämäki: Kilppeenjoen kirjatoimikunta.

Apter, E. 1991. *Feminizing the Fetish: Psychoanalysis and Narrative Obsession in Turn-of-the-Century France*, Ithaca: Cornell University Press.

Archives parlementaires 1, 39, 1892: Paris: P. Dupont.

Ardener, S. 1981. 'Ground Rules and Social Maps for Women: an introduction', in *Women and Space: Ground Rules and Social Maps*, ed. S. Ardener, New York: St Martin's Press, 11–34.

Arntzen, S. (trans.). 1997. *The Kagerô Diary*, Ann Arbor: Center for Japanese Studies, The University of Michigan.

Aulard, F.-A. (ed.). 1892. *La Société des Jacobins. Recueil de Documents pour l'histoire du club des Jacobins*, Vol. 4, Paris: Rouast, Noblet, Maison, Quantin.

Ayoub, J. and M. Grenon (eds). 1997. *Procès verbaux du Comité d'Instruction publique de l'Assemblée législative*, Paris-Montreal: l'Harmattan.

Bach, G. 1982. *Homosexualités,* Paris: Edition de Sycamore.

Baillie, K. and T. Salmon. 1993. *Paris. The Rough Guide,* London: The Penguin Group.

Balázs, B. and B. Bartók. 1979. *A kékszakállú herceg vára* [*Le Château de Barbe-Bleue*], Budapest, Zenemükiadó.

Balzac, H. de. 1931. *Mémoires de deux jeunes mariées*, in *Oeuvres complètes. La Comédie humaine*, Paris: L. Conard.

———. 1952. *Autre Étude de femme. La Comédie humaine*, III, Paris: Gallimard.

———. 1958. *Une ténébreuse affaire*, Paris: Gallimard.

———. 1961. *Le Lys dans la vallée*, Paris: Garnier.

Barrès, M. 1922. *Le Jardin de Bérénice*, Paris: Les Cent Bibliophiles.

Bataille, G. 1991. 'The Pineal Eye', in *Visions of Excess: Selected Writings 1927–1939*, Theory and History of Literature, 14, ed. A. Stoekl, Minneapolis: University of Minnesota Press.

Bendix, D.M. 1995. *Diabolical Designs: Paintings, Interiors and Exhibitions of James McNeill Whistler*, Washington and London: Smithsonian Institution Press.

Berg, R. 1997. *Histoire des Juifs à Paris,* Paris: Editions du Cerf.

Besançon, A. 1976. *The Soviet Syndrom*, New York: Harcourt Brace, Jovanowich.

Bettelheim, B. 1978. *The Uses of Enchantment*, Harmondsworth: Penguin.

Betterton, R. 1996. *An Intimate Distance, Women, Artists and the Body,* London: Routledge.

Bogusławski, A. 1994. *Sprawy słowa* ('Word Matters'), Warsaw: VEDA.

Boland, E. 1994. 'Mise Éire', in *Ireland's Women. Writings Past and Present*, eds K. Donovan, A. Norman Jeffares and B. Kennelly, Gill & Macmillan: Dublin, 375–6.

Bonnet, A.-M., Grudin, E.U. and K. Werner. 1996. *KriegsZustand. Völkerschlachtdenkmal, Leipzig*, Leipzig: Leipziger Galerie für Zeitgenössische Kunst.

Borges, J.L. 1972. 'The Aleph', in *A Personal Anthology by Jorge Luís Borges*, London: Picador.

Bourdon, D. 1968. 'The Razed Sites of Carl Andre', in *Minimal Art. A Critical Anthology*, ed. G. Battcock, New York: E.P. Dutton, 103–108.

Bourhis, R. 1982. 'Language policies and language attitudes: le monde de la francophonie', in *Attitudes towards language varia-*

tion: social and applied contexts, eds E. Ryan and H. Giles, London: Edward Arnold, 34–62.

Bouscayrol, R. (ed.). 1979. *Les Lettres de Miette Tailhand-Romme, 1787–1797*, Clermont-Ferrand: unnamed publisher.

Boyer d'Argens. 1992. *Thérèse philosophe*, Arles: Actes Sud-Labor-L'Aire.

Bralczyk, J. 1987. O języku polskiej propagandy lat siedemdziesiatych ('On the language of Polish propaganda in the 1970s'), Uppsalla.

Brownstein, R. 1994. *Becoming a Heroine: Reading about Women in Novels*, New York: Columbia University Press.

Buci-Glucksmann, C. 1987. 'Catastrophic Utopia: The Feminine as an Allegory of the Modern', in *The Making of the Modern Body: Sexuality and Society in the Nineteenth Century*, eds C. Gallagher and T. Laqueur, London: University of California Press.

Bulgakowa, O. 1991. 'Die Rebellion im Rock', in *Außerhalb von Mittendrin*, ed. A. Eckert, Berlin: Neue Gesellschaft für bildende Kunst e.V., 98–102.

Bundy, R. 1991. 'Japan's First Woman Diarist and the Beginnings of Prose Writings by Women in Japan', *Women's Studies*, Vol. 19, 79–97.

Bunreacht na hÉireann (the Irish Constitution), available in html format on the Internet at <http://www.maths.tcd.ie/pub/Constitution> (16 March 1997).

Butler, J. 1990. *Gender Trouble: Feminism and the Subversion of Identity*, London and New York: Routledge.

Byg, B. 1991. 'Parameters for institutional and thematic integration of filmmakers from the former GDR', in *What Remains? East German Culture and the Postwar Public*, ed. M. Silberman, (AICGS Report, 5), 64–74.

Cabanis. 1980. *Rapports du Physique et du Moral de l'Homme*, Paris-Geneva: Slatkine.

Callan, A. 1989. 'Sexual Division of Labour in the Arts and Crafts Movement', in *A View from the Interior: Feminism, Women and Design*, eds J. Attfield and P. Kirkham, London: The Women's Press.

Cameron, D. 1997. 'Demythologizing sociolinguistics', in *Sociolinguistics: a reader and coursebook*, eds N. Coupland and A. Jaworski, London: Macmillan, 55–67.

Cardinal, R. 1972. *Outsider Art*, London: Studio Vista.

Carson, F. 2000. 'Resculpting the Female Body', in *Feminist Visual Culture*, eds F. Carson and C. Pajaczkowska, Edinburgh: Edinburgh University Press.

Casteras, S.P. and C. Denney (eds). 1996. *The Grosvenor Gallery: A Palace of Art in Victorian England*, New Haven and London: Yale University Press.

Charrière, Mme de. 1981. *Oeuvres complètes 3*, Van Oorschot/Slatkine: Amsterdam/Geneva.

Chateaubriand. 1968. *Mémoires d'Outre-Tombe* 1, Lausanne: Rencontre.

———. 1978. *Essai sur les Révolutions*, Paris: Gallimard.

Chave, A.C. 1990. 'Minimalism and the rhetoric of power', *Arts Magazine*, 64 (January), 44–63.

———. 1992. 'Eva Hesse: A *"Girl Being a Sculpture"*', in *Eva Hesse: a Retrospective*, ed. H.A. Cooper, New Haven: Yale University Art Gallery, 99–117.

Cheal, D. 1991. *Family and the State of Theory*, New York: Harvester.

Cherry, D. 1993. *Painting Women: Victorian Women Artists*, London and New York: Routledge.

Chevalier, J. and A. Gheerbrant. 1982. *Dictionnaire des symboles*, Paris: Robert Laffont.

Chomsky, N. 1989. *Necessary Illusions: Thought Control in Democratic Societies*, Montreal: CBC Enterprises.

Christiansen, R. 1994. *Paris Babylon: the Story of the Paris Commune*, New York: Viking/ Penguin Group.

Coats, B.A. 1993. 'Buildings and Gardens in *The Tale of Genji*', in *Approaches to teaching Murasaki Shikibu's The Tale of Genji*, ed. E. Kamens, New York: Modern Language Association of America, 52–9.

Cocteau, J. 1965. *Les Enfants terribles*, Paris: Livre de Poche.

Comay, R. 1997. 'Memory block: Rachel Whiteread's proposal for a Holocaust Memorial in Vienna', *Art & Design*, 12 (July/August), 64–75.

Connolly, C. 1993. 'Culture or Citizenship? Notes from the *Gender and Colonialism* Conference, Galway, Ireland, May 1992', *Feminist Review*, 44.

Cooke, L. 1985. 'Alison Wilding', in *Alison Wilding*, Serpentine Gallery, London: Arts Council of Great Britain.

Copley, A. 1992. *Sexual Moralities in France 1780–1980*, London: Routledge.

Copley, W. 1969. 'The New Piece', *Art in America*, June/July.

Coxhead, E. 1965. *Daughters of Erin*, Gerard's Cross: Colin Smythe.

Crary, J. 1996. *Techniques of the Observer: On Vision and Modernity in the Nineteenth Century*, Cambridge, Mass.: MIT Press.

Crichton, F. 1980. *Eight Artists: Women: 1980*, London: Acme Gallery.

———. 1983a. 'When form engenders attitude', in *The Sculpture Show, Fifty Sculptors at the Serpentine and the South Bank*, London: Arts Council of Great Britain.

———. 1983b. *Guide to The Sculpture Show, 13 August – 9 October 1983, Fifty Sculptors at the Serpentine and the South Bank*, London: Arts Council of Great Britain.

Curtis, P. 1996. 'What is Left Unsaid', in *Barbara Hepworth Reconsidered*, ed. D. Thistlewood, Liverpool: Liverpool University Press and Tate Gallery Liverpool.

Dauzat, A., J. Dubois and H. Mitterand. 1973. *Nouveau Dictionnaire étymologique et historique*, Paris: Larousse.

Dellamora, R. 1990. *Masculine Desire: The Sexual Politics of Victorian Aestheticism*, Chapel Hill, NC: University of North Carolina Press.

Diderot. 1962. *Correspondance* 7: Paris: Minuit.
Didier, B. 1983. *Stendhal autobiographe*, Paris: PUF.
Dulwich Picture Gallery. 1992. *Palaces of Art: Art Galleries in Britain 1790–1990*, London: Lund Humphries.
Eleb-Vidal, M. and A. Debarre-Blanchard. 1989. *Architectures de la vie privée*, Brussels: Archives d'architecture moderne.
Ellmann, R. 1988. *Oscar Wilde*, London: Penguin.
Enloe, C. 1989. *Bananas, Beaches and Bases. Making Feminist Sense of International Politics*, Berkeley and Los Angeles: University of California Press.
Felman, S. and D. Laub. 1991. *Testimony: crises of witnessing in literature, psychoanalysis and history*, New York and London: Routledge.
Felski, R. 1995. *The Gender of Modernity*, Cambridge, Mass.: Harvard University Press.
Fer, B. 1997. 'Treading Blindly, or the Excessive Presence of the Object', *Art History*, 20 (June), 268–88.
Field, N. 1987. *The Splendor of Longing in the* Tale of Genji, Princeton: Princeton University Press.
Flaubert, G. 1971. *Madame Bovary*, Paris: Garnier.
———. 1984. *L'Éducation sentimentale*, Paris: Garnier.
Florence, P. 1996. 'Barbara Hepworth: the Odd Man Out? Preliminary Thoughts about a Public Artist', in *Barbara Hepworth Reconsidered*, ed. D. Thistlewood, Liverpool: Liverpool University Press and Tate Gallery Liverpool.
Fontana, A. (ed. and trans.). 1997. *Venise et la Révolution française. Les 470 dépêches des ambassadeurs de Venise au Doge*, Paris: Furlan, Saro, Laffont.
Forsberg, T. 1995. 'Karelia', in *Contested Territory. Border Disputes at the Edge of the Former Soviet Empire*, ed. T. Forsberg, Aldershot: Edward Elgar, 202–223.
Foucault, M. 1986. 'Of Other Spaces', in *Diacritics*, Spring, 22–25.
France, A. 1930. *Les Sept femmes de la Barbe-Bleue d'après des documents authentiques*, in *Oeuvres complètes illustrées 19*, Paris: Calmann-Lévy.
Franits, W. 1993. *Paragons of Virtue: Women in Seventeenth-Century Dutch Art*, Cambridge: Cambridge University Press.
——— (ed.). 1997. *Looking at Seventeenth-Century Dutch Art: Realism Reconsidered*, Cambridge, New York, Melbourne: Cambridge University Press.
Fray-Fournier, A. 1903. *Le Club des Jacobins de Limoges (1790–1795), d'après ses délibérations, sa correspondance et ses journaux*, Limoges: H.-C. Lavauzelle.
Freedberg, D. and J. de Vries (eds). 1991. *Art in History/History in Art: Studies in Seventeenth-Century Dutch Culture*, Santa Monica: Getty Center for the History of Art and the Humanities.
Fried, M. 1995. 'Art and Objecthood', in *Minimal Art*, ed. G. Battcock, Berkeley and Los Angeles: University of California Press.
Fromm, E. 1997. *The Fear of Freedom*, London and New York: Routledge.

Galland, A. (trans.). 1965. *Les Mille et une nuits* [The Thousand and One Nights] I–III, Paris: Garnier-Flammarion.
Gamboni, D. 1997. *The Destruction of Art. Iconoclasm and Vandalism since the French Revolution*, London: Reaktion.
'Gays on the Continental March', *The Economist*, 5 July 1997, 36.
Gehrmann, L. and M. Greber (eds). 1996. *Judenplatz Wien 1996. Wettbewerb Mahnmal und Gedenkstätte für die jüdischen Opfer des Naziregimes in Österreich 1938–1945*, Vienna: Stadt Wien, Kunsthalle Wien.
Gellner, E. 1994. *Encounters with Nationalism*, Oxford: Blackwell Publishers.
Genette, G. 1969. *Figures II*, Paris: Seuil.
Gilbert, S.M. and S. Gubar. 1979. *Madwoman in the Attic: The Woman Writer and the Nineteenth-Century Imagination*, New Haven: Yale University Press.
Gildea, R. 1994. *The Past in French History*, New Haven: Yale University Press.
Gillett, P. 1996. 'Art Audiences at the Grosvenor Gallery', in *The Grosvenor Gallery: A Palace of Art in Victorian England*, eds S.P. Casteras and C. Denney, New Haven and London: Yale University Press.
Giraudoux, J. 1990. *Oeuvres romanesques complètes*, I, Paris: Gallimard.
———. 1994. *Oeuvres romanesques complètes*, II, Paris: Gallimard.
Głowiński, M. 1990. *Nowomowa po polsku* ('Polish Newspeak'), Warsaw: PEN.
Golomstock, I. 1990. *Totalitarian Art in the Soviet Union, the Third Reich, Fascist Italy and the People's Republic of China*, New York: Icon Editions.
Gouhier, H. 1970. *Maine de Biran par lui-même*, Paris: Seuil.
Grandière, M. 1998. *L'Idéal pédagogique et France au dix-huitième siècle*, Oxford: Voltaire Foundation.
Green, M. 1995. *Celtic Goddesses*, London: British Museum Press.
Gresty, H. 1993. 'Bare', in *Bare: Alison Wilding Sculptures, 1982–1993*, Newlyn Art Gallery, Arts Council of Great Britain.
Guenier, N. et al. 1983. 'Les français devant la norme', in *La norme linguistique*, eds E. Bédard and J. Maurais, Québec: Conseil de la langue française, 763–787.
Gusdorf, G. 1969. *La Révolution galiléenne, Les Sciences humaines et la Pensée occidentale* 3, Paris: Payot.
———. 1973. *L'Avènement des Sciences humaines au Siècle des Lumières, Les Sciences humaines et la Pensée occidentale* 6, Paris: Payot.
———. 1976. *Naissance de la conscience romantique au Siècle des Lumières, Les Sciences humaines et la Pensée occidentale* 7, Paris: Payot.
———. 1982. *Fondements du Savoir romantique, Les Sciences humaines et la Pensée occidentale* 9, Paris: Payot.

———. 1984. *L'Homme romantique, Les Sciences humaines et la Pensée occidentale* 11, Paris: Payot.

Haataja, L. and M. Lintunen. 1990. *Karjala-Nostalgia*, Helsinki: WSOY.

Häkli, J. 1996. 'Borders in the Political Geography of Knowledge', in *The Dividing Line. Borders and National Peripheries*, eds L.-F. Landgren and M. Häyrynen, University of Helsinki, Renvall Institute, Publications Nr 9: 9–16.

Haltia, M. 1998a. *Venäläisten käsityksia Karjalasta*, University of Helsinki, Renvall Institute.

———. 1998b. 'Karjalan historiasta kerrotaan nykyasukkaille heidän omalla kielellään', *Karjala*, 7 May 1998.

Hämynen, T. 1994. 'Mikä Karjala?', in *Kahden Karjalan välillä, kahden riikin rintamalla*, eds A. Heikkinen, T. Hämynen and H. Sihvo, Joensuu: University of Joensuu, Studia Carelica Humanistica.

Heikkinen, K. 1989. *Karjalaisuus ja etninen itsetajunta*, Joensuu: University of Joensuu.

———. 1996. 'Suomen karjalaisten identiteetti ja sen alueellinen konteksti', in *Näkökulmia karjalaiseen perinteeseen*, ed. P. Hakamies, Helsinki: Suomalaisen Kirjallisuuden Seura, 13–35.

———. 1998. 'Paikan topografiaa. Paikka fyysisenä ja paikka merkityksinä', *Informaatio* 2, 1988, 86: 4–7.

Helvétius. 1988. *De l'Esprit*, Paris: Fayard.

———. 1989a & b. *De l'Homme* 1 & 2, Paris: Fayard.

Henttonen, A. 1985. *Muistojen kultainen Karjala*, Jyväskylä: Gummerus.

Herman, E. 1992. *Beyond Hypocrisy: Decoding News in the Age of Propaganda*, Boston: South End Press.

Heron, L. 1993. *Streets of Desire: Women's Fictions of the Twentieth Century*, London: Virago.

Hobsbawm, E. 1994. *Nationalismi*, Tampere: Vastapaino.

Hochmuth, D. (ed.). 1993. *DEFA NOVA – nach wie vor? Versuch einer Spurensicherung*. Berlin: Medienzentrum Treptower Park.

d'Holbach. 1990. *Système de la Nature* 1, Paris: Fayard.

Holland-Moritz, R. 1982. 'Eulenspiegel', *Kino-Eule*, 27 August.

Holmes, J. 1992. *An Introduction to Sociolinguistics*, London and New York: Longman.

Houdebine, A.-M. 1987. 'Le français au féminin', *La linguistique*, 23 (1), 13–34.

Hughes, A. 1996. 'The City and the Female Autograph', in *Parisian Fields*, ed. M. Sheringham, London: Reaktion, 115–32.

Hume, D. 1788. 'Enquiry into Human Understanding', in *Essays and Treatises on Several Subjects 2*, London: Cadell, Elliott & Kay.

Huysmans, J.-K. 1961. *Là-bas*, Paris: Plon.

Image et son. 1961. October, No. 144.

Innes, C.L. 1993. *Woman and Nation in Irish Literature and Society 1880–1935*, London: Harvester Wheatsheaf.

Jaatinen, M. 1997. *Karjalan kartat*, Helsinki: Tammi/Karjalan Liitto.

Jacobus, Mary et al. (eds). 1990. *Body/Politics, Women and the Discourse of Science*, London and New York: Routledge.
Jay, M. 1993. *Downcast Eyes: The Denigration of Vision in Twentieth-Century French Thought*, Berkeley: University of California Press.
Johnson, D. 1989. 'Next to Nothing: Uses of the Otherworld in Modern Irish Literature', in *New Irish Writing*, eds J.D. Brophy and E. Grennan, Boston: Iona College Press.
Jones, A. 1994. *Postmodernism and the En-Gendering of Marcel Duchamp*, New York, Cambridge: Cambridge University Press.
——— (ed.). 1996. *Sexual Politics: Judy Chicago's Dinner Party in Feminist Art History*, California: University of California Press.
———. 1998. *Body Art/Performing the Subject*, Minneapolis and London: University of Minnesota Press.
Jongh, E. de. 1991. 'Some Notes on Interpretation', in *Art in History/History in Art: Studies in Seventeenth-Century Dutch Culture*, eds D. Freedberg and J. de Vries, Santa Monica, 119–136.
———. 1995. *Kwesties van betekenis: Thema en motief in de Nederlandse schilderkunst van de zeventiende eeuw*, Leiden: Primavera Pers.
Joselit, D., J. Simon and R. Salecl. 1998. *Jenny Holzer*, London: Phaidon.
Judd, D. 1975. *Complete Writings, 1959–1975*, Halifax, N.S.: Press of the Nova Scotia College of Art and Design.
Kemppinen, H. (ed.). 1992. *Karjala, Matkaajan aakkoset*. Helsinki: Orient Express.
Kirkinen, H. 1976. *Karjala taistelukenttänä, Karjala idän ja lännen välissä II*, Helsinki: Kirjayhtymä.
Kiuru, P. 1981. *Ihmisiä Laatokan maisemissa*, Lohja: Karas-Sana.
Klemperer, V. 1947. *Lingua Tertii Imperii*, Berlin: Aufbau Verlag.
———. 1995. *Ich will Zeugnis ablegen bis zum letzten: Tagebücher 1933–1945*, Berlin: Aufbau Verlag.
Kortelainen, J. 1997. 'Crossing the Russian Border: Regional Development and Cross-Border Cooperation in Karelia', in Publication Nr 3. (TMR Course Report), Joensuu: University of Joensuu, Department of Geography.
Korzeniowska, V.B. 1999. 'L'Espace féminin dans *Choix des élues*', in *Et Giraudoux rêva la femme*, eds S. Coyault and C. Hallak, Clermont-Ferrand: Centre de Recherches sur les Littératures Modernes et Contemporaines, 207–15.
Kotitie, K. 1995. *'Hypihän ettet ala juurtumaan'*, Helsinki: University of Helsinki, Department of Folklore.
Krauss, R.E. 1977. *Passages in Modern Sculpture*, London: Thames and Hudson.
———. 1979. 'Sculpture in the Expanded Field', in *October*, 8, Spring.
———. 1993. *The Optical Unconscious*, Cambridge, Mass., London: MIT Press.
Kroó, G. 1962. *Bartók Béla szinpadi müvei* [Dramatic works of Béla Bartók], Budapest: Zenemükiadó.

Lacan, J. 1998. *The Four Fundamental Concepts of Psychoanalysis*, trans. A. Sheridan, London: Vintage.
Lakoff, R.T. 1990. *Talking Power*, New York: Basic Books.
Ledger, S. and S. McCracken (eds). 1995. *Cultural Politics at the Fin-de-Siècle*, Cambridge: Cambridge University Press.
Lee, J.J. 1989. *Ireland 1912–1985. Politics and Society*, Cambridge: Cambridge University Press.
Leiris, M. 1946. *L'Âge d'homme*, Paris: Gallimard.
de Ligne, Prince. 1989. *Mémoires, lettres et pensées*, Paris: F. Bourin.
Lilienthal, P. 1971. *Jakob von Gunten* (film).
Lindberg, D.C. 1976. *Theories of Vision from Al-Kindi to Kepler*, Chicago and London: University of Chicago Press.
Lindeperg, S. 1993. 'Images de la Seconde Guerre mondiale dans le cinéma français (1944–1969). Les usages cinématographiques du passé', Ph.D. diss., Institut d'Études politiques de Paris.
———. 1997. *Les Écrans de l'ombre. La Seconde Guerre mondiale dans le cinéma français (1944–1969)*, Paris: CNRS.
Lindström, J. 1979. *Karjala tänään*, Porvoo: WSOY.
Lippard, L. 1976. *Eva Hesse*, New York.
Lodge, A. 1993. *French: from dialect to standard*, London and New York: Routledge.
Lokin, D.H.A.C. 1996. 'Views in and of Delft 1650–1675', in *Delft Masters, Vermeer's Contemporaries: Illusionism through the Conquest of Light and Space*, Zwolle and Stedelijk Museum Het Prinsenhof, Delft: Waanders Publishers, 87–128.
Lyotard, J.-F. 1990. *Duchamp's TRANS/formers*, California: Lapis Press.
Mably. 1792. *De la Législation ou Principes des Loix*, in *Oeuvres complètes* 9, Lyon: Delamollière.
Maeterlinck, M. 1901. *Ariane et Barbe-Bleue ou la délivrance inutile*, in *Théâtre III*, Brussels: P. Lacomblez, Paris: Per Lamm.
Maine de Biran. 1955. *Journal II*, in *Etre et Penser. Cahiers de Philosophie* 42.
———. 1957. *Journal III, Agendas, Carnets et Notes*, in *Etre et Penser. Cahiers de Philosophie* 43.
Manigand, C. and I. Veyrat-Masson. 1982. 'Quelle Allemagne? Pour quels Français?', in *Télévision, nouvelle mémoire. Les magazines de grand reportage 1959–1968*, eds J.-N. Jeanneney and M. Sauvage, Paris: Seuil.
Marsh, J. 1998. 'Women and Art 1850–1900', in *Pre-Raphaelite Women Artists*, J. Marsh and P.Gerrish Nunn, Manchester: Manchester City Art Galleries.
Martel, F. 1996. *Le Rose et le Noir*, Paris: Editions Seuil.
Martin, X. 1993. 'Liberté, Egalité, Fraternité. Inventaire sommaire de l'idéal révolutionnaire français', in *Himeji International Forum of Law and Politics* 1: 3–25; 1991. N. Kanayama (Japanese trans.), in *Himeji Law Review* 8: 141–154; 1995. R. Isotton (Italian trans.), in *Rivista Internazionale dei Diritti dell'Uomo* 3: 586–605; 1999. P. A. Saenz (Spanish trans.), in *Gladius* 44: 85–102.

———. 1994. *Nature humaine et Révolution française. Du Siècle des Lumières au Code Napoléon*, Bouère, DMM/Forthcoming: *Human Nature and the French Revolution*, trans. P. Corcoran, Oxford: Berghahn.
Matsumura Sei'ichi, Kimura Masanori, and Imuta Tsunehisa (eds). 1973. *Tosa nikki Kagerô nikki*. Vol. 9 of *Nihon koten bungaku zenshû*, Tokyo: Shôgakkan.
Maupertius. 1752. *Lettre sur le Progrès des Sciences*, no place.
McCafferty, N. 1986. 'IRELAND(S): Coping with the Womb and the Border', in *Sisterhood is Powerful*, ed. R. Morgan, New York: Anchor Press, 347–352.
McCullough, H.C. 1990. *Classical Japanese Prose: An Anthology*, Stanford: Stanford University Press.
McEwan, J. 1983. 'Alison Wilding: The Stuff of Metaphor', in *Transformations: New Sculpture from Britain, XV11 Bienal de São Paulo 1983*, London: British Council.
Medbh, M. 1993. 'Easter 1991', *Feminist Review*, 44, 58–60.
Meehan, P. 1990. 'Don't Speak To Me of Martyrs', in *Wildish Things*, ed. A. Smyth, Attic Press: Dublin, 74–75.
Mercier, L.-S. 1994a & b. *Tableau de Paris* 1 & 2, Paris: Mercure de France.
Merleau-Ponty, M. 1962. *Phenomenology of Perception*, trans. C. Smith, London: Routledge & Kegan Paul.
———. 1964. *The Primacy of Perception and Other Essays*, Evenston, Illinois: Northwestern University Press.
Merrick, J. and B. Ragan. 1996. *Homosexuality in Modern France*, New York: OUP.
La Mettrie. 1975. *Discours sur le bonheur*, Banbury: J. Falvey, Voltaire Foundation.
Michalski, S. 1993. *The Reformation and the Visual Arts*, London: Routledge.
Michnik, A. 1991. *Z dziejów honoru w Polsce* ('From the history of honour in Poland'), Warsaw: Nowa.
Miller, N.K. 1988. 'Writing from the Pavilion: George Sand and the Novel of Female Pastoral', in *Subject to Change: Reading Feminist Writing*, New York: Columbia UP.
Mills, L. 1995. '"I Won't Go Back To It". Irish Women Poets and the Iconic Feminine', *Feminist Review*, 50, 69–88.
Mitchell, W.J.T. 1994. *Picture Theory: essays on verbal and visual representation*, Chicago: University of Chicago Press.
Miyake, L.K. 1989. 'Woman's Voice in Japanese Literature: Expanding the Feminine', *Women's Studies*, Vol. 17, 87–100.
Moniteur 203a, 2 Germinal, Year VII.
Moniteur 203b, 3 Nivôse, Year III, 23 December 1794.
Montesquieu. 1941: *Cahiers, 1716–1765*, Paris: Grasset.
Morley, D. and K. Robins. 1993. 'No Place Like Heimat: Images of Home(land) in European Culture', in *Space and Place, Theories of*

Identity and Location, eds E. Carter, D. James and J. Squires, London: Lawrence & Wishart.

Morris, I. 1985. *The World of the Shining Prince*, London: Penguin Books.

Mossman, C. 1993. *Politics and Narratives of Birth: Gynocolonization from Rousseau to Zola*, Cambridge: Cambridge University Press.

Nash, C. 1993. 'Remapping and Renaming: New Cartographies of Identity, Gender and Landscape in Ireland', *Feminist Review*, no.44, 39–57.

Nava, M. 1996. 'Modernity's Disavowal. Women, the city and the department store', in *Modern Times: Reflections on a Century of English Modernity*, eds M. Nava and A. O'Shea, London and New York: Routledge.

Neff, T.A. (ed.). 1987. *A Quiet Revolution, British Sculpture Since 1965*, London: Thames and Hudson.

Nemser, C. 1975. *Art Talk. Conversations with 15 Women Artists*, New York: Harper Collins.

———. 1990. 'An Interview with Eva Hesse' (May 1970), in *The New Sculpture, 1965–1975: between geometry and gesture*, eds R. Armstrong and R. Marshall, New York: Whitney Museum of American Art, 196–198.

Nesbit, M. 1993. 'Marcel Duchamp: *Etant donnés*', *Art Forum*, September.

Newall, C. 1995. *The Grosvenor Gallery Exhibitions: Changes and Continuity in the Victorian Art World*, Cambridge: Cambridge University Press.

Newman, M. 1982. 'New Sculpture in Britain', *Art in America*, September 1982, 104–179.

———. 1983. *Figures and Objects: Recent Developments in British Sculpture*, catalogue, John Hansard Gallery, University of Southampton: Southampton.

Nicolaïdis, D. (ed.). 1994. *Oublier nos crimes. L'amnésie nationale, une spécificité française?*, Paris: Autrement.

Nieminen, M. 1988. 'Vuokkiniemi ennen ja nyt, Kulttuurimatkailua Seesjärven Karjalaan' (articles published in *Kaleva*, July 1988).

Nochlin, L. 1971. 'Why Have there Been No Great Women Artists?' in *Art and Sexual Politics*, eds E. Baker and T. Hess, New York: Collier Books.

Nunn, P. Gerrish. 1987. *Victorian Women Artists*, London: Women's Press.

Ó hÓgaín, D. 1986. *The Hero in Irish Folk History*, Dublin: Gill & Macmillan.

Orłoś, K. 1973. *Cudowna melina*, Paris: Instytut Literacki.

———. 1985. *Przechowalnia*, London: Puls.

———. 1990. *Historia 'Cudownej meliny'; Cudowna melina*, Białystok: Versus.

———. 1998. 'Zgoda na kłamstwo' ('Consent to lies'), in a Warsaw newspaper *Zycie*, 24 July 1998, 14.

Orwell, G. 1946. 'Politics and the English language', reprinted in *Marxism and Art: Writings in Aesthetics and Criticism*, eds B. Lang and F. Williams, 1972, New York: David McKay Company.

———. 1949. *Nineteen Eighty-Four*, Martin Secker & Warburg.

Ozouf, M. 1984. *L'Ecole de la France. Essais sur la Révolution, l'Utopie et l'Enseignement*, Paris: Gallimard.

———. 1989. *L'Homme régénéré. Essais sur la Révolution française*, Paris: Gallimard.

Paasi, A. 1996. *Territories, Boundaries and Consciousness. The Changing Geographies of the Finnish–Russian Border*, Chichester: John Wiley.

Parker, R. and G. Pollock (eds). 1981. *Old Mistresses: Women, Art and Ideology*, London: Pandora.

——— (eds). 1987. *Framing Feminism: Art and the Women's Movement 1970–1985*, London: Pandora.

Paz, O. 1990. *Marcel Duchamp: Appearance Stripped Bare*, New York: Arcade.

Peel, E. 1993. 'Mediation and Mediators: Letters, Screens, and Other Go-Betweens in *The Tale of Genji*', in *Approaches to Teaching Murasaki Shikibu's* The Tale of Genji, ed. E. Kamens, New York: Modern Language Association of America, 108–14.

Perrault, C. 1981. *Contes*, Paris: Gallimard.

Phelan, P. 1993. *Unmarked: The Politics of Performance*, London and New York: Routledge.

———. 1997. *Mourning Sex: Performing Public Memories*, London and New York: Routledge.

Philippe, B. 1992. *Les Juifs à la Belle Epoque*, Paris: Editions Albin Michel.

Pollock, G. 1988. *Vision and Difference: Femininity, Feminism and the Histories of Art*, London and New York, Routledge.

———. 1998. 'Inscriptions in the Feminine', in *Inside The Visible, an elliptical traverse of 20th century art*, ed. M.C. de Zegher, London: MIT Press.

Portalis. 1834. *De l'Usage et de l'Abus de l'Esprit philosophique durant le dix-huitième siècle* 2, Paris: Moutardier.

Quay, T. and S. 1995. *Institute Benjamenta* (film).

Rabine, L. 1976. George Sand and the Myth of Femininity', *Women and Literature*, 4, 2–17.

Rancken, A.W. and K. Pirinen. 1949. *Suomen vaakunat ja kaupunginsinetit*, Porvoo: Werner Söderstöm Osakeyhtiö.

Ranum, O. 1968. *Paris in the Age of Absolutism*, New York: Wiley & Sons.

Rey, A. (ed.). 1998. *Dictionnaire historique de la langue française*, Paris: Robert.

Rhodes, C. 2000. *Outsider Art: Spontaneous Alternatives*, London: Thames & Hudson.

Rich, A. 1986. *Blood, Bread, Poetry. Selected Prose 1979–1985*, New York and London: W.W. Norton.

Ripatti, A.-K. 1985. 'Kävin Kalevalan mailla' (a series of articles published in *Kaleva*).

Rivarol. 1988. 'Lettre à M. Necker sur son livre De l'importance des opinions religieuses', in *Rivarol. Les plus belles pages*, no place: Mercure de France.

Robinson, H. (ed.). 1987. *Visibly Female: Feminism and Art Today*, London: Camden Press.

Ronchi, V. 1970. *The Nature of Light: An Historical Survey*, trans. V. Barocas, London: Heinemann.

Rose, G. 1996. *Mourning Becomes the Law. Philosophy and Representation*, Cambridge: Cambridge University Press.

Rosset, C. 1977. *Le Réel Traité de l'idiotie*, Paris: Minuit.

Rousseau, J.-J. 1966. *Emile ou de l'Education*, Paris: Flammarion.

———. 1969. *Correspondance complète* 10, Geneva/Madison: Institut et Musée Voltaire/University of Wisconsin Press.

———. 1979. *Discours sur l'Economie politique*, in *Oeuvres complètes* 3, Paris: Gallimard.

———. 1980 & 1981. *Correspondance complète* 37 & 38, Oxford: Voltaire Foundation.

———. 1991. *Confessions*, in *Oeuvres complètes* 1, Paris: Gallimard.

Ruf, B. 1997. *Jenny Holzer: Lustmord*, Warth: Kunstmuseum des Kantons Thurgau.

Saarelainen, P. 1994. *Karjalan tutkimus tänään*, Joensuu: University of Joensuu, Institute for Research on Rural Areas.

Sade. 1969. *Les Prospérités du vice*, Paris: Union Générale d'Editions, 10/18.

Salecl, R. 1994. *The Spoils of Freedom. Psychoanalysis and Feminism after the Fall of Socialism*, London: Routledge.

Sallinen-Gimpl, P. 1989. 'Karjalainen kulttuuri-identiteetti', in *Kansa kuvastimessa*, eds T. Korhonen and M. Räsänen, Helsinki: Suomalaisen Kirjallisuuden Seura, 209–226.

———. 1993. 'Karjalaisuus suomalaisuuden osana', in *Mitä on suomalaisuus*, ed. T. Korhonen, Helsinki: Suomen Antropologinen Seura, 135–160.

Sand, G. 1984. *Indiana*, Paris: Gallimard.

———. 1988. *Valentine*, Meylan: Les Éditions de l'Aurore.

Sapir, E. 1949. *Culture, Language and Personality*, Berkeley: University of California Press.

Schama, S. 1980. 'Wives and Wantons: Versions of Womanhood in Seventeenth Century Dutch Art', *The Oxford Art Journal*, 1 (1), April, 5–13.

———. 1991. *The Embarrassment of Riches*, London: Fontana Press.

Schepen, R.K. van. 1992. 'Duchamp as Pervert', *Art Criticism* 7/Part 2, 22.

Schieber, E. 1994. 'Anfang vom Ende oder Kontinuität des Argwohns 1980–1989', in *Das zweite Leben der Filmstadt Babelsberg 1946–92*, ed. R. Schenk, Berlin: Henschelverlag, 265–327.

Schmidt, E. 1982. 'Das Fahrrad als Stein des Anstosses. Interview mit Detlef Friedrich', *Berliner Zeitung*, 18 July.

Schor, N. 1986. 'Female Fetishism. The Case of George Sand', in *The Female Body in Western Culture*, ed. S. Suleiman, Cambridge, Mass.: Harvard UP, 363–72.

Schwarz, A. 1969. *The Complete Works of Marcel Duchamp*, London: Thames & Hudson.

Sedgwick, E. Kosofsky. 1985. *Between Men: English Literature and Male Homosocial Desire*, New York: Columbia University Press.

———. 1991: *Epistemology of the Closet*, Hemel Hempstead: Harvester Wheatsheaf.

Seidensticker, E. (trans.). 1964. *The Gossamer Years: The Diary of a Noblewoman of Heian Japan*, Rutland, Vermont: Charles E. Tuttle.

Sellainen on Viipuri. Viipuri ja Karjalankannas venäläisin silmin. 1993. Viipuri: PolyPlan.

Seymour, A. 1972. *The New Art*, Hayward Gallery, London: Arts Council of Great Britain.

Showalter, E. 1991. *Sexual Anarchy. Gender and Culture at the Fin-de-siècle*, London: Virago.

Sihvo, H. and K. Sallinen. 1990. *Karjalani*, Joensuu: Karjalaisen kulttuurin edistämissäätiö.

Silverman, K. 1996. *The Threshold of the Visible World*, New York & London: Routledge.

Simpson, M. 1996. *Anti-Gay*, London: Freedom Edition.

Smith, C. 1980. *Eight Artists: Women: 1980*, London: Acme Gallery.

Smolik, N. 1997. 'History Inscribed on Women's Bodies', in *Jenny Holzer: Lustmord*, B. Ruf, Warth: Kunstmuseum des Kantons Thurgau, 126–128.

Smyth, A. 1992. 'The Politics of Abortion in a Police State', in *Abortion Papers: Ireland*, ed. A. Smyth, Dublin: Attic Press, 138–149.

Solomon, A. 1991. *Irony Tower: Soviet artists in a time of glasnost*, New York: Knopf.

Solzhenitsyn, A.I. 1973a. *The Gulag Archipelago 1918–1956*, New York: Harper & Row.

———. 1973b. 'Nobel Lecture', in *Aleksandr Solzhenitsyn: Critical Essays and Documentary Materials*, eds J.B. Dunlop et al., London: Collier Macmillan, 557–575.

Soudet, P. 1979. 'Nécessité et limites du contrôle cinématographique', *Études et documents*, 30, Paris: Imprimerie nationale.

Spartacus International Gay Guide. 1997/98. Berlin: Bruno Gmünder Verlag.

Spencer, R. 1972. *The Aesthetic Movement. Theory and Practice*, London: Studio Vista.

Spoerri, E. et al. 1991. *Wölfli: Dessinateur – Compositeur*, Lausanne: L'Age d'Homme.

Spoerri, E. (ed.) 1997. *Adolf Wölfli: Draftsman, Writer, Poet, Composer*, Ithaca & London: Cornell University Press.

Stefan, V. 1975. *Häutungen*, Munich: Frauenoffensive.
———. 1993. *Es ist reich gewesen*, Frankfurt a.M.: Fischer.
Stendhal. 1952a. *Romans et Nouvelles* I, Paris: Pléiade.
———. 1952b. *Romans et Nouvelles* II, Paris: Pléiade.
———. 1960. *Le Rouge et Le Noir*, Paris: Garnier.
———. 1972. *Oeuvres complètes* 49, Geneva: Cercle du Bibliophile.
———. 1980. *De l'Amour*, Paris: Folio.
———. 1982. *Oeuvres intimes* II, Paris: Pléiade.
Stephenson, A. 2000. 'Refashioning modern masculinity: Whistler, aestheticism and national identity', in *Modernities and Identities in English Art 1860–1914*, eds D. Peters Corbett and L. Perry, Manchester: Manchester University Press.
Stroińska, M. 1994. 'Language that creates a social reality: linguistic relativism and the language of ideologies', in *Socialist Realism Revisited*, eds N. Kolesnikoff and W. Smyrniw, Hamilton: McMaster University, 59–72.
Stroińska, M.and B. Popovic. 1999. 'Discourse of black and white and stereotyping: some linguistic principles of hate-speech', in *Language and Ideology*, ed. J. Verschueren, Antwerp: IprA, 544–559.
Sutton, P.C. 1998. *Pieter de Hooch: 1629–1684* (exhibition catalogue), New Haven and London: Dulwich Picture Gallery, Wadsworth Atheneum in association with Yale University Press.
Sweeney, J.L. (ed.). 1989. *Henry James: The Painter's Eye, Notes and Essays on the Pictorial Arts*, Madison, Wisconsin: University of Wisconsin Press.
Szabolcsi, B. (ed). 1968. *Bartók, sa vie et son oeuvre*, Paris: Boosey and Hawkes.
Szerb, A. 1992. *Le Voyageur et le clair de lune*, trans. C. Zaremba and N. Zaremba-Huzsvai, Paris: Alinéa.
———. 1957. *A világirodalom története* [History of World Literature], Budapest: Bibliotheca.
Tanner, T. 1979. *Adultery in the Novel*, Baltimore and London: The John Hopkins UP.
Théry, J.-F. 1990. *Pour en finir une bonne fois pour toutes avec la censure*, Paris: Cerf.
Thévoz, M. 1976. *Art Brut*, New York: Rizzoli.
Tickner, L. 1978. 'The body politic: female sexuality and women artists since 1970', *Art History*, June 1978, Vol.1, No. 1, 236–49.
———. 1994. 'Men's work? Masculinity and Modernism', in *Visual Culture: Images and Interpretation*, eds N. Bryson, M.A. Holly and K. Moxey, Hanover NH.: Weslyan University Press.
Tocqueville. 1986a. *De la Démocratie en Amérique* 1, 2, Paris: R. Laffont.
———. 1986b. *L'Ancien Régime et la Révolution*, Paris: R. Laffont.
Trésor de la langue française. 1975. Paris: Editions du Centre National de la Recherche Scientifique.
Tuck, A. 'Gay, Proud – and Silent?', *The Independent on Sunday*, 29 June 1997, 16.

Turunen, A. 1998. 'Suomi Euroopan maantieteessä', in *Kansallisvaltion kielioppi*, ed. M. Keränen, Jyväskylä: SoPhi.
Tykkyläinen, M. (ed.). 1995. 'Russian Karelia – An Opportunity for the West', *Occasional Papers*, Nr 29. Joensuu: University of Joensuu, Human Geography and Planning.
Vanhanen, T. (ed.). 1993. *Vuoksenrannan mennyt maailma*, Jyväskylä: Vuoksenrannan Pitäjäseura.
——— (ed.). 1996. *Karjala, sua ikävöin, Vuoksenrantalaisten muistojen kirja*, Jyväskylä: Vuoksenrannan Pitäjäseura.
Vasseleu, C. 1998. *Textures of Light: Vision and Touch in Irigaray, Levinas and Merleau-Ponty*, London: Routledge.
Vidler, A. 1992. *The architectural uncanny: essays in the modern unhomely*, Cambridge, Mass. and London: The MIT Press.
Volkart, Y. 1997. 'I sing her a song about us', in *Jenny Holzer: Lustmord*, B. Ruf, Warth: Kunstmuseum des Kantons Thurgau, 115–120.
Voltaire. 1974. *Correspondence and Related Documents*, ed. T. Besterman, Banbury: Voltaire Foundation.
Voss, M. 1982. 'Ein zweiter Anlauf', *Film und Fernsehen*, 8.
Waldman, D. 1996. *Jenny Holzer*, London: Tate Gallery.
Walker, L. 1995. 'Vistas of Pleasure: Women consumers of urban space in the West End of London 1850–1900', in *Women in the Victorian Art World*, ed. C. Campbell Orr, Manchester: Manchester University Press.
Walser, R. 1967. *Das Gesamtwerk*, III, Geneva & Hamburg: Kossodo.
———. 1968. *Das Gesamtwerk*, X, Geneva & Hamburg: Kossodo.
———. 1995–96. *Aus dem Bleistiftgebiet*, 3 vols., Frankfurt a.M.: Suhrkamp.
Ward, M. 1991. 'Impressionist Installations and Private Exhibitions', *Art Bulletin*, 123, 2, December, 599–622.
Weinberg, D. 1977. *A Community on Trial*, Chicago: Chicago Press.
Wekerle, G.R., R. Peterson and D. Morley (eds). 1980. *New Space for Women*, Boulder, Colorado: Westview Press.
Westermann, M. 1996. *The Art of the Dutch Republic 1585–1718*, The Everyman Art Library, London: Calmann and King Ltd.
Wheelock, Jr., A. 1977. *Perspective, Optics and Delft Artists Around 1650*, New York and London: Garland Publishing.
Whiteread, R. 1997. *Rachel Whiteread: British Pavilion XLVII Venice Biennale 1997*, London: British Council.
Wilding, A. 5 January 1998. *Unpublished Interview by Fran Lloyd.*
———. 3 March 2000. *Unpublished Interview by Fran Lloyd.*
Wilks, C. and N. Brick. 1997. 'Langue non-sexiste et politique éditoriale', *Modern and Contemporary France*, 5(3), 297–308.
Wilson, E. 1991. *The Sphinx in the City*, Oxford: University of California Press.
Winchester, H. 1993. *Contemporary France*, London: Longman.
Wolff, J. 1990. 'Feminine Sentences', in *Essays on Women and Culture*, Cambridge: Polity Press.

Woolf, V. 1978. *Three Guineas*. London: Hogarth Press.
Young, J.E. 1993. *The Texture of Memory: Holocaust Memorials and Meaning*, New Haven and London: Yale University Press.
Young, J.W. 1991. *Totalitarian Language: Orwell's Newspeak and its Nazi and Communist Antecedents*, Charlottesville and London: University Press of Virginia.
Yuval-Davis, N. 1997. *Gender & Nation*, London: Sage.
Zegher, M.C. de (ed.). 1996. *Inside The Visible, an elliptical traverse of 20th century art*, London: MIT Press.
Žižek, S. 1989. *The Sublime Object of Ideology*, New York: London: Verso.
———. 1991. *Looking Awry. An Introduction to Jacques Lacan through Popular Culture*, Cambridge, Mass.: The MIT Press.
———. 1994. *The Metastases of Enjoyment. Six Essays on Woman and Causality*, London: Verso.
Zola, E. 1964. *Pot-Bouille. Les Rougon-Macquart*, III, Paris: Gallimard.

Index

C

D

E

N